9 9 9

The insider's guide to legal service.

Digital media & e-commerce

New City Media Books for Business

Editor: Mark Brandon
Assistant editor: Neil Dewhurst
Production manager: Simone Hermsen
Production assistant: Stephanie Sheppard
Researchers: Clarissa Fortescue, Stephanie Knight
Account executives: Edward Bannell, Chris Sevenoaks

For New City Media
Managing director: Mark Brandon
Editorial director: Catrin Griffiths
Managing editor: Mathew Lyons
Research and information manager: David Hall
Deputy research and information manager: Neil Hambley

This Insider's Guide is published by New City Media, 37-41 Bedford Row, London WC1R 4JH
Phone: 020 7405 6081 • Fax: 020 2831 3171 • email: ncmbs@ncm.uk.com

Printed by Alden Group
Second edition 1999
ISBN: 1 902514 06 8

Wiggin and Co

Media

WIGGIN AND CO

Solicitors

The Quadrangle, Imperial Square, Cheltenham, Glos GL50 1YX
Phone: 01242 224114 **Fax:** 01242 224223
Web: www.wiggin.co.uk **Email:** law@wiggin.co.uk
Head of department: Tim Osborne
Other offices: London (also a service centre in Los Angeles)
Firm: 12 partners, 10 assistants, 5 other fee-earners
Unit: 3 partners, 4 assistants, 1 other fee-earner

“Wiggin and Co was founded in 1973 as a 'City-type' practice with a strong international bias. Clients are drawn almost exclusively from London and overseas.

The firm has particular expertise in all aspects of media and entertainment law including cable, satellite and digital TV and internet online services.”

Recent highlights

- Advising on the establishment and operation of the Channel 5/S4C/SDN digital terrestrial television multi-plex, including carriage contracts and regulatory conditions and licences.
- Negotiating and advising on the carriage contracts for 4 BBC/Flextech channels on ONdigital's digital terrestrial television platform.
- Predominant supplier of legal services for Flextech Television and in particular advising on their new Interactive and online channels and services and issues on convergence.
- Advice on the establishment of a private European Certification Authority for Digital Signatures/encrypted email/documents transfers.
- Drafting a development agreement for bespoke European interest rate swaps trading software.
- Drafting listings data supply agreements for electronic programme guides for Digital TV.
- Drafting hypertext link agreements between e-businesses and website content supply and advertising agreements.
- Advising upon Internet transactions, the sale of products/services online and underlying contracts.
- Drafting for ISP's and their subscriber's contracts.

Related services

Computer games	☐	E-commerce	✓	Internet	✓	Multimedia publishing	✓
Digital TV	✓	'Hard' IT	✓	Litigation	✓	Telecoms	✓

key contacts

Wragge & Co

Computers & IT

Wragge&Co

55 Colmore Row, Birmingham B3 2AS
Phone: 0121 233 1000 **Fax:** 0121 214 1099
Website: www.wragge.com **Email:** mail@wragge.com
Head of group: Bill Jones
Other offices: Brussels
Firm: 72 partners, 71 assistants, 286 other fee-earners
Unit: 7 partners, 18 assistants

“Wragge & Co is renowned for having successfully and distinctively developed a national firm from a base in the Midlands. The firm has a strong, cohesive culture with a sharp focus on client service. Its philosophy is to provide a co-ordinated, responsive and highly tailored service for each client.”

Recent highlights

- Advising Vio Worldwide on the setting up of a global communications service in the publishing, printing and digital arts marketplace.
- Completing the £75m outsourcing contract on behalf of the Driving Standards Agency. This was an interesting project since it required full commitment to the European Procurement regime, it was a second generation outsourcing project and it also involved technology refreshment whereby the written theory of the driving test was converted to a computerised system.
- Advising Unique Broadcasting on its joint venture with Ginger Media Group to form a new production company G One Ltd. The deal combines Ginger's access to talent with Unique's production management skills and positions G One as a major player in the independent radio sector.
- Advising AT&T on various IT and M&A related projects as well as in relation to the IT aspects of the PFI funded Norfolk and Norwich NHS Trust hospital project, one of the first NHS PFI funded transactions to be completed.

key contacts

Related services

Computer games	✓	E-commerce	✓	Internet	✓	Multimedia publishing	✓
Digital TV	✓	'Hard' IT	✓	Litigation	✓	Telecoms	✓

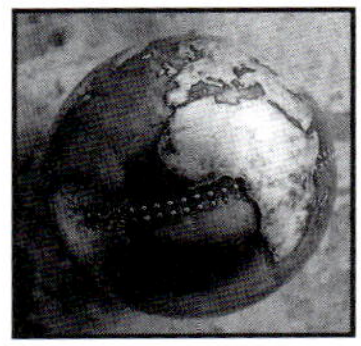

Where do I find a lawyer?

Contact details and profiles of some of the top lawyers in the digital media & e-commerce sector

Nick Aleksander
Travers Smith Braithwaite

Melanie Allen
Harbottle & Lewis

Gill Andrews
Sidley & Austin

John Angel
Clifford Chance

Quentin Archer
Lovell White Durrant

John Armstrong
Cameron McKenna

Jonathan Armstrong
Keeble Hawson Moorhouse

Michael Arnold
Eversheds

Tim Ashdown
Donne Mileham & Haddock

Tim Aspinall
Donne Mileham & Haddock

Philip Atkinson
Cobbetts

Rafi Azim-Khan
Theodore Goddard

Richard Barratt
Norton Rose

Elizabeth Barrett
Slaughter and May

Richard Barrie
MacRoberts

Paul Barton
Simmons & Simmons

Wendy Batchelor
Lawrence Graham

Martin Bazen
Clark Holt

Sebastian Belcher
Harbottle & Lewis

Nigel Bellis
Dickinson Dees

David Berry
Charles Russell

Joanna Berry
Eversheds

Catherine Bingham
Denton Hall

Cathleen Blackburn
Manches & Co

Joanna Boag-Thomson
MacRoberts

Mark Bolt
Morgan Cole

Robert Bond
Hobson Audley Hopkins & Wood

Julia Bracewell
Brobeck Hale and Dorr

Andrew Braithwaite
Osborne Clarke

Nick Braithwaite
Bindman & Partners

Nicholas Aleksander

Travers Smith Braithwaite

Tax department

Snow Hill, London, EC1A 2AL

Phone: 020 7295 3000

Fax: 020 7295 3500

Email: Nicholas.Aleksander@TraversSmith.co.uk

Nicholas has been a partner in the Travers Smith Braithwaite tax department since 1993 and has specialised in the taxation of business affairs for 12 years. His background having studied engineering at Cambridge University gives him a unique insight into understanding the underlying technology of e-commerce. Nicholas regularly lectures on taxation matters and writes for the technical press. He is a consultant editor to Croner Publications and a member of the International Fiscal Association.

Recent work

- Advising on the structuring of a joint venture for provision of e-commerce services.
- Advising venture capital funds on investment in an Internet service provider and on its subsequent trade sale.
- Advising on the establishment of a company providing sports-related websites.
- Advising on VAT and corporation tax consequences of e-commerce transactions.
- Advising on tax issues relating to siting of web servers.

Areas of expertise

Computer games		Internet	✓
Digital TV	✓	Litigation	
E-commerce	✓	Multimedia publishing	✓
'Hard' IT	✓	Telecoms	✓

Rafi Azim-Khan

Theodore Goddard

Media & entertainment

150 Aldersgate Street, London EC1A 4EJ

Phone: 020 7606 8855

Fax: 020 7606 4390

Email: rafiazimkhan@theodoregoddard.co.uk

Manager of Theodore Goddard's Advertising Law and E-commerce groups and acknowledged as one of the UK's leading marketing lawyers. Previously with Lewis Silkin and Cameron McKenna, Rafi has extensive experience of advising on all aspects of e-commerce, particularly in relation to conducting full legal 'audits,' site design and ISP startup, including agreements with third party partners, electronic shopping, 'webvertising' and Internet sales promotions and competitions, Internet gaming/betting, site disclaimers, terms and conditions, domain and trade mark protection.

Recent work

- Full e-commerce 'audit' for General Motors Corporation (Vauxhall in the UK).
- Advising New International's new ISP venture on disclaimers, terms of access, domain names, data protection, contracts with partners.
- Internet gaming and betting issues.
- Setting up new e-trade music site.
- Internet advertising contracts/legal issues.
- E-trade terms and Distance Selling Directive.
- Setting up computer games sites.

Areas of expertise

Computer games	✓	Internet	✓
Digital TV		Litigation	
E-commerce	✓	Multimedia publishing	✓
'Hard' IT		Telecoms	

Paul Barton

Simmons & Simmons

Commercial & trade dept/IP

21 Wilson Street, London EC2M 2TX

Phone: 020 7825 4174

Fax: 020 7628 2070

Email: paul.barton@simmon-simmons.com

Paul trained with Simmons & Simmons and has specialised in IP/IT law since 1991. He has also worked in the firm's Hong Kong and New York offices. Regularly advises on the establishment of websites, Internet liability issues, contracting online, issues arising from business to business e-commerce, the protection and exploitation of IPR's in cyber space and the resolution of Internet disputes.

Recent work

- Advising Telewest on a PC-based high speed Internet access service.
- Advising a professional body on an online system for use throughout one of the leading professions.
- Advising on the development and introduction of a computerised system for metals traded on the London Metal Exchange.
- Advising one of Europe's leading logistics organisations on the implementation of a supply chain information system.
- Advising a major insurance broker on e-publishing agreements.
- Advising one of the leading cable operators on the implementation of a digital television project.

Areas of expertise

Computer games		Internet	✓
Digital TV	✓	Litigation	
E-commerce	✓	Multimedia publishing	✓
'Hard' IT	✓	Telecoms	

Joanna Boag-Thomson

MacRoberts

IP and technology law group

152 Bath Street, Glasgow G2 4TB

Phone: 0141 332 9988

Fax: 0141 332 8886

Email: joannab@macroberts.co.uk

Qualified in 1990 and has specialised in IP/IT since 1991. Handles a wide range of IP and IT work with an emphasis on electronic commerce and legal issues arising from commercial activities on the Internet. Has considerable experience in multimedia and games fields, and also advises on data protection.

Recent work

- Advice to AIM-listed games company and drafting/negotiating contracts for exploitation of several titles.
- Acquisition of rights from publishers to enable production of multimedia versions of children's books.
- Advice to employers regarding email/software policies and data protection.
- Contracts for exploitation of leading multimedia product in financial services sector.
- Advice regarding domain name disputes.
- Contracts for website designers (design, maintenance and ownership of rights).
- Contracts for design of company intranets.

Areas of expertise

Computer games	✓	Internet	✓
Digital TV		Litigation	
E-commerce	✓	Multimedia publishing	✓
'Hard' IT		Telecoms	

Nick Braithwaite

Bindman & Partners

Media department

275 Gray's Inn Road, London WC1X 8QE
Phone: 020 7833 4433
Fax: 020 7837 9792
Email: nbraithwai@aol.com

Nick Braithwaite is a partner and director of digital media at Bindman & Partners. Before joining the firm, he worked at a major City law firm. He has been an in-house lawyer for Reuters and the BBC. He is editor of the *International Libel Handbook* and has written widely on Internet-related issues.

Recent work

- Acting in *Godfrey v Demon Internet* (the first Internet libel case against an Internet service provider in the UK).
- Advising in five other Internet libel claims.
- Advising on a private banking service for a major US bank.
- An international confidentiality claim for a Middle Eastern corporation.
- Advising on computer retailers' websites.

Areas of expertise

Computer games		Internet	✓
Digital TV		Litigation	✓
E-commerce	✓	Multimedia publishing	✓
'Hard' IT	✓	Telecoms	

Robin Bynoe

Charles Russell Solicitors

Media & communications group

8-10 Fetter Lane, London EC4A 1RS
Phone: 020 7203 5191
Fax: 020 7203 5302
Email: robinb@cr-law.co.uk

Oxford University graduate. Articled with Jaques & Lewis (now Eversheds); remained with firm on qualifying becoming partner and head of IP and media. Joined Charles Russell in 1996 as partner and head of IP/IT. Non-contentious IP work with emphasis on IT; also media and franchising.

Recent work

- Installed and responsible for Charles Russell domain name registration service.
- Documentation for designers and suppliers of software systems employing neural networks.
- Setting up documentation for e-commerce acting for major provider of enabling software.
- Regular columnist for *ZDNet*: online computer magazine.

Areas of expertise

Computer games		Internet	✓
Digital TV		Litigation	
E-commerce	✓	Multimedia publishing	✓
'Hard' IT	✓	Telecoms	

Patrick Cantrill
Walker Morris

Intellectual property group

Kings Court, King Street, Leeds LS1 2HL
Phone: 0113 2832591
Fax: 0113 2459412
Email: pxc@walkermorris.co.uk

1984 – Admitted in England
1986 – Admitted in Hong Kong
1986-89 – Deacons, Graham & James – Hong Kong
1989–92 – Crossman Block – London
1992-date – Walker Morris – Leeds

Recent work

- Advising on the Distance Selling Directive.
- Acting in the first UK High Court action under the Database Regulations 1997.
- Advising on Internet trading.
- Preparing commercial agreements for website facilities.
- Advising on data protection.
- Negotiating and drafting complex software licences, hardware contracts and other procurements and outsourcing arrangements.

Areas of expertise

Computer games	✓	Internet	✓
Digital TV	✓	Litigation	✓
E-commerce	✓	Multimedia publishing	
'Hard' IT	✓	Telecoms	

Peter Carey
Rakisons

IT & Telecoms group

Clements House, 14/18 Gresham Street, London EC2V 7JE
Phone: 020 7367 8000
Fax: 020 7367 8001
Email: peter.carey@rakisons.co.uk

Peter Carey is a leading expert on content and media issues. He graduated in law from Nottingham Law School and after practising media law for a few years, gained a Masters degree in Comparative and International Business Law in Texas. He recently joined the group at Rakisons following a period spent as a senior lecturer at The College of Law where he set up the country's first professional Media and Entertainment Law course. Peter's work in data protection is widely recognised and he brings specialist media knowledge to the group. He is the author of *Media and Entertainment, The Law and Business, Blackstone's Guide to the Data Protection Act 1998* and is a visiting professor at The College of Law.

Recent work

- Advising various Internet based business on data protection and IP issues.

Areas of expertise

Computer games		Internet	✓
Digital TV	✓	Litigation	✓
E-commerce	✓	Multimedia publishing	✓
'Hard' IT		Telecoms	

Robert Carolina

Tarlo Lyons Solicitors

E-commerce & digital media

Watchmaker Court, 33 St John's Lane, London EC1M 4DB

Phone: 020 7814 5461

Fax: 020 7814 9421

Email: rac@tarlo-lyons.com

Robert routinely represents users, purchasers, developers and vendors of related products and services and regularly advises on electronic commerce transactions and projects.

Recent work

- Advised an international financial institution on the legal risks related to the use of an online derivatives order placement and matching service.
- Advised a financial data value-added reseller concerning its new Internet based financial data service and drafted a new licensing agreement for its 'purchase' of raw financial data from an international data vendor.
- Provided emergency advice to an international financial institution following an Internet related employee incident with significant financial ramifications and provided substantial drafting advice related to its Internet acceptable use policy document.
- Provides regular advice to an international financial institution concerning Internet risk management.

Areas of expertise

Computer games		Internet	✓
Digital TV	✓	Litigation	
E-commerce	✓	Multimedia publishing	✓
'Hard' IT	✓	Telecoms	✓

Clive Davies

D J Freeman

IT & telecoms

43 Fetter Lane, London, EC4A 1JU

Phone: 020 7556 4564

Fax: 020 7583 1056

Email: cid@djfreeman.co.uk

Clive Davies is D J Freeman's lead partner and adviser on all aspects of information technology and communications law, including the application of law to the internet. He worked as a lawyer in industry for ICL for a number of years before joining D J Freeman in 1990, becoming a partner in 1991. Clive is on the editorial team of Tolley's Professonal Journal, *Communications Law*.

Recent work

- Advising Bull Information Systems on 5 PFI government procurement contracts.

Areas of expertise

Computer games		Internet	✓
Digital TV	✓	Litigation	
E-commerce	✓	Multimedia publishing	✓
'Hard' IT	✓	Telecoms	✓

Margaret Briffa
Briffa & Co

Michael Burden
Eversheds

Robin Bynoe
Charles Russell

Duncan Calow
Denton Hall

Gillian Cameron
Maclay Murray & Spens

Jonathan Cameron
Paisner & Co

Mike Camps
Thomas Eggar Church Adams

Patrick Cantrill
Walker Morris

Peter Carey
Rakisons

Robert Carolina
Tarlo Lyons

James Chesterman
Weil Gotshal & Manges

Michael Chissick
Field Fisher Waterhouse

Paul Cooke
Bristows

Ellen Cooper-de-Groote
Charles Russell

Chris Coulter
Ashurst Morris Crisp

Mark Crichard
Garretts

Peter Crockford
Titmuss Sainer Dechert

John Crozier
Linklaters

Bina Cunningham
Willoughby & Partners

Mimi Curran
Paisner & Co

Clive Davies
DJ Freeman

Simon Deane-Johns
Dibb Lupton Alsop

John Deech
Linnells

Graham DeFries
Bird & Bird

Peter Dickinson
Rowe & Maw

Stephen Digby
Davenport Lyons

Danelle Dinsdale
Dibb Lupton Alsop

Natasha Doman
McNeive

Robbie Downing
Baker & McKenzie

Charles Drayson
Eversheds

Peter Dickinson

Rowe & Maw

IT & telecoms

20 Black Friars Lane, London EC4V 6HD

Phone: 020 7782 8747

Fax: 020 7248 2009

Email: pdickinson@roweandmaw.co.uk

Peter graduated from Southampton University in 1983. He qualified as a solicitor in 1988, and practised in the corporate finance department of Clifford Chance until 1993. Peter then joined Mercury Communications Ltd, as a senior legal advisor, specialising in mergers and acquisitions. He has been a partner at Rowe & Maw since 1995, shortly after having joined the firm. Peter leads Rowe & Maw's Communications Group.

Recent work

- Led team on behalf of Cable & Wireless Communications in relation to the outsource of its IT systems to IBM.
- Acting for Reuters Investments Ltd in relation to its acquisition of Liberty SA, a subsidiary of Cedel International SA, which company carries on the business of automated order routing of securities transactions.
- Acting on behalf of GE Information Systems Ltd in relation to various joint ventures relating to electronic commerce.

Areas of expertise

Computer games		Internet	
Digital TV	✓	Litigation	
E-commerce		Multimedia publishing	
'Hard' IT		Telecoms	✓

Robbie Downing

Baker & McKenzie

IT/Communications department

100 New Bridge Street, London EC4V 6JA

Phone: 020 7919 1161

Fax: 020 7919 1999

Email: robbie.downing@bakernet.com

Robbie Downing qualified at Baker & McKenzie in 1988, working in the EC/Competition Group in London and Brussels. After stints as an in-house lawyer at IBM and a lecturer at King's College, London, he returned to Baker & McKenzie in 1995, becoming a partner in 1998. He specialises in IT, telecoms and convergence.

Recent work

Recent projects involving online services include:

- Advising Bolero Association on membership structure for online international trade documentation system.
- Advising World Insurance Network on system for trading insurance online.
- Advising Cisco on transactions involving online trading.
- Advising telco on telecoms services agreement with ISP to enable free Internet access service.

Areas of expertise

Computer games		Internet	✓
Digital TV	✓	Litigation	
E-commerce	✓	Multimedia publishing	
'Hard' IT	✓	Telecoms	✓

Robyn Durie

Linklaters & Alliance

Communications group

One Silk Street, London EC2Y 8HQ
Phone: 020 7456 2000
Fax: 020 7456 2222
Email: rdurie@linklaters.com

Robyn joined Linklaters & Paines, a member firm of Linklaters & Alliance, in 1987 and became a partner with the firm in 1990.

She is currently co-head of the communications practice, as well as a member of the Management Group of Linklaters & Alliance Information Technology and Communication Law Practice Group.

Robyn specialises in telecommunications, broadcasting, data protection and information technology. She has worked on a number of significant transactions.

Recent work

- Drafting an electronic commerce law for Bermuda.
- The initial offering of Telecom Eireann.
- The rail journey information system for the British rail network.

Areas of expertise

Computer games		Internet	✓
Digital TV	✓	Litigation	✓
E-commerce	✓	Multimedia publishing	✓
'Hard' IT	✓	Telecoms	✓

Justin Ellis

Donne Mileham & Haddock

Innovation & media

100 Queens Road, Brighton, East Sussex, BN1 3YB
Phone: 01273 744249
Fax: 01273 202105
Email: justin.ellis@dmh.co.uk

Solicitor in Innovation & Media Group. Previously with a major city firm for four years until 1997. Joined DM&H to build non-contentious IP/IT work to add to firm's existing litigation practice in this field. Majority of work now digital media, Internet/e-commerce related. Regularly invited to speak at seminars on legal issues on the Internet. Mainly represents fast growing companies, at lower rates than most London firms.

Recent work

- Regularly advises ISP clients on contract and liability issues with their customers and telecoms suppliers.
- Currently advising on web-based global freight tracking system.
- Advised on US/German/UK domain name dispute.
- Advised on copyright issues of marketing DVD products from other regions into Europe via Internet.
- Advised on IP/IT issues on purchase of Internet/magazine publishing company.

Areas of expertise

Computer games	✓	Internet	✓
Digital TV		Litigation	
E-commerce	✓	Multimedia publishing	✓
'Hard' IT	✓	Telecoms	

Pierre-Andre Dubois
Brobeck Hale and Dorr

Andrew Dunlop
Shaw Pittman

Robyn Durie
Linklaters

Patrick Duxbury
Wragge & Co

John Edwards
Sidley & Austin

Sara Ellacott
Nabarro Nathanson

Justin Ellis
Donne Mileham & Haddock

David Engel
Theodore Goddard

John Enser
Olswang

Lloyd Evans
Berwin Leighton

Linda Fazzani
Paisner & Co

Iain Ferguson
Allen & Overy

Robin Fletcher
Ledingham Chalmers

David Flint
MacRoberts

Mike Francies
Weil Gotshal & Manges

Suzanne Garben
Denton Hall

George Gardiner
Tarlo Lyons Solicitors

Nick Gardner
Herbert Smith

Paul Gardner
Osborne Clarke

Shelagh Gaskill
Masons

Tony Ghee
Ashurst Morris Crisp

Lindy Golding
Lovell White Durrant

Paul Golding
Nabarro Nathanson

Ben Goodger
Willoughby & Partners

Roddy Gordon
Robert Muckle

Rory Graham
Osborne Clarke

Gill Grassie
Maclay Murray & Spens

Christopher Grew
Brobeck Hale and Dorr

Mike Grierson
Cobbetts

David Griffiths
Clifford Chance

John Enser

Olswang

90 Long Acre, London WC2E 9TT

Phone: 020 7208 8716

Fax: 020 7208 8800

Email: jxe@olswang.co.uk

John has been a solicitor for ten years and a partner at Olswang since 1996. He provides commercial, regulatory and competition law advice to clients active in all aspects of electronic media, particularly those involved in the Internet and cable and satellite delivered content. The areas advised upon by John include copyright protection, specification and design of websites, ISP liability, CD-ROM development, music rights, advertising and competition.

Recent work

Commercial and regulatory issues for digital and interactive television on behalf of:

- MTV Europe
- Bloomberg
- Microsoft Web TV
- Two Way TV Ltd
- Channel 4

Advice on Internet projects for:

- United Broadcasting
- Carphone Warehouse
- Blueberry New Media
- confetti.co.uk
- BPI

Areas of expertise

Computer games	✓	Internet	✓
Digital TV	✓	Litigation	
E-commerce	✓	Multimedia publishing	✓
'Hard' IT		Telecoms	

David Flint

MacRoberts

IP & technology law group

152 Bath Street Glasgow, G2 4TB

Phone: 0141 332 9988

Fax: 0141 332 8886

Email: df@macroberts.co.uk

Partner in MacRoberts since 1984. Specialises in all aspects of IP and IT with a particular emphasis on Internet technology and law, both in the UK and internationally.

Recent work

- Co-author of *Proposal for a CyberMark(®)*.
- Advised on first Scottish domain name case.
- Member of Scottish Chapter of ISOC Executive Board.
- Member of Nominet Dispute Resolution Experts Panel.
- Advised on Internet service provider and website hosting agreements.
- Advised on Clickwrap licensing for a major academic institution.

Areas of expertise

Computer games	✓	Internet	✓
Digital TV		Litigation	
E-commerce	✓	Multimedia publishing	✓
'Hard' IT	✓	Telecoms	

George Gardiner

Tarlo Lyons Solicitors

E-commerce & digital media group

Watchmaker Court, 33 St John's Lane, London
EC1M 4DB

Phone: 020 7814 5447

Fax: 020 7814 9421

Email: gjg@tarlo-lyons.com

George specialises in IT law including software licensing, outsourcing and facilities management for big software systems; developments agreements; Internet and e-commerce; trade marks and branding (including domain names); data protection; data and email networks; web development and hosting agreements.

Recent work

- Advised a publisher of technical journals and an online recruitment agency on web development and hosting agreements for e-commerce sites.
- Provided a global data and communications intra-structure service contract for an international bank.
- Securitisation aspects of investment in IT/technology companies.
- Advised on IP issues relating to AIM listing for a high tech Internet company.
- Advising on a domain name dispute and passing of claim and branding/trade marks on the Internet.

Areas of expertise

Computer games		Internet	✓
Digital TV	✓	Litigation	
E-commerce	✓	Multimedia publishing	✓
'Hard' IT	✓	Telecoms	✓

Paul Gardner

Osborne Clarke

IT & telecoms

Hillgate House, 26 Old Bailey, London
EC4M 7HW

Phone: 020 7809 1062

Fax: 020 7809 1005

Email: paul.gardner@osborne-clarke.co.uk

Handles all aspects of intellectual property and commercial law relating to the digital media industries with particular emphasis on the computer games and educational software industries. He also advises a variety of organisations in connection with the legal aspects of e-commerce.

Recent work

- Representing a leading computer game developer in connection with a ground breaking technology development and licence agreement with a computer game publisher.
- Reviewing and modifying the data protection policies and procedures of a leading US based computer game publisher.
- Advising a computer game publisher in connection with the establishment of an online shop.
- Advising an educational software publisher in connection with the exploitation of its products as part of an online database.
- Advising a leading advertising agency in relation to advertising on the Internet.

Areas of expertise

Computer games	✓	Internet	✓
Digital TV	✓	Litigation	
E-commerce	✓	Multimedia publishing	✓
'Hard' IT		Telecoms	

Shelagh Gaskill

Masons

Information & technology

Springfield House, 76 Wellington Street, Leeds LS1 2AY

Phone: 0113 233 8905

Fax: 0113 245 4285

Email: shelagh.gaskill@masons.com

Shelagh Gaskill is a partner and practice area manager for IT/IP in Masons. She specialises in information law and the commercial exploitation of data including their valuation, sale and exchange. She designs databases from a legal point of view and devises worldwide and group company data flows.

Recent work

- Drafting email policies for a financial services group and a major retail organisation.
- Designing a global knowledge system and Intranet for an international paperless trader.
- Designing anti-fraud shared information databases for two sectors of industry.
- Drafting standard terms and conditions for online business for a multi-media company.
- Advising an international chemical company on all aspects of e-commerce.

Areas of expertise

Computer games		Internet	✓
Digital TV		Litigation	
E-commerce	✓	Multimedia publishing	✓
'Hard' IT	✓	Telecoms	✓

Lindy Golding

Lovell White Durrant

Computers, communications and media

65 Holborn Viaduct, London EC1A 2DY

Phone: 020 7236 0066

Fax: 020 7248 4212

Email: lindy.golding@lovellwhitedurrant.com

Qualified in Australia and the UK. LLM from Cambridge University and Diploma in Intellectual Property from Bristol University. Lindy's work encompasses a broad range of digital media work, both contentious and non-contentious, including advice on rights clearances and licences, development agreements, multimedia publishing, digital broadcasting, intellectual property and IT aspects of the Internet, litigation in connection with domain names, intellectual property and technology aspects of new media.

Recent work

- Advising a major free to air broadcaster on the protection of electronic programme guides.
- Advising a major media company on the setting up of an ISP service.
- Advice on ISP subscriber terms and conditions.
- Advice to a major computer games manufacturer on infringements over the Internet.

Areas of expertise

Computer games	✓	Internet	✓
Digital TV	✓	Litigation	✓
E-commerce	✓	Multimedia publishing	✓
'Hard' IT	✓	Telecoms	✓

Paul Golding

Nabarro Nathanson

IT/IP

50 Stratton Street, London W1X 6NX
(until September 1999) thereafter:
Lacon House, Theoblads Road, London WC1X 8SA
Phone: 020 7518 3711 (until September 1999)
Fax: 020 7629 7900 (until September 1999)
Email: p.golding@nabarro.com

Paul is the head of the firm's IT, Communications and New Media Group in London and specialises in commercial work involving IT/IP. Paul advises on all legal issues relating to digital media and e-commerce. Paul is a regular speaker at seminars on topics including.

- The legal aspects of IT security.
- Information in the electronic age.
- The Internet – avoiding the traps.
- Data protection – the new law.

Recent work

- Issues relating to an Internet property mall including preparation of terms governing membership of the mall and access by the public.
- The establishment of and hosting arrangements for the official Manchester United website.
- Advising a consortium of the Examination Awarding Bodies of England on the legal aspects of establishing a combined online database of examination awards.

Areas of expertise

Computer games		Internet	✓
Digital TV		Litigation	
E-commerce	✓	Multimedia publishing	✓
'Hard' IT	✓	Telecoms	✓

Rory Graham

Osborne Clarke

IT & Telecoms

Hillgate House, 26 Old Bailey, London
EC4M 7HW
Phone: 020 7809 1116
Fax: 020 7809 1005
Email: rory.graham@osborne-clarke.co.uk

Corporate and commercial lawyer focusing on the technology industry. Trained at Stephenson Harwood in London and Hong Kong. Spent eight years at Bird & Bird, four as a partner. Co-author of *Internet Law and Regulation (1997).* Particular expertise in EDI, e-commence and website design and hosting agreements.

Recent work

- Advised trusted third party on Internet publishing and encryption agreements.
- Advised financial institutions on liability issues surrounding Internet trading.
- Advised major Internet advertising agency on 'push' technology.
- Advised Internet news agency on transaction with leading US ISP.
- Advised major internet software publisher on global distribution and licensing strategy.
- Advised providers of digital teletext services on commercial agreements.
- Advised international digital video processing company on structural, intellectual property and corporate finance issues.

Areas of expertise

Computer games		Internet	✓
Digital TV		Litigation	
E-commerce	✓	Multimedia publishing	✓
'Hard' IT	✓	Telecoms	✓

David Grossman

Berwin Leighton

Information & communications technology

Adelaide House, London Bridge, London
EC4R 9HA
Phone: 020 7760 4373
Fax: 020 7760 1111
Email: david.grossman@berwinleighton.com

David is an experienced technology lawyer recognised as a leading e-commerce specialist. He advises major UK and global corporates as well as key emerging names in the Internet industry. He is closely involved in the development of the Electronic Communications Bill and other e-commerce legislation. David joined Berwin Leighton in 1994.

Recent work

- Acted for NatWest on a range of e-commerce projects.
- Advised leading corporates on the establishment of public key infrastructures (PKI) including drafting certification practice statements and certificate policies.
- Acted for United News & Media in its joint venture with BT to operate LineOne, a leading ISP and portal.
- Advised on projects involving smart cards, digital signatures and secure electronic payment systems.
- Advised FTSE 250 companies on the establishment of online retailing schemes.

Areas of expertise

Computer games		Internet	✓
Digital TV	✓	Litigation	
E-commerce	✓	Multimedia publishing	
'Hard' IT	✓	Telecoms	

Nicholas Higham

Denton Hall

Media, information & technology group

Five Chancery Lane, Clifford's Inn, London
EC4A 1BU
Phone: 020 7320 6479
Fax: 020 7320 6470
Email: nach@dentonhall.com

Nicholas Higham, an experienced partner in Denton Hall's media, information and technology group, is adviser to some of the world's leading technology and telecoms companies and a number of governments. He has gained particular recognition for his expertise on both regulation and complex commercial issues and heads a 25-lawyer strong practice at Denton Hall which is rated number one in Digital Media by *Chambers and Partners Directory 1998/1999*. He is also co-author with colleagues, Alan Williams and Duncan Calow, of *Digital Media: Contracts, Rights and Licensing* (Sweet and Maxwell, 2nd edition, 1998).

Recent work

- Conducting a review of the Internet Watch Foundation (IWF) for DTI/Home office.
- Advising Springboard Internet Services, on all aspects of the operation of the LineOne service including content agreements, transaction contracts and advertising issues.
- Advised the British Library on digitisation of its archive.

Areas of expertise

Computer games	✓	Internet	✓
Digital TV		Litigation	
E-commerce	✓	Multimedia publishing	
'Hard' IT	✓	Telecoms	✓

Paul Hosford

Rakisons

IT & Telecoms group

Clements House, 14/18 Gresham Street, London EC2V 7JE

Phone: 020 7367 8000

Fax: 020 7367 8001

Email: paul.hosford@rakisons.co.uk

A partner in the Group, Paul has been involved in the technology sector for many years and his work encompasses the commercial and transactional aspects of IT and the Internet. He focuses in particular on software companies, large scale users of technology products and services and e-commerce start-ups, acting for a wide variety of clients. His work includes IT and telecoms outsourcing, online content provision and contracting, data protection, technology supply and sourcing, digital signatures and encryption and intellectual property issues.

Recent work

- Advising several businesses in relation to establishing e-commerce.
- Advising .com emerging growth companies on IT/IP issues, corporate structure and public offerings.
- Advising an Internet software house on development agreements and strategic partnering.

Areas of expertise

Computer games	✓	Internet	✓
Digital TV	✓	Litigation	✓
E-commerce	✓	Multimedia publishing	✓
'Hard' IT	✓	Telecoms	✓

Sean James

Wiggin and Co

Media

The Quadrangle, Imperial Square, Cheltenham, Glos GL50 1YX

Phone: 01242 631211

Fax: 01242 224223

Email: sstjj@wiggin.co.uk

Partner specialising in all cable, satellite, terrestrial, online and other television operations and programming issues including satellite uplink, encryption, facilities, conditional access and subscriber management contracts.

Recent work

- Advising on the establishment and operation of the Channel 5/S4C/SDN digital terrestrial television multi-plex, including carriage contracts and regulatory conditions and licences.
- Advising on the carriage contracts for four BBC channels/Flextech channels on ONdigital's digital terrestrial television platform.
- Advising Flextech Television on their new Interactive and online channels and services.
- Advising S4C on digital satellite, uplink, EPG, conditional access and subscriber management contracts.

Areas of expertise

Computer games		Internet	✓
Digital TV	✓	Litigation	
E-commerce	✓	Multimedia publishing	✓
'Hard' IT		Telecoms	✓

Bill Jones

Wragge and Co

Computers & IT

55 Colmore Road, Birmingham B3 2AS
Phone: 0121 214 1058
Fax: 0121 214 1099
Email: bill_jones@wragge.com

Bill joined Wragge & Co in 1982 and became a partner in 1990. He specialises in IP, IT and telecoms law, both contentious and non-contentious. He has acted in connection with many large scale computer system development and facilities management projects based in the UK and overseas, including publicly quoted companies and well known financial services businesses.

Recent work

- Advising several banks and building societies on their IT strategies including software development contracts and data protection compliance.
- Advising a major retailer on several IT-related ventures, most notably the acquisition of a new merchandise management and electronic tagging system.
- Advising a telecoms company on its commercial agreements.
- Advising on an innovative outsourcing deal involving transmission masts that could become commonplace in the telecoms industry.
- Advising start-up IT businesses in all areas including neural networking software and encryption technology.

Areas of expertise

Computer games	✓	Internet	✓
Digital TV	✓	Litigation	✓
E-commerce	✓	Multimedia publishing	✓
'Hard' IT	✓	Telecoms	✓

Caroline Kean

Wiggin and Co

Media

The Quadrangle, Imperial Square, Cheltenham, Glos GL50 1YX
Phone: 01242 631210
Fax: 01242 224223
Email: cmk@wiggin.co.uk

Caroline Joined Wiggin and Co as Head of Litigation in 1995. Since qualifying in December 1984, Caroline has specialised in commercial litigation with particular expertise in the fields of 'media' litigation, defamation, copyright and trade marks. She is a member of the Council of the Media Society and Legal Adviser to Women in Journalism.

Recent work

- Advised on an injunction against a satellite provider in order to restrain them from declining access to a satellite for a digital TV company.
- Advised on one of the first defamation cases on the internet.
- Advice on contract disputes between satellite providers and digital TV companies.
- Advice on libel claims on email.
- Advice on disputes on software licensing.
- Advice on copyright infringement on the Internet.

Areas of expertise

Computer games		Internet	
Digital TV		Litigation	✓
E-commerce		Multimedia publishing	
'Hard' IT		Telecoms	

David Grossman
Berwin Leighton

Melanie Haddad
Davenport Lyons

Mark Haftke
Bird & Bird

Angus Hamilton
Hamiltons

Michael Hart
Baker & McKenzie

Margaret Harvey
Shaw Pittman

Alan Hawley
Hobson Audley Hopkins & Wood

Mark Headley
Marriott Harrison

Chris Hickson
Slaughter and May

Elizabeth Hiester
Clifford Chance

Nicholas Higham
Denton Hall

David Hinde
Marriott Harrison

Christopher Holder
Shaw Pittman

Jeremy Holt
Clark Holt

Paul Hosford
Rakisons

Christopher Hoyle
Rakisons

Andrew Inglis
Olswang

Laurence Jacobs
Allen & Overy

Sean James
Wiggin and Co

Don Jerrard
Baker & McKenzie

Tim Johnson
SJ Berwin & Co

Bill Jones
Wragge & Co

Gareth Jones
Bevan Ashford

Lawrence Kaye
Paisner & Co

Caroline Kean
Wiggin and Co

Colleen Keck
Allen & Overy

Richard Kemp
Kemp & Co

Richard Kempner
Addleshaw Booth & Co

David Kent
Taylor Joynson Garrett

Sarah Kirk
Nicholson Graham & Jones

Richard Kemp

Kemp & Co

IT & multimedia

Saddlers House, Gutter Lane, London EC2V 6BR
Phone: 020 7710 1610
Fax: 020 7600 7878
Email: richardk@comlegal.com

Before setting up Kemp & Co in November 1997 as 'a law firm for the .com world', Richard Kemp was head of European IP/IT practice of the Arthur Anderson legal network. He was the only IT lawyer listed in Legal Business' survey of *40 lawyers under 40* in 1996.

Recent work

- Acts for Microsoft Expedia in the UK/Europe, the largest online business by turnover.
- Is currently acting on the European roll-out of the online sales system for a major PC manufacturer.
- Acts for Netlife UK, a major Internet banking software company.
- Acts on a wide variety of digital media, e-commerce and convergence legal matters for major technology suppliers and acquirers integrating Internet and e-commerce applications into their business strategies and systems.
- For further information, see the firm's Review of 1998 on our website at www.comlegal.com

Areas of expertise

Computer games	✓	Internet	✓
Digital TV		Litigation	
E-commerce	✓	Multimedia publishing	✓
'Hard' IT	✓	Telecoms	✓

David Kent

Taylor Joynson Garrett

IT/Telecoms group

Carmelite, 50 Victoria Embankment,
Blackfriars, London EC4Y 0DX
Phone: 020 7353 1234
Fax: 020 7936 2666
Email: dkent@tjg.co.uk

Partner leading a team specialising in advising US and Canadian e-commerce and Internet companies in the UK on: M&A and joint ventures; strategic alliances; distribution and licensing agreements; establishment and operation of business in the UK and Europe and capital raising.

David specialises in advising US and UK digital media and e-commerce companies and his team comprises probably the leading practice of UK lawyers advising North American Internet companies.

Recent work

- Acting for Infospace.com, Inc, Multex.com, Inc and Marimba, Inc in their recent IPO and UK activities.
- Advising ebay, Inc, e-gain, e-Toys and four other major US e-companies and a further 34 US Internet companies in their UK start up, joint ventures, distribution and capital raising activities.

Areas of expertise

Computer games	✓	Internet	✓
Digital TV	✓	Litigation	
E-commerce	✓	Multimedia publishing	✓
'Hard' IT	✓	Telecoms	✓

Philip Krauss

Thomas Eggar Church Adams

Intellectual property

Fulwood House, Fulwood Place, London
WC1V 6HR
Phone: 0207 242 0841
Fax: 0207 831 9609
Email: philip.krauss@teca.co.uk

Previously a legal adviser in industry (chemicals and computers) he now has 15 years experience in computer related matters in a private practice context. Many years experience in electronic banking has led to an interest and involvement in e-commerce.

Recent work

He has advised on the following:

- Website development.
- Online trading including internet shopping.
- Liability of service providers.
- Domain name problems.
- Regulatory matters.
- Online business start-ups.
- Electronic banking – all aspects of major network operations.

Has written articles eg *Financial Times* and attended and given seminars on this subject. The firm is an active member of e-centre (formerly the electronic commerce association) and through working with technical consultants has easy access to technical advice in this area.

Areas of expertise

Computer games		Internet	✓
Digital TV		Litigation	
E-commerce	✓	Multimedia publishing	
'Hard' IT		Telecoms	

Emyr Lewis

Morgan Cole

Business services

Princess House, Princess Way, Swansea, SA1 3LJ
Phone: 01792 634634
Fax: 01792 634634
Email: emyr.lewis@mogan-cole.com

Emyr is commercial litigator and experienced Welsh language advisor. He is head of the firm's media group of which digital media is a part. Has expertise in all areas of media, telecommunications and the digital movement means he advises many types of client. An area of specialism for Emyr is animation.

Recent work

- Advising Internet service providers on contracts and legal structures.
- Advised on agreements for the retailing of Internet services.
- Advised a prospective digital TV channel as to all aspects of business and regulatory matters and TV programme makers as to the impact of DTT on supply contracts, commissioning agreements, co-production agreements and rights acquisition agreements.
- Advised in relation to digital and interactive exploitation of cartoon characters TV programmes and databases.
- Involved in major transactions involving two Cardiff-based animation companies on projects with budgets in excess of £1m.

Areas of expertise

Computer games	✓	Internet	✓
Digital TV	✓	Litigation	✓
E-commerce	✓	Multimedia publishing	✓
'Hard' IT	✓	Telecoms	✓

Mike Lindsey

Morgan Cole

Business services

Bradley Court, Park Place, Cardiff CF10 3DR
Phone: 01222 385385
Fax: 01222 385300
Email: mike.lyndsay@morgan-cole.com

Mike deals in all aspects of intellectual property law and is the leader of the Wales leader of the IPR group of which digital media is a part. Mike deals in all aspects of intellectual property law, advising companies, public bodies and individuals in respect of both contentious and non-contenious matters.

Recent work

- Advising a statutory agency in respect of the protection of rights in databases, a data model and software.
- Acting for a company in the multi million pound development and licensing of electrosurgical medical instrumentations to major US Corporations.
- Acting for a company in the exploitation of compact disc hologram patents.
- Advising a university and various NHS trusts in respect of the licensing of patents and confidential information.
- Acting for a major software house, various public bodies and a statutory agency in connection with software development, licensing and support agreements and IT.

Areas of expertise

Computer games	✓	Internet	✓
Digital TV	✓	Litigation	
E-commerce	✓	Multimedia publishing	✓
'Hard' IT	✓	Telecoms	✓

Shaun Lowde

Wiggin and Co

Media

The Quadrangle, Imperial Square, Cheltenham, Glos GL50 1YX
Phone: 01242 631215
Fax: 01242 224223
Email: srl@wiggin.co.uk

Shaun specialises in IT and IP work with emphasis in online and internet related transactions, digital media rights and products, interactive television and associated aspects of technology convergence, copyright, designs, music and trade marks.

Recent work

- Advice on and establishment of a private European Certification Authority for Digital Signatures.
- Negotiating/drafting a development agreement for bespoke European interest rate swaps trading software.
- Negotiating/drafting website development, content supply and hypertext link agreements. Negotiating/drafting listings data supply agreements for Digital TV electronic programme guides.
- Advising on IP, Digital TV and Internet aspects of interactive television.
- Advising on the use of the Internet transactions, the sale of products/services online and the underlying contracts.

Areas of expertise

Computer games	✓	Internet	✓
Digital TV		Litigation	
E-commerce	✓	Multimedia publishing	✓
'Hard' IT	✓	Telecoms	

Where to find a lawyer

Robb Klein
SJ Berwin & Co

Philip Krauss
Thomas Eggar Church Adams

Edward Lee
Linnells

Tony Leifer
DJ Freeman

Simon Leonard
Titmuss Sainer Dechert

Simon Levine
Denton Hall

Amanda Lewis
Berwin Leighton

Emyr Lewis
Morgan Cole

Mike Lindsey
Morgan Cole

Richard Lister
Freshfields

Jonathon Little
Kemp & Co

Jonathon Lloyd Jones
Linnells

Colin Long
Olswang

Shaun Lowde
Wiggin and Co

Mark Lubbock
Ashurst Morris Crisp

Morag Macdonald
Bird & Bird

Mary Anne Macharg
Robert Muckle

Michael Mahoney
Hammond Suddards

Steven Maier
Manches & Co

Renzo Marchini
Titmuss Sainer Dechert

Vanessa Marsland
Clifford Chance

Avril Martindale
Freshfields

Rosemary Martin-Jones
Nabarro Nathanson

Nick Mason
Edge Ellison

Alistair Maughan
Shaw Pittman

John Mawhood
Tarlo Lyons

Peter McBride
Nicholson Graham & Jones

Robert McCallough
Masons

Tom McGuire
Taylor Vinters

Liam McNeive
McNeive

Nicolas Mason

edge ellison

Marketing & media

18 Southampton Place, London WC1A 2AJ
Phone: 020 7400 7919
Fax: 020 7400 7997
Email: nickm@edge.co.uk

Qualified 1987, partner 1991. Specialises in intellectual property litigation (copyright, trade mark, passing off, design right), advertising clearance, Internet and e-commerce. Considerable experience of High Court commercial litigation, including search and seize orders, freezing assets and international disputes. Has given seminars on e-commerce, email policies and legal issues in advertising.

Recent work

- Acted for Defendant in *Matel Inc (1), JW Spear (2), v Aspect Internet*. One of the first domain name disputes.
- Advising high tech manufacturer in dispute over competitor trade marks in keyword lists on website.
- Advising major advertising agencies on numerous occasions in relation to design of websites for major international brands (health & beauty products, motor manufacturers, drinks & beverage conglomerates) – in particular, intellectual property issues.
- Advising new media development agency in relation to dispute with publishing house.

Areas of expertise

Computer games		Internet	✓
Digital TV		Litigation	✓
E-commerce	✓	Multimedia publishing	✓
'Hard' IT		Telecoms	

John Mawhood

Tarlo Lyons Solicitors

E-commerce & digital media group

Watchmaker Court, 33 St John's Lane, London EC1M 4DB
Phone: 020 7814 5433
Fax: 020 7814 9421
Email: jnm@tarlo-lyons.com

John advises clients internationally whose business involves the sale, purchase use and protection of all types of information systems and related technologies. He has advised on a wide range of transactions or disputes affecting IT purchasers and suppliers from global Year 2000 programs to global outsourcing; software protection, licensing and distribution, EC competition law, electronic commerce, broadcasting and telecommunications.

Recent work

- Advised a UK based financial institution on strategic software vendor issues relating to Internet use and pricing.
- Global penetration testing for a bank with internet business (testing system access of global networks).
- Advises numerous Internet based vendor companies for a range of services and markets.
- Worked on an Initial Public Offering for an Internet company on the UK market.

Areas of expertise

Computer games		Internet	✓
Digital TV	✓	Litigation	
E-commerce	✓	Multimedia publishing	✓
'Hard' IT	✓	Telecoms	✓

Iain Monaghan

Masons

Information & technology

30 Aylesbury Street, London EC1R 0ER
Phone: 020 7490 6239
Fax: 020 7490 2545
Email: iain.monaghan@masons.com

Iain has worked in commerce and IT for 20 years. A partner in Masons since 1983, Iain heads up the transactional side of Masons' I&T group in London. Particular expertise in the use of the web as a medium for the sale of financial products, procurement of IT in commercial and financial services, joint ventures for the exploitation of rights.

Recent work

- Advised bank on sales of financial products and other banking services on the internet.
- Advised supplier in connection with major public sector contract for e-commerce services.
- Advised issuer concerning the risks and liabilities arising from the issue of smartcards.
- Participated in two collaborative public/private sector projects designed to promote secure e-commerce in the City.
- Provided the legal input to EU study on the use of electronic tendering in a paneuropean procurement environment.
- Retained to provide legal services to consortium bidding to develop e-commerce legislation for a Far Eastern government.

Areas of expertise

Computer games		Internet	✓
Digital TV		Litigation	
E-commerce	✓	Multimedia publishing	
'Hard' IT	✓	Telecoms	✓

Mark Moncreiffe

Charles Russell Solicitors

Media & communications group

8-10 Fetter Lane, London EC4A 1RS
Phone: 020 7203 5113
Fax: 020 7203 0202
Email: markm@cr-law.co.uk

Qualified in 1978. Joined Charles Russell in 1984 and became a partner in 1985. Head of Charles Russell's media and communications group. His main area of specialisation is the corporate, commercial and regulatory aspects of communications, both in the UK and internationally.

Recent work

- Acquisition by WAM!NET Inc (a provider of high speed data transmission service) of 4-Sight Ltd. He acted for WAM!NET.
- Global strategic alliance between our client, National Telecommunications Ltd and Williams Communications Inc involving a range of long term commercial transactions relating to amongst other things the acquisiton and use of transatlantic cables and satellite capacity.
- Obtaining a provisional order under the Telecommunications Act 1984 from OFTEL against BT Talking Pages. We acted for Scoot.com plc.
- He has also acted for Scoot.com plc in relation to numerous corporate and commercial transactions.

Areas of expertise

Computer games		Internet	
Digital TV		Litigation	
E-commerce		Multimedia publishing	
'Hard' IT		Telecoms	✓

Suzanne Mercer
Eversheds

Christopher Millard
Clifford Chance

Iain Monaghan
Masons

Mark Moncreiffe
Charles Russell

Bill Moodie
Herbert Smith

Glyn Morgan
Taylor Joynson Garrett

Leon Morgan
Davenport Lyons

Tony Morris
Marriott Harrison

Jeremy Morton
Simmons & Simmons

Andrew Moyle
Shaw Pittman

Kenneth Mullen
Kemp & Co

David Naylor
Weil Gotshal & Manges

Jeremy Newton
Cameron McKenna

Kim Nicholson
Olswang

Fiona Nicolson
Maclay Murray & Spens

Dinah Nissen
Freshfields

Bernard Nyman
Manches & Co

Norman Oliver
Bird Semple

Alistair Orr
Maclay Murray & Spens

Tim Osborne
Wiggin and Co

Nigel Palmer
SJ Berwin & Co

Raj Parkash
Clifford Chance

Rex Parry
Eversheds

Jamie Pass
Dickinson Dees

Lawrence Phillips
Tarlo Lyons

Mark Phillips
Harbottle & Lewis

Claire Poll
Hobson Audley Hopkins & Wood

Alisdair Poore
Mills & Reeve

Selina Potter
Olswang

Daniel Preiskel
Rakisons

Tony Morris

Marriott Harrison

New media

12 Great James Street, London WC1N 3DR
Phone: 020 7209 2093
Fax: 020 7209 2001
Email: tony.morris@marriottharrison.co.uk

Recent work

- Generally retained by leading publishers of educational software and computer games, The Learning Company and Mindscape for UK/EU commercio-legal advice.
- Generally retained by many developers and publishers of commercial software including Asset Control (knowledge warehousing systems), Global Recall (document management systems) and Right Track Solutions (royalty tracking systems).
- Advised Eagle Rock Entertainment plc on its arrangements with Fantastic Corp for establishment of a Broadband television network scheduled for launch in January 2000.
- Advised on numerous e-commerce arrangements for exploitation of entertainment related products including compact discs, computer games and branded merchandise.
- Course director of the Interactive Media Business School, an initiative of the EU Media II programme.

Areas of expertise

Computer games	✓	Internet	✓
Digital TV		Litigation	✓
E-commerce	✓	Multimedia publishing	✓
'Hard' IT		Telecoms	

Jeremy Morton

Simmons & Simmons

Commercial & trade department/IP

21 Wilson Street, London EC2M 2TX
Phone: 020 7825 4140
Fax: 020 7628 2070
Email: jeremy.morton@simmon-simmons.com

Jeremy has been a solicitor with Simmons & Simmons since 1991 and in 1998 became a partner. He advises on contentious and non-contentious aspects of intellectual property and electronic commerce. His clients include service providers, network operators, web consultants and content providers in addition to more traditional businesses engaging in new e-commerce initiatives. He has also advised many clients on the implications of the new European data protection laws on their businesses. Jeremy combines a wide range of specialist legal skills with an understanding of the business issues fo- industry.

Recent work

- Advice on terms for the joint supply of broadband interactive services.
- Due diligence in proposed mergers and acquisitions concerning businesses such as ISP's and game providers.
- *Samsung v Fujitsu* (High Court patent action concerning DRAM's).
- Setting a US web company up in business in the UK.

Areas of expertise

Computer games	✓	Internet	✓
Digital TV		Litigation	✓
E-commerce	✓	Multimedia publishing	
'Hard' IT		Telecoms	

Kenneth Mullen

Kemp & Co

IT & multimedia

Saddlers House, Gutter Lane, London EC2V 6BR
Phone: 020 7710 1606
Fax: 020 7600 7878
Email: kennethm@comlegal.com

Kenneth joined the practice in January 1998 from McGrigor Donald in Glasgow. He also took his law degree and LLM in Glasgow (where he specialised in public law and competition law). He qualified as a solicitor in Scotland in 1995. Kenneth specialises in commercial, competition, intellectual property and regulatory law for computer and information industry clients.

Recent work

- Kenneth acts for Digital River Ltd, the UK subsidiary of Digital River Inc, the largest electronics software distributor.
- Acts for a range of growing Internet consultancy companies, including e technology associates and netdecisions.
- Acts on contract, content and rights clearance matters for a major software manufacturer.

Areas of expertise

Computer games	✓	Internet	✓
Digital TV		Litigation	
E-commerce	✓	Multimedia publishing	✓
'Hard' IT	✓	Telecoms	

Kim Nicholson

Olswang

90 Long Acre, London WC2E 9TT
Phone: 020 7208 8731
Fax: 020 7208 8800
Email: kan@olswang.co.uk

Kim has been a lawyer for 14 years and a partner at Olswang since March 1993 when she joined to establish and develop the firm's technology and telecoms practice. She now heads the e-commerce team and specialises in communications transactions in the online and telecoms industries. Her clients range from small start-ups raising their first tranche of venture capital through to fully listed organisations doing worldwide equity issues.

Recent work

Commercial arrangements for:

- Freeserve (content, joint ventures, licensing, exploitation)
- UUNet (liability and commercial infrastructure arrangements)
- Demon (carrier liability, network contracts)
- Pangolin (content purchasing and licensing)

Corporate:

- Whitaker (restructuring and disposal of publishing and multimedia business)
- Pangolin (venture capital funding)
- Head New Media (joint venture and recapitalisation)

Areas of expertise

Computer games	✓	Internet	✓
Digital TV		Litigation	
E-commerce	✓	Multimedia publishing	✓
'Hard' IT	✓	Telecoms	✓

Tim Osborne

Wiggin and Co

Media

The Quadrangle, Imperial Square, Cheltenham, Glos GL50 1YX
Phone: 01242 631203
Fax: 01242 224223
Email: two@wiggin.co.uk

Tim joined Wiggin and Co from Lovell White King in 1979 and became a partner in 1980. He is head of the firm's Media and Entertainment Group and was responsible for Wiggin and Co becoming involved in the media sector.

Areas of expertise

Computer games		Internet	
Digital TV	✓	Litigation	
E-commerce		Multimedia publishing	
'Hard' IT		Telecoms	✓

Mark Phillips

Harbottle & Lewis

New media & interactive entertainment

Hanover House, 14 Hanover Square, London W1R 0BE
Phone: 020 7667 5000
Fax: 020 7667 5100
Email: mphillips@harbottle.co.uk

Head of new media and interactive entertainment group. Deals with all commercial and corporate concerns of clients ranging from small online start-ups to leading US, European and Japanese software publishers, development houses, portals, service and content providers and e-commerce businesses.

Recent work

- Publishing, distribution, licensing, joint venture and marketing arrangements for leading industry businesses.
- Key industry acquisitions by several NASDAQ quoted companies and management buy out of international publisher.
- Dealing with regulatory authorities in respect of a 'banned' video game.
- Advising NASDAQ digital entertainment company regarding online auction business.
- Exploitation of innovative video imaging technology by Israeli development company.
- Commercial development of EU funded consortium project relating to online rights exploitation.

Areas of expertise

Computer games	✓	Internet	✓
Digital TV	✓	Litigation	
E-commerce	✓	Multimedia publishing	✓
'Hard' IT		Telecoms	

Mark Prinsley

Rowe & Maw

IP/IT

20 Black Friars Lane, London EC4V 6HD

Phone: 020 7248 4282

Fax: 020 7248 2009

Email: mprinsley@roweandmaw.co.uk

Partner in Rowe & Maw since 1987 and has practised exclusively in the area of information technology and intellectual property since qualification.

Recent work

- Acting for Cable & Wireless Communications plc in the outsourcing of much of its IT functions to IBM – the biggest outsource done by IBM outside the USA.
- Acting for the Tradition Group of companies in *Cantor Fitzgerald v Tradition & Others.*
- Work for internet businesses such as Vignette Corporation & Netgravity on licensing e-commerce solutions, data protection and related e-commerce issues.

Areas of expertise

Computer games	✓	Internet	✓
Digital TV	✓	Litigation	✓
E-commerce	✓	Multimedia publishing	✓
'Hard' IT	✓	Telecoms	✓

Christine Reid

Manches

IT group

3 Worcester Street, Oxford

Phone: 01865 813604

Fax: 01865 201012

Email: christine.reid@manches.co.uk

Christine read Classics at St Hilda's College, Oxford, trained with Morrell, Peel & Gamlen, became a partner in that firm in 1986 and a partner in Manches when the two firms merged in 1997. Specialised in IT work since the early 1980s, advising multi-national organisations on IT procurement, intellectual property rights, software licensing and development, oursourcing, consultancy, the Internet and agency and distribution.

Recent work

- Facilities management arrangements for global investment manager.
- Advising a multi-national company on the legal risks associated with its product development.
- The development of foreign exchange and trading systems.
- Terms and conditions for Internet service providers, IT consultancies, online data providers, software developers and software distributors.
- Value added reseller agreements for a major international systems integrator.
- Information security and acceptable use policies.

Areas of expertise

Computer games	✓	Internet	✓
Digital TV		Litigation	
E-commerce	✓	Multimedia publishing	✓
'Hard' IT	✓	Telecoms	

Paul Renney

Theodore Goddard

Media & entertainment

150 Aldersgate Street, London EC1A 4EJ
Phone: 020 7606 8855
Fax: 020 7606 4390
Email: paulrenney@theodoregoddard.co.uk

Partner in Theodore Goddard's Entertainment group since 1997 and joint head of e-commerce group. Paul's experience was initially in advising clients operating in the music business and this extended to advising clients on corporate media acquisitions and disposals. In addition he advises on IP rights generally and especially on commercial arrangements relating to the theatre, magazine and book publishing businesses and on promotions. He advises on all commercial arrangements and acquiring and exploiting IP rights for clients in the entertainment industries and on all matters relating to data protection.

Recent work

- Advising on an online shopping mall.
- Advising a free-access Internet provider on all legal arrangements for their site.
- Advising a software development house on website design and maintenance arrangements.
- Advising a new sports venture for online retailing.

Areas of expertise

Computer games		Internet	✓
Digital TV		Litigation	
E-commerce	✓	Multimedia publishing	✓
'Hard' IT		Telecoms	

Andrew Rigby

Tarlo Lyons Solicitors

E-commerce & digital media

Watchmaker Court, 33 St John's Lane, London EC1M 4DB
Phone: 020 7814 5456
Fax: 020 7814 9421
Email: adr@tarlo-lyons.com

Andrew heads the e-commerce & digital media group. He acts for a number of global businesses and advises them on all aspects of Internet and e-commerce law. Andrew provides regular legal comments for the legal press and speaks regularly at UK and International Conferences. He has been asked to co-ordinate the legal section and speak at the E-Commerce Summit in Rome in October 1999.

Recent work

- Appointed as the e-commerce & digital media lawyer for an international bank, for whom he has previously given advice on the development of a global online banking service. He has also provided advice on data protection and transborder data flows, digital signatures and cryptography and regulatory issues.
- Acting for a new venture setting up an online web based real time video and audio subscription channel.
- Advising a TV and film music publisher on an interactive website providing audio streaming and downloading of music.

Areas of expertise

Computer games		Internet	✓
Digital TV	✓	Litigation	
E-commerce	✓	Multimedia publishing	✓
'Hard' IT	✓	Telecoms	✓

Mark Prinsley
Rowe & Maw

Mike Rebeiro
Slaughter and May

Christine Reid
Manches & Co

Simon Rendell
Osborne Clarke

Paul Renney
Theodore Goddard

Andrew Rigby
Tarlo Lyons

Jonathan Riley
Lawrence Graham

Lisa Roberts
Bristows

Robert Roper
Cobbetts

Adam Rose
Paisner & Co

Nick Rose
Field Fisher Waterhouse

Heather Rowe
Lovell White Durrant

Howard Rubin
Bird & Bird

John Rubinstein
Manches & Co

Ian Sampson
Addleshaw Booth & Co

Paul Sampson
Eversheds

Daniel Sandelson
Clifford Chance

Kiran Sandford
Taylor Joynson Garrett

Alison Sarsfield-Hall
Morgan Cole

Sarah Sasse
Wragge & Co

Joss Saunders
Linnells

Clive Seddon
Masons

Arnold Segal
Theodore Goddard

Chris Shelley
Manches & Co

Scott Singer
Sinclair Roche & Temperley

Harry Small
Baker & McKenzie

Graham Smith
Bird & Bird

Quentin Solt
Berwin Leighton

Andrew Somper
Berwin Leighton

Julian Stait
Dibb Lupton Alsop

Heather Rowe

Lovell White Durrant

Computers, communications and media

65 Holborn Viaduct, London EC1A 2DY
Phone: 020 7236 0066 **Fax:** 020 7248 4212
Email: heather.rowe@lovellwhitedurrant.com

Heather, a former banking lawyer, specialised for many years in non contentious telecommunications and IT advice, particularly for the financial services sector.

Heather is now a partner in the firm's Computers, Communications and Media Unit specialising in telecommunications, the Internet, and all aspects of electronic commerce. She is Co-Chairman of Committee R of the International Bar Association (International Computers and Technology Law) and Chairman of the International Chamber of Commerce, UK, Commission on Telecommunications and IT.

Recent work

- Advising a major UK clearing bank on the establishment of Internet portal services.
- Advising two UK clearing banks in relation to online banking products.
- Advising corporate clients on information security policies and email guidelines.
- Advising a number of financial institutions on PKI projects.
- Advising multinational companies on the legal implications of the new Data Protection Act 1998.

Areas of expertise

Computer games		Internet	✓
Digital TV		Litigation	
E-commerce	✓	Multimedia publishing	✓
'Hard' IT		Telecoms	✓

Alison Sarsfield-Hall

Morgan Cole

Business services

3 West Way, Buxton Court, Oxford OX2 0SZ
Phone: 01865 262600
Fax: 01865 721367
Email: alison.sarsfield-hall@morgan-cole.com

Alison Sarsfield-Hall is an Oxford-based partner and she is head of the firm's intellectual property law group, of which digital media is a part.

Alison has a special interest in IT law and advises a range of computer companies, including developers, distributors and maintenance companies on all aspects of their business, particularly development and licensing agreements and issues surrounding the Year 2000 and e-commerce.

Recent work

- Drafting Internet and email security issues.
- Advising on UK and European law and their impact on commercial contracts.
- Advising a wide range of clients from individuals to multi-national corporations, educational establishments, NHS trusts and research authorities.
- Identifying and protection of IP, including trade mark, patent and design right registration, the commercialisation of such rights by way of licensing or assignment and enforcement of the rights.

Areas of expertise

Computer games	✓	Internet	✓
Digital TV	✓	Litigation	✓
E-commerce	✓	Multimedia publishing	✓
'Hard' IT	✓	Telecoms	✓

Kiran Sandford

Taylor Joynson Garrett

IT/Telecoms group

Carmelite, 50 Victoria Embankment,
Blackfriars, London EC4Y 0DX
Phone: 020 7353 1234
Fax: 020 7936 2666
Email: ksandford@tjg.co.uk

Partner in IT/Telecoms group specialising in all types of computer, communications and technology law, including licensing, software development, computer games and strategic alliances. Main areas of work are in IT and Telecommunications.

Recent work

- Advised Eidos plc in relation to their subscription free access to online Internet service in conjunction with Easynet.
- Also advised Eidos plc on the intellectual property aspects of its publishing deal with Michael Crichton's Timeline Studios. The agreement is a long term deal for Eidos plc to publish games based on material written by Crichton.

Areas of expertise

Computer games	✓	Internet	✓
Digital TV	✓	Litigation	✓
E-commerce	✓	Multimedia publishing	✓
'Hard' IT	✓	Telecoms	✓

Arnold Segal

Theodore Goddard

Corporate rescue & IT

150 Aldersgate Street, London EC1A 4EJ
Phone: 020 7606 8855
Fax: 020 7606 4390
Email: arnoldsegal@theodoregoddard.co.uk

Head of Theodore Goddard's IT law group and acknowledged as a leading IT lawyer. Arnold was in-house counsel for five years and has been advising and negotiating in the IT field for over 20 years. He has extensive experience in a wide range of IT and related issues.

Recent work

- Advising Computacenter's intelligent e-business solutions division on its proposed contract with Intertrust Corp.
- Advising Pilot Network Services on UK and European issues relating to dynamically secure Internet services.
- Advising a major publisher on computer games hotlinking issues.
- Negotiating numerous IT-related contracts.

Areas of expertise

Computer games	✓	Internet	✓
Digital TV		Litigation	
E-commerce	✓	Multimedia publishing	✓
'Hard' IT	✓	Telecoms	

Harry Small

Baker & McKenzie

IT/Communications department

100 New Bridge Street, London EC4V 6JA

Phone: 020 7919 1914

Fax: 020 7919 1999

Email: harry.small@bakernet.com

Harry Small qualified at Linklaters & Paines in 1981, working in the IT Group there. He transferred to Baker & McKenzie in 1986, becoming a partner in 1989. He specialises in IT, convergence and IP.

Recent work

Recent projects involving online services include:

- Advising palmtop computer operating system provider on contracts with handset manufacturers, to provide bandwidth to the new generation of handheld devices;
- Advising major car rental company on setting up of web-based Europe-wide trading system;
- Advising trusted third party on liability for certificates.

Areas of expertise

Computer games		Internet	✓
Digital TV		Litigation	
E-commerce	✓	Multimedia publishing	
'Hard' IT	✓	Telecoms	✓

Quentin Solt

Berwin Leighton

Information & communications technology and corporate finance specialist

Adelaide House, London Bridge, London EC4R 9HA

Phone: 020 7760 4203

Fax: 020 7760 1111

Email: quentin.solt@berwinleighton.com

Quentin joined Berwin Leighton as a solicitor in 1990 and has been a partner since 1997. He leads the ICT group of IP, IT, commercial, employment, tax, litigation and corporate finance lawyers.

As well as acting as an 'advising angel' to a number of high profile entrepreneurs' networking groups, he is editor of Sweet & Maxwell's *Commercial Transaction Checklists* and contributes specialist sections of the leading loose-leaf publication, *Company Directors: Law and Liability.*

Recent work

- LineOne ISP and portal joint venture.
- Sale of Bookpages, the UK based Internet bookstore, to Amazon.com.
- $10.4m joint venture between Harnischfeger Industries, Inc and SI Technologies.
- Micro Focus Group Plc's $534m merger with Intersolv Inc to form Merant.
- Incorporation and funding advice to emergent companies.

Areas of expertise

Computer games		Internet	✓
Digital TV	✓	Litigation	
E-commerce	✓	Multimedia publishing	
'Hard' IT	✓	Telecoms	

Nigel Stamp

Baker & McKenzie

IT/Communications department

100 New Bridge Street, London EC4V 6JA

Phone: 0171 919 1979

Fax: 0171 919 1999

Email: nigel.stamp@bakernet.com

Nigel is an information and communications technology lawyer specialising in digital interactive television services, the Internet and other online services, electronic commerce and other new media and technology. Before qualifying as a solicitor, Nigel worked for ten years in the IT industry. He joined Baker & McKenzie in Hong Kong in 1995 and transferred to the London office in 1997.

Recent work

- Five months secondment at NTL advising and assisting in particular with the launch of its digital interactive services project including the drafting and negotiation of agreements with content partners for that service.
- Advising a major telecommunications provider in Hong Kong on the launch of its own ISP service and the launch of its digital interactive television service including drafting and negotiating technology, content and operational agreements for these services.

Areas of expertise

Computer games	✓	Internet	✓
Digital TV	✓	Litigation	
E-commerce	✓	Multimedia publishing	✓
'Hard' IT	✓	Telecoms	✓

Peter Stevens

Manches

IT group

Aldwych House, 81 Aldwych, London WC2B 4RP

Phone: 020 7404 4433

Fax: 020 7430 1133

Email: peter.stevens@manches.co.uk

Commercial partner specialising in IT/IP and all aspects of Internet/e-commerce. Trained at Allison & Humphreys, joined Rubinstein Callingham on qualifying in 1979, became a partner there in 1983 and in Manches on merger in 1994. Associate of the Institute of Taxation 1986.

Recent work

- Advising on creation and development of e-shopping site for leading department store.
- Advising on establishment of portal sites.
- Advising Lloyds underwriters on Internet insurance policy wardings.
- Advising photographic agencies on licensing stock photographs over Internet.
- Terms and conditions for web hosting.
- Computer games contracts for leading publisher quoted on Stock Exchange.
- Data protection issues affecting major US suppliers of software over the Internet.

Areas of expertise

Computer games	✓	Internet	✓
Digital TV		Litigation	
E-commerce	✓	Multimedia publishing	✓
'Hard' IT	✓	Telecoms	

Nigel Stamp
Baker & McKenzie

Iain Stansfield
Hobson Audley Hopkins & Wood

Paul Stevens
Olswang

Peter Stevens
Manches & Co

Robert Stoker
Addleshaw Booth & Co

Peter Strivens
Baker & McKenzie

Nigel Swycher
Slaughter and May

Richard Talbot
Nicholson Graham & Jones

Trystan Tether
Bird & Bird

David Tighe
Manches & Co

Victor Timon
Olswang

Simon Tracey
Titmuss Sainer Dechert

Mark Turner
Herbert Smith

Lucy Vernall
Kemp & Co

Toni Vitale
Cylde & Co

Gerald Wakefield
Rakisons

Kim Walker
Biddle

Simon Walker
Taylor Joynson Garrett

Justin Walkey
Bird & Bird

Conor Ward
Lovell White Durrant

James Ware
Davenport Lyons

Matthew Warren
Bristows

Christopher Watson
Simmons & Simmons

Michael Webster
Rowe & Maw

Robert Wegenek
Edge Ellison

Hugh Welch
Robert Muckle

Nicholas West
Denton Hall

Philip Westmacott
Bristows

Robin Whaite
Linklaters

Tom Wheadon
Simmons & Simmons

Victor Timon

Olswang

90 Long Acre, London WC2E 9TT
Phone: 020 7208 8744
Fax: 020 7208 8800
Email: vwt@olswang.co.uk

Victor has been a lawyer for 17 years and a partner at Olswang since April 1995 when he joined the firm's technology and telecommunications practice. He is a member of the e-commerce team and focuses on communications transactions involving the online and telecoms industries, and in particular, in the areas of portals and interactive television. His clients include some of the most innovative players in e-commerce.

Recent work

E-commerce projects:

- Freeserve (content, joint ventures, licensing, exploitation)
- Pangolin (sports content purchasing and licensing)
- Open (content)
- BBC Worldwide (beeb.com, access)
- MARS (content, licensing)
- Telstar (content, licensing)
- Carphone Warehouse (website development)
- Trinity International Holdings (content development, licensing, hosting)

Areas of expertise

Computer games	✓	Internet	✓
Digital TV		Litigation	
E-commerce	✓	Multimedia publishing	✓
'Hard' IT	✓	Telecoms	✓

Toni Vitale

Clyde & Co

Business law group

51 Eastcheap, London EC3M 1JP
Phone: 020 7623 1244
Fax: 020 7623 5427
Email: toni.vitale@clyde.co.uk

Toni Vitale qualified in 1990 and joined Clyde & Co in January 1999 as a senior assistant in the corporate group. He has particular experience of media law, advertising, broadcasting and branding. He has negotiated and many commercial agreements relating to business acquisitions, disposals, management and corporate recoveries. He has particular experience in outsourcing and has worked on a number of PFI projects.

Recent work

- Advised extensively on software and hardware procurement licensing and outsourcing.
- Advised extensively on electronic information, e-commerce, EDI, databases and related Internet/technology issues, as well as data protection.
- Experience of trade marks and branding issues.
- Advised in merchandising and franchising.
- Handled passing off interlocutory injunctions.
- Assisted in a major patent damages inquiry and handled other trade mark, copyright and media related disputes.

Areas of expertise

Computer games	✓	Internet	✓
Digital TV	✓	Litigation	✓
E-commerce	✓	Multimedia publishing	✓
'Hard' IT	✓	Telecoms	✓

Kim Walker

Biddle

Media & publishing group

1 Gresham Street, London EC2V 7BU
Phone: 020 7606 9301
Fax: 020 7606 3305
Email: Kim.Walker@Biddle.co.uk

Partner specialising in commercial work involving intellectual property, IT and new media. Acts for individuals and companies on specialist contracts, joint ventures, use of the internet, online services and content regulation, data protection and licensing.

Recent work

- Advising ITN and ITN Archive on Internet issues, including website disclaimer wording, content regulation, rights to use under 'fair dealing' and online terms and conditions for the ordering of footage.
- Advising Storage Technology Inc (StorageTek) on the Data Protection Act 1998.
- Acting for The Associated Press and The Press Association on various internet-related matters.
- CD-Rom publishing and development agreements for Bertelsmann and others.
- Preparing and negotiating supply and licensing agreements for the use of content in third party websites.

Areas of expertise

Computer games	✓	Internet	✓
Digital TV	✓	Litigation	
E-commerce	✓	Multimedia publishing	✓
'Hard' IT	✓	Telecoms	

Simon Walker

Taylor Joynson Garrett

IT/Telecoms group

Carmelite, 50 Victoria Embankment,
Blackfriars, London EC4Y 0DX
Phone: 020 7353 1234
Fax: 020 7936 2666
Email: swalker@tjg.co.uk

Simon deals in all aspects of corporate finance, specialising in flotations, public and private company takeovers and joint ventures, in particular in the information technology and bio-technology sectors.

Recent work

- Client partner for Eidos plc, one of the world's leading developers and publishers of interactive entertainment, acting on various transactions including the purchase of Crystal Dynamics Inc for £28.5m.
- Advised the consortium of investors Amadeus I, Amadeus I Affiliates Fund LP, Gilde IT Fund and 3i Group plc that have committed to provide investment backing of up to $10m to Cambridge Silicon Radio, the first company to market the 'radio chip,' the vital component of tomorrow's wire-free world.

Areas of expertise

Computer games	✓	Internet	✓
Digital TV	✓	Litigation	
E-commerce	✓	Multimedia publishing	✓
'Hard' IT	✓	Telecoms	✓

Chris Watson

Simmons & Simmons

Communications Practice

21 Wilson Street, London EC2M 2TX

Phone: 020 7825 4735

Fax: 020 7628 2070

Email: chris.watson@simmon-simmons.com

Chris joined Simmons & Simmons in 1981 and became a partner in 1989. He specialises in commercial, administrative, regulatory and EEC law. Chris opened and ran the Paris office for seven years before becoming acting head of Regulatory and Legal Affairs at General Cable plc for eight months in 1995. Chris is a qualified avocat á la cour and a member of the International Bar Association.

Recent work

- Advice to Merrill Lynch and CSFB on Spanish and EU telecoms regulation for Jazztel high yield funding.
- Called as an expert before Irish court on comparative study of licensing procedures in several EU countries.
- Successful judicial review of OFTEL/DTI on publication of MMC report into prices of calls to mobiles based on EU and competition arguments.
- Multi-country advice on acquisition by client GTS of Esprit Telecom.
- Leading in the creation of a multi-national International Communications Law Group throughout Europe.

Areas of expertise

Computer games		Internet	
Digital TV	✓	Litigation	✓
E-commerce	✓	Multimedia publishing	
'Hard' IT		Telecoms	✓

Michael Webster

Rowe & Maw

IT & communications group

20 Black Friars Lane, London EC4V 6HD

Phone: 020 7782 8862

Fax: 020 7248 2009

Email: mwebster@roweandmaw.co.uk

Partner since 1973. Core experience in corporate finance including venture capital investments, acquisitions and disposals, reconstructions and joint ventures and a full range of commercial agreements for and with the IT, telecoms and the electronic publishing sectors. He advises on software and systems procurement, licensing and distribution and on IT and telecoms outsourcing.

Founder member of the Computer Law Group and member of the Worshipful Company of Information Technologists.

Recent work

- E-commerce software development procurement arrangements for HMV from IBM.
- Standard conditions of website supply.
- Turnkey IT and systems procurement contracts advice for the Pensions Trust and M&G.
- Outsourcing of IT and telecoms facilities viz Cable & Wireless Communications outsourcing to IBM.
- Advising various publishing companies on their migration into electronic publishing.
- Financing and refinancing of companies in these market sectors.

Areas of expertise

Computer games		Internet	✓
Digital TV		Litigation	
E-commerce	✓	Multimedia publishing	✓
'Hard' IT	✓	Telecoms	✓

Robert Wegenek

edge ellison

Marketing & media

18 Southampton Place, London WC1A 2AJ

Phone: 020 7400 7934

Fax: 020 7400 1636

Email: robert.wegenek@edge.co.uk

A background based on high profile advertising and marketing client base led to some of the earliest opportunities to explore the legal issues involved in Internet usage. Continues as an advertising and content specialist but also acts for a number of other household names, particularly in the retail sector.

Recent work

- Vetting legal content of websites operated in respect of a number of household names.
- Advising on a series of joint ventures between creative agencies and website producers.
- Acting for a large number of specialist developers of websites.
- Advising on e-commerce strategies, from FTSE 100 companies down to new business start-ups.
- Clients in this sector include WPP Group plc, B&Q plc, The Football League, Bartle Bogle Hegarty, Mindshare Digital, Clever Media, OgilvyOne Interactive.

Areas of expertise

Computer games		Internet	✓
Digital TV		Litigation	
E-commerce	✓	Multimedia publishing	✓
'Hard' IT		Telecoms	

Robin Whaite

Linklaters & Alliance

Intellectual property & technology

One Silk Street, London EC2Y 8HQ

Phone: 020 7456 2000

Fax: 020 7456 2222

Email: rwhaite@linklaters.com

Robin joined Linklaters & Paines, a member firm of Linklaters & Alliance, in 1986 and became a partner with the firm's Intellectual Property and Technology department in 1989.

He represents a wide range of clients in the IT and multi-media sectors and other high-tech areas, from start-up companies to leading multi-nationals.

Robin is a committee member of the IP Lawyers Association, and he also represents the British Chamber of Commerce on the UK Government's Standing Advisory Committee on IP. He speaks and writes widely on IT and IP subjects, and is on the editorial board of *Managing Intellectual Property.*

Recent work

- Handling the IT aspects of the flotation of a software company.
- Major outsourcing transactions.
- A number of IT joint ventures.
- Patent disputes in the multi-media field.
- A number of software development disputes.
- Various electronic publishing and e-commerce deals.

Areas of expertise

Computer games		Internet	✓
Digital TV		Litigation	✓
E-commerce	✓	Multimedia publishing	✓
'Hard' IT	✓	Telecoms	

Tom Wheadon

Simmons & Simmons

Communications Practice

21 Wilson Street, London EC2M 2TX

Phone: 020 7825 3603

Fax: 020 7628 2070

Email: tom.wheadon@simmon-simmons.com

Tom is a partner in the Communications Practice. He has a specialisation in the law, regulation and policy of telecommunications and is regarded as a leading individual in the field. The 1997 edition of *Chambers & Partners Guide to the Legal Profession* described Tom as one of the 25 best business lawyers in the UK.

Recent work

- Advising a major Internet company on a cross-border data flow agreement involving consideration of the international and regional and framework for data protection.
- Advising one of the largest Internet service providers in connection with trading, regulatory and licensing issues.
- At the request of OFTEL set up the Service Providers Interest Group (SPIG) and subsequently a European Service Providers Interest Group (ESPIG) and regularly attends meetings.

Areas of expertise

Computer games		Internet	✓
Digital TV	✓	Litigation	
E-commerce	✓	Multimedia publishing	✓
'Hard' IT	✓	Telecoms	✓

Alistair Wilson

Travers Smith Braithwaite

Commercial group

Snow Hill, London, EC1A 2AL

Phone: 020 7248 9133

Fax: 020 7236 3728

Email: Alistair.Wilson@TraversSmith.co.uk

Partner in the commercial group (which deals with IT, IP, competition and joint ventures/strategic alliances). Previously a senior legal adviser at Unilever plc and then a partner with Manches & Co. His experience includes extensive IT work including outsourcing, licensing, development agreements, software and hardware acquisition, computer games and data protection.

Recent work

- Development agreement for an intranet based training program for a major bank.
- Financial services regulation and design of compliant websites.
- Agreement for a digital online banking service.
- Joint venture to set up a web-based learning product.
- Sale of a web-based publisher including relevant domain names
- Contract for website design and hosting.
- Sale of Internet service provider.
- Internet trading agreements including linking and referral/commission agreements.

Areas of expertise

Computer games	✓	Internet	✓
Digital TV		Litigation	
E-commerce	✓	Mult media publishing	✓
'Hard' IT	✓	Telecoms	

John Worthy

Denton Hall

Media, information & technology group

Five Chancery Lane, Clifford's Inn, London
EC4A 1BU

Phone: 020 7320 6354

Fax: 020 7320 6470

Email: jnw@dentonhall.com

John is a partner in the media, information and technology group and a leading adviser in e-commerce. In recent years he has worked with a range of large commercial organisations including financial institutions, online retailers, publishing houses and internet service providers on the setting up of their electronic business operations. With an understanding of the convergent information technology and telecommunications worlds, John has worked on ground-breaking projects advising on internet transactions, encryption issues, data protection and a range of regulatory issues.

Recent work

- Advising major European and US banks on their electronic banking operations.
- Advising Europay International SA on its agreements with Mastercard.
- Advising a leading insurance broker on its online broking services.
- Advising on the launch of a major internet bookshop.

Areas of expertise

Computer games		Internet	✓
Digital TV		Litigation	
E-commerce	✓	Multimedia publishing	
'Hard' IT	✓	Telecoms	✓

Stuart Whitfield
Bevan Ashford

James Wilders
Dickinson Dees

Nigel Wildish
Field Fisher Waterhouse

Alan Williams
Denton Hall

Alistair Wilson
Travers Smith Braithwaite

Ashley Winton
Osborne Clarke

Graham Wood
Cobbetts

David Woods
Eversheds

Paul Woolf
Manches & Co

John Worthy
Denton Hall

Clare Wright
Allen & Overy

John Yates
Oxley & Coward

Ian Yonge
Manches & Co

Stephen York
Hammond Suddards

David Zeffman
Olswang

key contacts

Appendix

Law firm website addresses

Addleshaw Booth & Co
www.addleshaw-booth.co.uk

Allen & Overy
www.allenovery.com

Ashurst Morris
www.ashursts.co.uk

Baker & McKenzie
www.bakerinfo.com

Berwin Leighton
www.berwinleighton.com

Bevan Ashford
www.bevanashford.co.uk

Biddle
www.biddle.co.uk

Bindman & Partners
No website, according to the switchboard

Bird & Bird
www.twobirds.com

Bird Semple
www.birdsemple.co.uk

Briffa & Co
www.briffa.com

Bristows
www.bristows.com

Brobeck Hale and Dorr
www.bhd.com

Cameron McKenna
www.mckenna.co.uk

Charles Russell
www.charlesrussell.co.uk
or www.cr-law.co.uk

Clark Holt
www.clarkholt.co.uk

Clifford Chance
www.cliffordchance.com

Cobbetts
No website

Davenport Lyons
www.davenportlyons.com

Davies Arnold Cooper
No website

Denton Hall
www.dentonhall.com
or www.dentonhall.co.uk

Dibb Lupton Alsop
www.dibbluptonalsop.co.uk
or www.dla-law.co.uk

Dickinson Dees
www.dickinson-dees.com

DJ Freeman
www.djfreeman.co.uk

Donne Mileham & Haddock
www.dmh.co.uk

Edge Ellison
www.edge.co.uk

Eversheds
www.eversheds.co.uk

Field Fisher Waterhouse
www.ffwlaw.com

Freshfields
www.freshfields.com

Garretts
www.arthurandersen.com

Hamiltons
www.btInternet.com/~hamiltons/

Hammond Suddards
www.hammondsuddards.co.uk

Harbottle & Lewis
www.harbottle.co.uk

Henry Hepworth
No website

Herbert Smith
www.herbertsmith.com

Hobson Audley Hopkins & Wood
www.hobsonaudley.co.uk

Keeble Hawson Moorhouse
www.keeblehawson.co.uk

Kemp & Co
www.comlegal.com

Lawrence Graham
www.lawgram.com

Ledingham Chalmers
www.ledingham-chalmers.co.uk

Linklaters & Alliance
www.linklaters.com

Linnells
www.linnells.co.uk Under construction.

Lovell White
www.lovellwhitedurrant.com

Maclay Murray & Spens
www.maclaymurrayspens.co.uk

MacRoberts
www.macroberts.co.uk

Manches & Co
www.manches.co.uk

Marriott Harrison
www.marriottharrison.com

Masons
www.masons.com

McNeive
www.mcneive.com

Mills & Reeve
www.mills-reeve.com

Morgan Cole
www.morgan-cole.com

Nabarro Nathanson
www.nabarro.co.uk

Nicholson Graham & Jones
www.ngj.co.uk

Norton Rose
www.nortonrose.com

Olswang
www.olswang.co.uk

Osborne Clarke
www.osborneclarke.com

Oxley & Coward
www.oxcow.co.uk

Paisner & Co
www.paisner.co.uk

Rakisons
www.rakisons.co.uk

Robert Muckle
www.robertmuckle.co.uk

Rowe & Maw
www.roweandmaw.co.uk

Shaw Pittman
www.shawpittman.com

Sidley & Austin
www.sidley.com

Simmons & Simmons
www.simmons-simmons.com

Sinclair Roche & Temperley
www.sinclair-roche.com

SJ Berwin & Co
www.sjberwin.com

Slaughter and May
www.slaughterandmay.com

Tarlo Lyons
www.tarlo-lyons.co.uk

Taylor Joynson Garrett
www.tjg.co.uk

Taylor Vinters
www.taylor-vinters.co.uk

Theodore Goddard
www.theodoregoddard.com

Thomas Eggar Church Adams
www.teca.co.uk

Titmuss Sainer Dechert
www.titmuss-sainer-dechert.com

Travers Smith Braithwaite
www.traverssmith.co.uk

Walker Morris
www.walkermorris.co.uk

Weil Gotshal & Manges
www.weil.com

Wiggin and Co
www.wiggin.co.uk

Willoughby & Partners (Rouse & Co International
www.iprights.com

Wragge & Co
www.wragge.co.uk

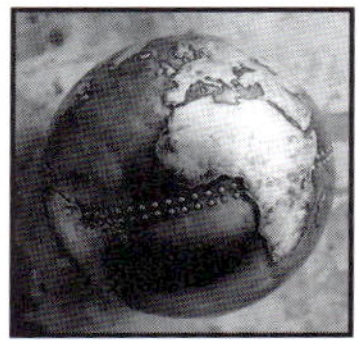

Index

Index

Index

Index

Index

Index

Index

Index

Index

Index

Contents

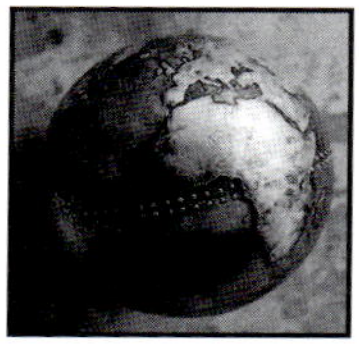

Foreword

Introduction by Dr Nick Palmer MP

Foreword by Dr Nick Palmer MP

The rise of the Internet has brought together three types of people who normally studiously ignore each other: technofreaks, politicians and lawyers. Like a party hosted by an office colleague who insists on making you meet all his ghastly friends from other parts of his life, the Internet makes it essential that each of this wildly disparate groups understands the others.

As a politician (and secretary of the all-party Internet group in Parliament) and ex-technofreak (my last pre-election job was Internet manager for Novartis, a Swiss-based multinational), I was keen to complete the set by talking to lawyers, and this guide provides an ideal introduction to the specialists in the area. The launch of the Government's new e-commerce Bill makes it even more topical and timely.

As the e-commerce tidal wave crests, it would be natural to ask whether we can't just pull the sheet over our heads and hope the thing will go away. If you run a factory producing mock-Edwardian wine glasses, for instance, do you really need or expect customers in Bogota or Shanghai, and should you care if you miss out on the Internet market altogether?

The answer is, I'm afraid, a very clear 'Yes'. At the moment, the Internet merely presents itself as an opportunity: hundreds of millions of potential customers out there who can reach you with no advertising expenditure needed. It will rather soon become a commercial necessity: hundred of millions of potential customers who will refuse to buy from you if you don't have an e-commerce option. This is already starting to happen in the USA, and in technological areas the Americans are usually an accurate guide to our own future. Quite soon, not offering your products and services via the Internet is going to seem charmingly archaic, like refusing to have a fax or insisting that your company's phone number should be ex-directory. A bit further down the line, it will stop seeming charming and simply label you as out of touch.

Enter the politicians. The e-commerce Bill is needed to make possible e-sales on a large scale. First, it seeks to define exactly what an 'electronic signature' is, so that contracts can be agreed over the Internet without the farcical extra requirement that the people post each other letters with their illegible scrawl at the bottom. This is widely agreed to be a good idea, and although there may be quibbles over the precise approach it's basically non-controversial. Not so the rules on encryrption.

To summarise the argument on this: commercial partners often want encryption of transactions. It is technically possible to make these virtually impossible to break with any known technique. This sounds a good thing too, but not to law enforcement bodies, who are less than enthusiastic about the Mafia having channels of communication unreadable by anyone else. So perhaps we need 'trusted third parties', who will keep encryption details secretly registered, only to be revealed on order from a judge, like a search warrant? But how much do you really trust a third party to lock up all your secrets? A criminal infiltrating the 'trusted party' could gain access to a vast range of commercial data. As I write, the debate is still continuing.

Enter the lawyers. The Internet suddenly makes your products and services available around the globe. But this means (perhaps) that you have to obey every law and regulation on the planet. Do your product labels fulfil the requirements in Germany? Does your advertising offend the sensibilities of consumers in Singapore? Have you infringed the copyright of an unsuspected rival in Canada? Worried?

In fact, the likelihood of your being successfully sued by a Canadian company or As in medicine, so in law: prevention is better than cure. Taking timely advice to find out what the risks to you might be is infinitely better (and much, much cheaper) than picking up the phone to your lawyers when it all goes horribly wrong. Chances are it might even be too late for them to recover the situation. I wouldn't necessarily endorse every recommendation lawyers have to give: in particular, I have yet to see the company which even tries to implement the suggestion that every email be checked by a responsible authorised officer before dispatch. But taking good advice from recognised experts in the field – something the exhaustive research in this guide can help you identify – is an excellent investment in these times of uncertainty.

I'll conclude with a final example of the way in which the Internet can hit you unawares. I was contacted by an elderly couple in Beeston in my constituency who were persistently being woken up by people eager to engage in telephone sex. After hanging up a few times, they paused for long enough to ask the next caller what made him think that they were likely partners. It turned out that an American website had been advertising a sex line based in Guyana (whose rules for these matters are not as strict as you and I might wish). From America, the Guyanan number was 0115925... However, as websites are equally accessible from Britain, overheated British teenagers were looking at the alluring people on the site and reaching for the phone, and if you ring 0115925... in Britain, you will get not Guyana but Beeston. I solved the problem with a polite email to the vendors, pointing out that they were losing business, since my constituents were not minded to pay them for the privilege of getting their calls. The next day, the website had separate instructions for non-US customers.

Read this guide, find some decent lawyers, and you will avoid such embarrassments with your products.

Dr Nick Palmer MP (Labour MP for Broxtowe)

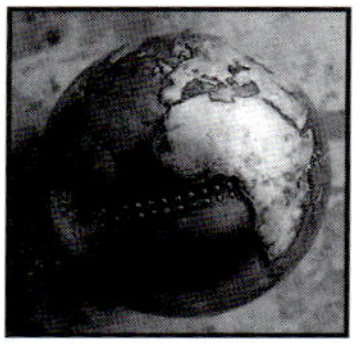

Views from the industry

A letter to (some of) the lawyers...
by Charles Christian

Where goes the law of England in an Internet enabled society
by Christian de Larringa of ISOC

Internet = IT revolution by David Finn of Oracle UK

The work of the Internet Watch Foundation
by Ruth Dixon of the IWF

The work of Nominet UK by
Dr Willie Black

Online and e-commerce: a legal insider's view
by Clare Gilbert of AOL

A letter to (some of) the lawyers...

by Charles Christian

Every day, or so it seems, I receive a press release from yet another law firm announcing that they have set a new practice division specialising in telecoms, new media, digital technology or even – cliche alert – 'cyber-law'. Without exception, these press releases are on paper and arrive by post. And, almost equally without exception, I can be certain that if I fire off an email message containing the journalistic equivalent of a request for further and better particulars, it will be several days before anyone replies to my questions.

Why? Because although we now have plenty of lawyers practising digital media law, there are still relatively few law firms out there actually using digital media technology to assist with their practice of law or help deliver the legal services they offer.

That is why email still appears to be something lawyers check and deal with on a Friday afternoon, if they happen to have some spare time on their hands – and then only after they have completed their time sheets and expenses forms for the week.

That is why so many law firms are still launching websites that are little more than ill-conceived and poorly executed unimaginative first-generation brochureware.

That is why although it is now nearly five years since the first English solicitors' practices established websites – Clifford Chance and Jeffrey Green Russell share the honours for going 'live' in the autumn of 1994 – there are still only about 500 firms in the UK with their own Internet presence.

Considering there are about 80,000 solicitors practising in approximately 10,000 law firms in England and Wales alone, we are looking at a less than 5 per cent wired and web-enabled rate. If this was the telephone we were talking about, it would be a national scandal. Sadly, the point far too many lawyers have so far failed to grasp is that the Internet and related digital media is the new telephone system.

And, that is also why we still hear so much about the Linklaters 'Blue Flag' service – because three years on from its launch Linklaters, and a handful of other firms, still have the online delivery of legal services market almost exclusively to themselves.

Perhaps the worst example of a new media lawyer failing to practice what he preaches is a certain senior-ish partner in the West End of London who still has his secretary print off his incoming email messages and then dictates his replies for her key-in and dispatch. This however does not stop another member of his firm from regular extolling the virtues of the legal Internet at the seminars and conferences he speaks at around the country.

Of course you are perfectly free to ignore the Internet – after all, it is not compulsory.

You do not have promote your services on the web. You do not have to invest in interactive web sites or extranets that can handle e-commerce transactions or new instructions from clients. You do not even have to offer your clients the convenience of email access. But, if you do take this course of inaction, don't then complain when you find yourself running a sunset practice, where the only light at the end of tunnel proves to be the sun setting upon your once promising legal career.

This may seem a harsh judgment but it is quite clear that many lawyers still do not 'get' the Internet and the whole digital media revolution.

Within the space of five years this has progressed from being a playground for academics and techie enthusiasts into a mainstream business medium that is already worth billions of dollars a year and looks set to become the pervasive commercial technology of the opening years of the 21st century. (Prediction: the Freeserve Desktop Lawyer service is set to become massive and is likely to have the same effect on high street law firms' private client bases that the May 1997 general election had on the Conservative Party.)

Such remarks inevitably prompt a response from solicitors along the lines of: 'Well we haven't got email and we have had no complaints from our clients!' Fair comment but do you actually know how many of your existing clients would contact you by email if you gave them the option? Or, how many prospective clients took their instructions elsewhere because you could not offer online services?

As the digital media revolution rolls on its way, the market for legal services is changing. When the Internet was still the preserve of a relatively small numbers of IT enthusiasts, early adopters and aficionados – the so-called 'digerati' – law firms could afford to ignore the more outrageous demands from those men in deconstructed Armani suits with offices near the Groucho Club. But, we are now seeing the emergence of a far broader digitally street-wise audience, what have been termed the 'Martini generation'.

They have the technology, they understand how to use it and they know it has the ability to deliver the right answers to the right people at 'any time, any place, anywhere'.

They are cash-rich and time-poor. They are in particular need of access to services outside normal office hours. They are now coming to expect the prospective suppliers of the services they are interested in to be equally wired up and web-enabled as they are. And if their suppliers are not sufficiently digitally aware to be able to provide the interactive service levels demanded, they are likely to switch their allegiance to suppliers who can.

If you can search the web for new insurance cover, computer software suppliers and even pizza delivery services, why can't you also search it for details of solicitors' practices and other providers of legal services?

If you can order and pay for books and computers via the web, why can't you also send new instructions online to a solicitor or obtain a quotation on how much it will cost to have a firm handle a contractual dispute for you?

If you can monitor the progress of a parcel as it makes its way from Seattle to Savannah, why can't you use the web to find out if the company you are suing for bad debts has paid up, made an offer or otherwise responded to the 'letter before action' from your lawyers?

If you can communicate with a supplier via email or an interactive website from anywhere in the world and at any time of the day or night, why can't you contact your lawyer after 5.00pm on a Friday evening until sometime during the following Monday morning?

And, if you can log on to your bank's website to see if your salary cheque has been paid into your account, why can't you also log on to your lawyer's client account records to see how much of your money has already been spent pursuing some ongoing litigation?

What we are seeing is a revolution in communications. Just as face-to-face meetings and correspondence by post has been superseded on a day-to-day basis by fax and telephone communications, so we are now moving into an era when Internet email, interactive websites and other forms of digital communications, such as video conferencing, are becoming the expected norm.

Of course the quality of the legal services you offer will always be important but, and here's the rub, they are still 'services' and, as with any other form of service, it is the way you deliver them that ultimately differentiates one law firm from another and establishes a sufficiently high degree of client satisfaction to ensure a reasonable likelihood of them returning to you with more legal work.

Or, to put it another way, not matter how good the quality of your digital media legal advice, if clients find day-to-day dealings with your firm anything less than convenient, they will go elsewhere.

Charles Christian is the editor of Legal Technology Insider *and author of* Legal Practice in the Digital Age
Email: info@legaltechnology.co.uk
http://www.legaltechnology.co.uk

Where goes the law of England in an Internet enabled society?

By Christian de Larringa of ISOC

The Internet is a formidable opportunity for England's legal system. Yet the problem of defining jurisdiction in relation to Internet cases is being cited as why our legal institutions will be sidelined or forced to change from a national to a global legal system. So are we witnessing the death of over 1,000 years of English law at the hands of the Internet? Or does English law have qualities which will be strengthened by the Internet? How can we find out and where can we go to achieve an authoritative understanding of the Internet?

For me, the best definition of the Internet is that it is a 'relationship' medium. A medium where human contact and transactions are enabled without recourse to distance or human boundary. There is no parallel development in our history to help us prejudge the consequences of such an invention. Everybody involved with the Internet is seeking out how best to approach it.

As global Internet trade reaches $3 trillion in the early years of the next century, the legal profession can expect to see their slice of this business. In particular as it is 'early days' the level of business for lawyers is likely to be proportionately higher for Internet-related business than conventional. Now is a good time for lawyers to develop their Internet skills and practices.

How serious a threat is the issue of jurisdiction on the Internet to the law? English law is an impressive social technology. By combining acts of Parliament with precedent, we have systematised consistency with flexibility in determining cases. Jurisdiction issues are well understood in England with centuries of experience dealing with shipping, insurance, banking and other industries. English courts are frequently used by foreign nationals to judge disputes with no element of English territoriality, on account of the perceived expertise and fairness of our jurisdiction.

Recent Internet cases suggest that jurisdiction is applied vigorously. Internet pornographer Graham Waddon found Judge Hardy ruling for English jurisdiction when he copied the material from his computer in England to an American computer for distribution. Last year people who broke into a UK-based computer were extradited from the US to face trial in England.

The high standing and expertise of English law may be a major beneficiary of the Internet and contribute significantly to the future invisible earnings of the country. As businesses and organisations study the issues that e-commerce brings a further dimension comes into focus – the consumer.

It is one thing dealing with professional trading houses disputing million pound transactions. But what of a situation where you need to determine millions – even billions – of international transactions whose average value may be less than $1 to millions of individuals? How ready and how interested are English lawyers for the potential deluge that this aspect of Internet will bring? Is there an opportunity here which the legal profession are able to respond to?

What is the Government view? Not surprisingly there have been calls on Government to legislate to ensure that transactions on the Net are treated equivalently and transparently to traditional trading systems without having to resort to case law or wait for precedent from the courts. Yet the UK Government's e-commerce legislative process has been highly contentious.

It is clear that any legislation which reduced the perception of English jurisdiction as a natural home for Internet trade would have potentially damaging consequences to our legal profession's future prospects. It is clear that the White Paper has been viewed as damaging to these prospects by both business and the legal profession. Nevertheless people have not widely appreciated the high stakes threatening the profession's own future through inappropriate inward-looking legislation damaging the reputation of English jurisdiction.

One of the main difficulties in devising an effective Internet policy is in coming to understand the Internet and how it works. It is not controlled by a single authority. Nor is it owned or regulated by a single nation or institution.

Yet there is an organisation which is at the heart of the global Internet. The Internet Society (ISOC). This society contains the founders, inventors and principle movers in the Internet. It also promotes and manages the main standards making processes of the Internet through its associated organisations, IETF, IAB, and IRTF. It is at the centre of a global process allowing the technology to develop in a systematic and democratic manner.

ISOC already a leading authority on the technical core of Internet has recently established the Internet Societal Task Force (ISTF) to further develop links between the professions and organisations working in social issues of the Internet.

The English Chapter of ISOC (http://www.england.isoc.org) has a standing committee for Legal and Regulatory Affairs which is open to lawyers, legal organisations and fora. It is important to meet one's peers in an environment dedicated to the task at hand with reference to the global specialist technical knowledge to empower that debate. That place is the Internet Society.

I believe that we have the opportunity to secure the next 1,000 years of English legal jurisdiction within an expanding international legal market and with it the future of English law. But it is an opportunity other jurisdictions are already seeking to exploit.

Christian de Larrinaga is the founder chairman of The Internet Society of England.
http://www.england.isoc.org; The Internet Society http://www.isoc.org;
Sample e- commerce White Paper submissions http://www.fipr.og

Internet = IT revolution

By David Finn of Oracle UK

The rapid take-up of the Internet continues to surpass predictions, and professionals in every walk of life are having to come to terms with the potential of the networked society.

The most commonly quoted statistic to assess the speed with which the Internet is beginning to permeate our business and domestic lives compares the adoption rates for previous emergent technologies with the rise of the Internet. While it took 38 years for the telephone to gain over 10 million users, and nine years for the cellular phone, it has taken just three years for the Internet to reach a similar level of use.

The US Department of Commerce has forecast that over $350bn of goods will be traded over the Internet by the year 2002, and businesses such as Amazon.com which trade exclusively through the medium of their websites are the success stories of the late 20th century, despite their fluctuating stock values. It is clear that something profound is happening which will impact all areas of business and society over the next ten years.

The advent of the Internet and the technologies which will allow widespread access to information for citizens – through digital television in the home and through public access kiosks and community-based services – will also herald a revolution in the way in which public services are provided, and in people's expectations of how they will interact with the state.

The Government is committed to surfing this wave of technological change. The recent white paper on the Modernising Government programme sets out a radical agenda for transforming services to citizens. The targets for ensuring that 100 per cent of public services are capable of being provided electronically by 2008 will impact both individuals themselves, and all professionals such as accountants and lawyers who provide services to citizens or to the state.

The key themes of the Internet age are information and access. For too long, the citizen has had to surmount physical and social barriers to get access to information – typically having to visit a variety of central and local governmental offices to access the services they need, and to explain how their circumstances qualify them for assistance. The advisory sector has developed to help the public through the maze of services provided and to explain their rights and obligations.

Last autumn the Lord Chancellor's Department anticipated the release of the full electronic government agenda by publishing its own consultation paper – Civil Justice:

Resolving and Avoiding Disputes in the Information Age. It foresaw that technology could be brought into use at almost every stage of the civil justice process. The consultation paper is radical and innovative – but the technology to support the changes discussed is available today.

One of the main areas of change envisaged is in the provision of information and advice. Online information sources have great potential to replace the current favoured means of communication – the advisory leaflet. We are moving from a 'push' society to a 'pull' society where the individual will chose for themselves when and how they access services – and seek information. The increasing use of the Internet in education is producing a generation whose first instinct will be to access the web to ask a question or to solicit information, and who will resort to the telephone or request a personal interview with an advisor only when they have exhausted their first means of enquiry or established for themselves that the type of assistance they need requires professional input.

An example of the new style of information advisory service has been developed for the National Association of Citizens Advice Bureaux (NACAB) with assistance from Oracle. Situated at www.adviceguide.org.uk the service covers employment, housing, family, legal and consumer issues.

The Citizens Advice Bureaux handle around six million cases each year. David Harker Chief Executive of NACAB, said 'We are aiming the Internet service at people who would not normally consult a Citizens Advice Bureau. Adviceguide is not a substitute for a human adviser, but for many people it will be a convenient starting point to solving problems and a link to other advice.'

The NACAB site also addresses one of the public's key concerns about use of the Internet, through the concept of the 'trusted provider'. One of the most common criticisms of Internet usage is the sheer volume of information which can be produced from a single search – for example a search on the word 'housing queries' via a typical Internet search engine would generate hundreds of thousands of references. But by providing structured access routes to meet the needs of its clients a site such as adviceguide can become the first point of reference for people who understand the functions of the Citizens Advice Bureau and have trust in the information and service to be provided.

Where will this lead to in the future? Initial users of Internet sites giving information on legal and advisory issues will access from their workplace and from their home personal computers. Broader access to the general public will be available through advice centres, and many local authorities are looking at the use of kiosks and 'one stop shops' to provide information services on a wide range of issues at the touch of a button. Before long the availability of digital television in the home will bring immediate access to online information services within reach of the majority of the population.

David Finn is the head of public sector consulting for Oracle UK

The Work of the Internet Watch Foundation

By Ruth Dixon of the IWF

The Internet Watch Foundation was set up in the autumn of 1996 in response to growing public concern about illegal and offensive material on the Internet. The Foundation is an independent organisation established to implement proposals jointly agreed by the government, the police and the UK Internet service provider industry (the Safety-Net agreement[1]). It is funded and managed by the industry, with an independent Policy Board representing a wide range of interest groups[2].

The stated aims of IWF are twofold: to hinder the use of the Internet to transmit illegal material, particularly child pornography; and to encourage the classification of legal material on the Net in order to enable users to customise the nature of their experience of the Net to their own requirements.

Just ten weeks after the Safety-Net discussions IWF launched its hotline[3] to enable Internet users to report illegal content. The hotline can be contacted by email at report@iwf.org.uk, online via the website at http://www.iwf.org.uk/hotline/report.html or by phone on 08456 008844. The volume of reports to the hotline has built up steadily, and currently IWF receives about 300 messages a month. In the first two years of IWF's activity over 13,000 items[4] were referred to the police and UK ISPs were alerted and advised to remove them. The majority of these involved child pornography.

The success of recent police operations shows that effective international action can be taken to curb illegal use of the Internet and to bring those responsible to justice. An example was Operation Cathedral in September 1998, which led to the arrest of 40 members of an international paedophile network, 11 of them in the UK.

Experience with the hotline soon showed that much of the material about which users express concern, chiefly in the area of adult pornography, is unlikely to be subject to prosecution under UK law. Given the basic Safety-Net principle that if something is illegal offline it will also be illegal online, and vice versa, such material does not fall under the remit of the IWF hotline. However, this has confirmed the need to develop tools to enable users to choose what they do and don't wish to view, as set out in the second of IWF's core aims.

In January 1997 an Advisory Board5 was established to propose specifications for a UK system of rating Internet content in order for individual users to filter their own access. The Board's findings were published in March 1998 along with a public consultation paper.

In view of the global nature of the Internet it is essential that any proposed solutions to issues of content – whether illegal or legal – be implemented on the widest possible basis. The Internet Watch Foundation has taken a leading role in promoting international cooperation in both the hotline and rating fields.

Early in 1997, IWF and other hotlines in Europe were drawn together in the INHOPE forum (Internet Hotline Providers in Europe)[7] to share information and expertise. This forum is now being constituted as an association to continue this exchange and to support the establishment of new hotlines. There is also informal dialogue with the Cyber Tipline[8] in the United States.

Over the past couple of years the European Union has carried out extensive policy reviews on regulation of the Internet. In response to the findings[9] and in order to develop a practical programme to deliver some of the proposed policies IWF drew together a range of European organisations in March 1997 to form INCORE (Internet Content Rating for Europe)[10]. INCORE has received funding from the European Commission to develop an Internet content rating and filtering system for Europe.

Looking further afield, IWF has also been working with partners in North America and the Asia Pacific region, and is a founding member of the Internet Content Rating Association[11]. ICRA has been formed to develop an internationally acceptable system of rating. This will be based on the RSACi content rating system[12] which is already incorporated in latest versions of the major browsers.

In the spring of 1998 Barbara Roche, the then DTI Minister responsible for Internet issues, announced a review of IWF's work, which was carried out by a team from KPMG and Denton Hall. The results[13] were published earlier this year. The review was broadly supportive both of the UK model of industry self-regulation and of the effectiveness of IWF's operation. At the same time it poses challenging questions about possible future extensions of the role of the Internet Watch Foundation. An extensive internal debate is under way to examine these questions and their implications for the IWF's structure and resources.

Within just two and a half years the Internet Watch Foundation has become established as a leading player in the Internet world in both the domestic and international arenas, and continues to respond swiftly and innovatively to new challenges in the fast changing world of this powerful global medium.

Ruth Dixon is acting chief executive of the Internet Watch Foundation

Useful websites

1 http://www.iwf.org.uk/about/R3Safety.html

2 http://www.iwf.org.uk/about/policy.html

3 http://www.iwf.org.uk/hotline/hotline.html

4 http://www.iwf.org.uk/stats/stats.html

5 http://www.iwf.org.uk/rating/rating.html#advisory

6 http://www.iwf.org.uk/rating/rating_r.html

7 http://www.childnet-int.org/hotlines/index.html

8 http://www.missingkids.com/cybertip/

9 http://www2.echo.lu/legal/en/internet/communic.html and http://www2.echo.lu/legal/en/internet/gpen-toc.html

10 http://www.incore.org/

11 http://www.iwf.org.uk/press/archives/p120599.html

12 http://www.rsac.org/

13 http://www.dti.gov.uk/iwfreview/

The work of Nominet UK

By Dr Willie Black

Every computer (or server) connected to the Internet is identified by an Internet Protocol (IP) address, which comprises four numbers separated by dots eg 123.45.6.78. However, the human brain does not remember long numbers particularly well and so the Domain Name System (DNS) was introduced to associate easily remembered and convenient names with the IP addresses. Within the DNS each country has a Top Level Domain (TLD) which uses an automatic electronic mechanism to match names with IP addresses. Each country stores its names and IP addresses in a central Register Database.

Until 1996 the registration process for domain names in the .uk TLD was managed on a voluntary basis. However, once registrations were running at 200 per week, it became obvious that a permanent organisation was required. Nominet UK was set up to maintain the .uk Register Database, provide search facilities and administer other necessary functions. It is incorporated as an English not-for profit company, limited by guarantee.

The .uk TLD is divided into about 12 Second Level Domains (SLDs). Nominet also has a remit, in co-operation with the Governmental and non-Governmental organisations concerned, to manage and control the use of these SLDs, including administering rules for the use of the .uk TLD and SLDs. The most common SLDs are .co.uk for commercial enterprises (the largest SLD in the UK); .org.uk for non-commercial organisations; .plc.uk and .ltd.uk for registered companies only; and .net.uk for the host machines of network providers.

Disputes

Nominet UK does not and cannot determine the legality of competing rights in relation to Applicants' requests for the registration and delegation of domain names. If two applications are received for the same domain name, the rule which normally applies is that the one which arrives first has priority. However, Nominet requires all applicants for domain names to warrant that their registration of the name does not infringe the rights of a third party.

There are no statutes in English law specifically governing domain name registration but existing law can be applied to the process. Examples include trade mark infringement and contract law.

Trade mark infringement

The rules which underpin Nominet's Dispute Resolution Service (DRS), (http://www.nic.uk/rules/rup2.html) are by now familiar to many brand owners and their professional advisers, both in the UK and overseas. Many of those who use Nominet's DRS make submissions based on English and foreign case law in the field of trade mark infringement. They are nevertheless advised that Nominet does not and cannot act as an intellectual property tribunal.

Nominet believes it should not in any way trespass on the jurisdiction of the English Court and other Courts of competent jurisdiction. It is quite clearly not equipped to deal with trade mark issues, which touch on international relations and the conflict of laws as well as domestic legislation.

There have been approximately 400 cases dealt with under Nominet's DRS, whereas some 30 cases have come before the English or Scottish Court. Nominet is not aware of any domain name litigation in the Northern Ireland Court.

There has only been a handful of instances of Nominet UK being joined as a party in civil litigation in England relating to domain name registrations. Two of the cases have been reported in the English Law Reports and copies of the official transcripts of the decisions are available on the Nominet website (http://www.nic.uk/news/index.html). The earliest reported case, relating to the pitman.co.uk domain name concerned errors of registration inherited by Nominet from its predecessor, the UK Naming Committee.

The second case related to one registration in the .co.uk SLD (and almost ten other registrations in the .com generic Top Level Domain) by the English registered company One In A Million Ltd and its shareholders or directors. The plaintiffs were Marks & Spencer plc and others. Nominet UK was not a co-defendant with the Registrant of the domain name. There was nevertheless solicitors' correspondence between Nominet's advisors and the in-house legal department of Marks & Spencer plc. Nominet sought to intervene under procedural rules of the Court of Appeal in the appeals in June/July1998. Had the application for Leave to Intervene been granted, Nominet would have submitted that the decision of the California Court in *Lockheed Martin v Network Solutions Inc* should be followed in English law. The issue of alleged liability of TLD managers for causing or enabling passing off or trade mark infringement has yet to be determined by the English Courts.

Disputes Resolved

Nominet believes that its successful intervention in several hundred cases since 1996 may account for the low level of case law relating to domain name disputes before the UK Courts. It is frequently the case that when a mutually acceptable resolution of the dispute is sought by the impartial intervention of Nominet staff, a settlement is rapidly reached without any need for court action, or even for Nominet to act under its rules.

Dr Willie Black is managing director of Nominet UK
Nominet UK is the national Registry for all Internet Domain Names ending .uk.

Online and e-commerce: a legal insider's view

By Clare Gilbert, AOL

Summarising the 'hot' legal issues faced by the Internet and online industry is a difficult and ever-changing task. When I first started to work for AOL back in 1995 as their external lawyer in the UK, with my former colleague Liam McNeive, I think neither of us had any idea that our new work would bring us into regular contact with bodies as diverse as the Gaming Board, Scotland Yard's paedophile unit and OFTEL. Yet it has done and continues to throw new and exciting challenges to me and my department – which now stretches across Europe, reflecting the growth of our services and operations – on a daily basis.

The nature of our work in fact merely reflects the fast-evolving medium in which our business operates. This medium has moved from being only a few years ago the exclusive domain of 'geeks' in anoraks, to becoming the mass medium for consumers to inform, entertain and educate themselves as well as to buy their groceries and build up whole online communities with people of similar interests across the globe. The Internet is also now the focus of furious Government and media attention, with the Government ambitious to make the UK the focus for e-commerce on a global basis and the media obsessed with the mega-bucks to be made as Internet start-ups move into the European stock-markets.

In this environment the job of the in-house lawyer is not an easy one. A typical day might include the following:

- Arrive at the office at 8.30am – clutching indispensable Americano from Coffee Republic – and trawl through the 20 or so emails which have arrived since I left the office last night. These may include bulletins from subscription online news services, requests from my colleagues in America Online Inc in the States for information about the latest EU Commission statement or decision, as well as lots of new instructions for the latest pan-European e-commerce deals.

- Attend internal senior management meeting where all the latest trends, industry activities and intra-group issues are thrashed out by the European managers and key action items identified. In these meetings I may well be called upon to provide updates on matters as diverse as the UK interconnect revenue structure and DT's latest tariff structure; progress in the difficult negotiations with rights holders on a compromise for the draft Copyright Directive; legal issues raised by any new e-commerce proposals.

- Return to my office to deal with numerous requests from my colleagues for advice on subjects

View from the industry

ranging from a potential problem with allegedly defamatory content, marketing material which needs approval and sign-off, an essential domain name which has been registered by a cybersquatter and a couple of messages from journalists who want to talk about unmetered telephone access charges for the Internet.

Amid all of this, it is essential to find the time to focus on the key issues which impact AOL Europe's business. While there are many issues which affect us, those highest on our list are those which may/could impair the growth of the business in the future or our ability to compete on a level playing field.

In the current environment of a continuous stream of draft legislation coming out of Europe and increased interest in this industry from large players such as the telcos and media companies, regulatory and public policy issues are of prime importance.

So, for example we have an increasing dialogue with OFTEL and the German regulator as well as the EU Commission on the issue of call access charges for the Internet: European access charges are, in general, extremely high and accrue on a per minute basis. They have been identified by independent analysts, such as Jupiter Communications, as the largest inhibitor to growth of the Internet in Europe. Feedback from our members certainly shows that call charges are a big disincentive to them spending more time online. It is a primary objective of AOL Europe to see these rates of access come down to an affordable and preferably capped level to encourage users to come online and stay online longer. Only then will the Internet truly become a part of people's lives and sufficient trust in the medium develop so as to enable e-commerce really to grow in Europe.

We are also closely involved in ongoing negotiations and discussions over the draft Copyright and E-Commerce Directives, the IOCA consultation and the UK E-commerce Bill.

Even with an excellent in-house team of lawyers, security specialists and lobbyists, the volume and breadth of our work makes us heavily reliant on expert external advisors.

Our experience has shown us the large disparity between the number of lawyers who claim to have expertise in the online sector and those who actually practise in this area in any depth and are able to offer well-informed, business-orientated advice.

We move in Internet time and it is essential that our advisors stay up-to-date with the many legal developments affecting us, that they can respond quickly to our queries and that they understand the potential ramifications of their advice on the different components of our business.

Finally, people really matter to us: we want the people we meet to be responsible for our work rather than passing it down to invisible assistants and we place a great deal of value on the personal interaction as well as professional relationships we develop with our advisors. To date we have fulfilled our requirements by building on long-term relationships with key individuals. These have – we hope – proved fruitful on both sides; as the breadth of our work increases our need to find more of these key players in different areas of expertise grows with it.

Clare Gilbert is vice president and general counsel for AOL Europe

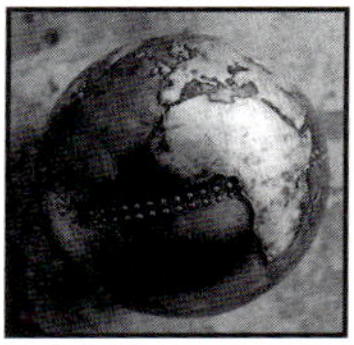

Commercial solutions

The search for funding: finding the right partners
by Quentin Solt of Berwin Leighton

The search for funding: finding the right partners

By Quentin Solt of Berwin Leighton

All expanding businesses need money to fund development and growth. information and communications technology (ICT) businesses are no exception, indeed because they usually have a higher 'burn rate' than other businesses they often need more funding. The different sources of funding available to ICT entrepreneurs can be bewildering, and finding the best funders can be a daunting task.

This article discusses the different types of funding which may be available to entrepreneurs, gives some practical suggestions of things to bear in mind when looking to raise funding and, finally, looks at the role of professional advisers.

Before we start, it is worth remembering that the funding market is just like the market for new graduates seeking jobs – the best graduates will have the choice of the best employers. If yours is truly an unmissable investment opportunity – a brilliant concept implemented by a blue chip team – funders will find you. If it is less exciting, you will need to work harder to raise money.

Sources of funding?

There are three main sources of funding for new ICT businesses. These are debt finance, equity finance and 'venturing' opportunities. Traditionally debt finance is provided by banks, although debt may be provided as part of an equity or venturing package. Equity capital is most commonly provided by private equity funds, venture capital institutions or wealthy individuals (often called 'business angels'). Venturing, which is described in more detail below, involves support from trading partners.

Because of the relative merits of different types of funding, and funders' requirements, businesses typically take a cocktail of debt and equity finance. The properly structured funding arrangement will ensure both that cash is available when the business needs it and that it is available as cheaply as possible. Since interest is payable on debt but not on equity the way in which the business is funded will itself influence the funding requirements. The importance of managing cash and funding flows, in the context not only of raising finance but also in running the business, can hardly be overstated.

For these purposes we are assuming that the entrepreneur has decided to 'incorporate the business', that is to transfer the business into a company. The company, which is usually initially owned by the entrepreneur, has a separate legal identity and the entrepreneur is not automatically liable for it's debts. The entrepreneur may, of course, assume liability by guaranteeing that the company meets specific obligations or – in certain limited circumstances, usually involving a misdemeanor or recklessness – by operation of law.

Debt financing

It is worth hunting around for the best deal. We have found a lot of funding deals have their genesis at networking events (such as, in the Internet world, First Tuesday and, in the wider technological space, Digital People) where entrepreneurs share their aspirations with others.

An individual may have different types of debt – ranging from the informal fiver lent by a colleague at lunch time, through the overdraft and the credit card loan to the mortgage. In the same way a wide range of debt facilities is available to the ICT entrepreneur setting up or expanding his business.

The requirements of lenders are fundamentally the same. They look for a secure 'passive' investment, and a return on their funds. Lenders are not charitable organisations. They want to be repaid in full, together with interest to cover the cost of money and to reward them for accepting the risk of their 'investment' with limited upside. All lenders will want to see how and when they will be repaid and what 'security' they have to guard against the unforeseen.

Different lenders will be more willing to lend (or to lend on better terms) to some types of business than others. Failing to persuade a particular lender to fund your business may not mean that the business is fundamentally flawed, but may simply reflect the lender's aversion to a business which it doesn't understand or with a risk profile which it is not prepared to accept.

'Servicing' debt

Debt must be 'serviced', that is to say that interest and finance charges must be paid. A prudent bank will only lend if it is confident that the business will be able to repay the debt through its cash revenues. The well prepared business plan (see below) will help the entrepreneur assess how much debt the business can afford and persuade the lender that yours is a business proposition that can work.

Channelling cash revenue to pay the bank can be frustrating for the entrepreneur who knows that the business' prospects would be enhanced by investing the revenue in new resources, IT and people rather than paying the bank. The value of cash today, as against equity tomorrow, is one of the drivers in deciding the debt/equity split.

Security

The comfort that the lender will be repaid even if the venture fails has traditionally been given in the form of charges over the business and its assets. These charges, often referred to as 'debentures' or 'security interests', are from the same legal family as the mortgage over your home. Unfortunately, few start-up ICT businesses have valuable assets which they can charge. Usually the greatest assets are two 'intangibles': its (often unproven) intellectual property rights (IPRs) and its people. IPRs are ideas and distinguishing marks which have more or less valuable connotations. Charges over unproven IPRs are unlikely to the give a lender much comfort. Put simply, if the IPRs are valuable the business is more likely to succeed and the bank will be paid: if the IPRs are not valuable the bank will not have improved its position by taking security over them. (Taking security over people died out in this country when Lord Wilberforce and the abolitionist movement succeeded.)

To 'get comfortable', the bank may require the entrepreneur to put up personal security, such as a second charge over his home or a guarantee from a relative (to 'help focus his mind' and 'demonstrate personal commitment'). The requirement to give a personal guarantee can also be pretty unpalatable, but with a bank staking its money on your entrepreneurial skills, is it unreasonable for it to ask you to share some of the risk?

Equity finance

Most companies have 'shares' (the Americans refer to shares as 'stock', hence 'stock options' – options to buy shares, usually at a cheap price, often granted to employees to incentivise them). 'Equity' is the term investors use to describe a holding of shares.

Shares have rights attaching to them, the most important of these are to share in the company's profits and to influence important decisions made by the company by voting at meetings. A company may have different 'classes' of share, each class or type of share having distinct voting and economic rights. Commonly an equity investor will want a separate class of shares, with particular rights. For example, the funder may require shares with a right to receive a fixed rate of dividend in priority to shares held by the entrepreneur.

An entrepreneur who allows the company which owns the business to issue new equity will retain a smaller slice of the business 'cake' in the hope that his retained slice will become more valuable as the business grows. He will also acquire a business partner, and a source of funding which does not usually need to be serviced.

Equity funders often accept more risk and are prepared to be more actively involved in the business than the passive debt funder. In return, the equity funder will expect a higher potential 'upside' than the debt funder.

What the equity investor is looking for

Equity investors' concerns are similar to those of the debt provider, but may be tempered by the facts that they have a greater understanding of the business, are more actively involved in it and will have the opportunity to share in profits. The equity investor faces the risk of failure, just like other shareholders. This commitment may mean that the investor will be more likely to assist (and continue to support) the business if it runs into difficulty than the bank which has the benefit of its security and guarantees.

Typically the equity investor will look for an 'attractive return' within a given time scale, traditionally between three and seven years but increasingly with ICT businesses a shorter period. The return is achieved by selling shares at a gain. The sale is usually referred to as an 'exit', commonly a sale of the investment to a trade investor or a flotation of the business on a stock exchange (often called an Initial Public Offering, or simply an IPO).

Investors may be prepared to state their targeted level of return - often expressed as a percentage internal rate of return (IRR) figure – and, if asked, may agree to share any excess over that level of return with the entrepreneurs. This 'sharing of excess' sweetens the investment terms for the entrepreneurs, and incentivises them to exceed the desired rate of IRR.

The equity investors 'security' – control of the business

To protect their investment, equity investors usually require the right to appoint a representative to the board and a right to veto certain actions which fall outside the parameters of the approved business plan. They will also seek to have input in relation to strategic issues and the right to adopt 'hands on' management control if the business significantly underperforms the business plan projections.

Entrepreneurs must consider the degree to which they are prepared to cede control to funders. This is one of the issues which the entrepreneurs ought to discuss with their professional advisers at an early stage. Perhaps the realistic approach is to accept that if the business flounders, the entrepreneurs face the 'rock and hard place' choice of allowing the business to become insolvent, or losing control to its funders. Funders may require that control should pass to them if, for example, targets are not achieved. If this is accepted by the entrepreneurs, they should argue to retain a right to buy-out the funders so that if the entrepreneurs see an alternative option they will at least have an opportunity to persuade another funder to champion their cause, and buy out the original funders.

Venturing

We are finding that venturing, although still relatively rare in Europe, is increasing in popularity. Venturing usually involves trading partners - typically an established industry player and a 'newbie' – exploiting opportunities to their mutual advantages. The established co-venturing partner will be looking both to make a worthwhile investment and enhance its own business position.

Commonly one venturer will provide cash funding, in the form of debt or equity, combined with access to an additional 'special contribution'. The special contribution is something which a non-industry player could not provide. It may be access to research and development facilities, joint marketing opportunities or resource and management support. The special contribution may present the opportunity to grow at a rate or in a direction which would otherwise simply not be possible. This may outweigh the fact that the terms of the debt or equity funding which the co-venturer offers are less advantageous in financial terms than those offered by the 'pure' debt or equity funders.

Industry giants, such as Microsoft, Intel and Reuters, have proved to be strong venturing partners for those businesses which they have backed. We are also seeing successful ventures involving smaller companies, too. The success of the venturing may be attributed to the common cultures – often involving a shared history – and ambitions of the companies involved.

Venturing partners providing funding have concerns similar to those of the debt and equity providers, and will often seek security and control rights. In addition, venturers with valuable brands will be concerned to ensure that the integrity and value of the brand is at least maintained, and hopefully enhanced. The venture partners are also in business for their own benefit, so will negotiate the best deal they can: although the experienced players will know that a 'win-win' deal is always better in the long term that the short-sighted 'win-lose' deal. The weaker partner must make sure that it is adequately protected from the aggressive co-venturer, whose agenda may well change over time.

Will funders be interested in me?

All funders will look for a well-prepared management team, with a sound business proposition. Funders will be attracted to businesses with the right commercial ingredients. They may turn tail if their due diligence (pre-investment investigation) reveals unexpected difficulties. This means that when selling their business idea to the funders the entrepreneurs must demonstrate that the business has the correct commercial ingredients without skeletons in the cupboard.

The successful business is likely to have leadership potential in a market segment and own the intellectual property rights essential to the business. It should also have a strong management team, clear marketing strategy and ability to fulfil orders placed on it.

The successful ICT entrepreneur will anticipate the areas that investors will look at and plan ahead to prepare the business for investment. For example, it is often easier to raise funds for a business which has adhered to the 'keep it simple' maxim. Funders may be scared off by complex arrangements and 'clever' schemes which are not easily understood or may fly slightly too close to the wind for the blue-chip investor's taste.

Preparation and communication are fundamental to raising funds

In business terms it is vital to capitalise on the moment. The time bidden phrase 'today's opportunity is tomorrow's news' may be trite, but arguably it is more apt in the ICT world than in any other. While delay can cause the business to crater, planning and preparation – particularly in structuring the business vehicle, optimising tax breaks, ensuring ownership of intellectual property rights and putting appropriate incentive arrangements in place – will pay dividends if the business achieves its potential.

Failing to take advice early enough can be costly. Acting for funders we have encountered businesses which depended on the right to use consumers' personal data, but where the consumers had never consented to the use of the data and where the whole business concept and process was founded on an idea which somebody else owned. In each case the value of the business plummeted.

Entrepreneurs and funders should ensure that they delineate their respective contributions and identify the pitfalls, as well as the benefits, of their contributions to the union. Transparency engenders trust and avoids misunderstandings. Where parties trust and understand one another they will go the extra mile to promote the business – and that is in everyone's interests.

To help focus the team on these key issues and also to show potential funders that the issues have been addressed, entrepreneurs of the ICT business should prepare a business plan.

Catching the funders' interest – the business plan

The preparation of a business plan is essential to raise finance. A well prepared business plan will inform investors of the business, its operations, people, markets, competition and opportunities. The plan should articulate management's strategy and persuade the funders that they have an opportunity to make an investment which is capable of yielding high returns.

1 Key questions which entrepreneurs should be prepared to answer:

- how much money will be needed, and when it will be required
- how the business expects to create value and make money, and when
- what the growth prospects of the business are, and how it is proposed that those prospects should be realised
- what competitive edge or 'unique selling points' the business offers
- whether the management team has the requisite skill sets – in terms of financial discipline, as well as on the technical and marketing sides
- are proper contracts with customers and key suppliers are in place (preferably these contracts will be written plainly, so that they are easy to understand)
- have risks and potential liabilities been identified and appropriate contingencies made
- does the business own the assets it uses, for example are intellectual property rights properly registered
- are the financial accounts of the business (including revenue, costs and order books) in order
- have cash flow projections and staged funding requirements been properly prepared and include sensitivity analyses based on realistic assumptions
- are marketing and brand strategies in place
- do the contracts of employment for key employees include appropriate incentives and enforceable restrictions to protect the business

- are the premises of the business are occupied on appropriate terms: for example in an expanding business it may be necessary to be able to relocate to bigger premises within a relatively short timescale without incurring extensive liabilities in relation to existing premises
- have applicable consents been obtained and regulations complied with – for example have customers given appropriate 'informed consent' for the business to use their personal data

The business plan – Box 1 gives a list of some of the questions which it may be appropriate for the business plan to address – should be clear and concise. It should address the needs of the business and the competition and their relative strengths and weaknesses. The plan should identify critical success factors, barriers to market entry, and what must be done to achieve profitable growth. Relevant in this context will be the marketing strategy, funding and staffing requirements and steps necessary to register title to intellectual property rights.

The plan should also append historical (if available) and projected financial information including profit and loss accounts, cashflows and balance sheets. The projections will help form the basis for determining the funding structure for the business.

No business is perfect, the business plan should identify the shortcomings and the proposed solutions or 'work arounds'. The plan may legitimately ask the funder to contribute more than cash – perhaps the funder can help fill a hole in the management structure? The business should also identify the entrepreneurs' own role – has the business outgrown its founder?

Finally, the plan should demonstrate its purpose to investors, particularly equity participators, by postulating potential exit scenarios.

Preparation is only the first step, once prepared the business plan should be reviewed on a regular basis: it is essential that it is kept up to date during the negotiating process so that it can be seen to be dynamic, changing with the ICT business as it grows. The process forces management to analyse the business, its structure and markets.

The business plan gets the entrepreneur's foot in the door. Once face to face with the funder, listen to his comments, criticisms and advice. Address the funder's concerns and, if necessary, start the process again.

What should an ICT business be looking for in its search for equity funders and venturing partners?

In choosing equity funders or venturing partners, the best deal is not necessarily the one that gives the entrepreneur the cheapest financial terms. Other factors, such as personal relationships, understanding the business and ability to continue to fund the business through its various stages of development are also critical to the decision. ICT businesses are in many ways unique. For example, evidence suggests that the ICT business cycle is seven times faster than the 'traditional' business cycle. The funder who understands this accelerated cycle may be more sympathetic to the business's cash requirements than the investor who has not ventured into the area before.

There is a wide range of potential equity investors and venturing partners, with differing investment requirements and offerings – the best investors contribute far more than just capital. Box 2 lists some of the add-ons that a funder may offer.

2 In the search for funding an ICT business should seek investors who:

- have adequate funding to satisfy both the immediate and future cash requirement of the business,
- understand the business in which they are investing,
- share values, compatible goals and strategies with the entrepreneurs,
- show themselves to be willing and able to maintain open communications,
- are prepared to adopt a flexible approach during the relationship, in order to allow the ICT business to shape opportunities (rather than react to them as they arise)
- have good contacts and offer opportunities for networking, venturing, partnering and making strategic alliances and being able to introduce the ICT business to its other investments

A good relationship with equity partners and co-venturers will improve communication and understanding of the business and usually results in more support in times of difficulty and greater interest if an expansion or diversification opportunity comes along.

The role of professional advisers

It is in the interest of ICT entrepreneurs seeking funding to appoint advisers with appropriate market and corporate finance experience. Accountants must understand the business and accounting conventions, lawyers also need to understand the commercial environment and the way in which the market operates.

As with investors, the right advisers will bring far more to the table than mere technical expertise. By being sensitive to the requirements, pitfalls and opportunities in this unique business sector, the right professional team can open new financing opportunities and help strengthen the business, even at the planning stage.They will help spot the commercial opportunities, open a network of contacts and help the business to achieve its potential. They should also optimise tax breaks and be alive to opportunities for grants to be obtained.

Accountants can help the management team prepare the business plan and identify the business's cash requirements (both amounts and timings). They will also help ensure that financial projections are properly compiled and presented in a manner readily appreciated by potential investors. They will help value the business to determine the value at which equity investors should be invited to subscribe for shares.

Lawyers will work with entrepreneurs, they will explain the process and help to ensure the process runs smoothly. For example, they will help co-ordinate replies to the funder's due diligence enquiries and its core business-related issues. Berwin Leighton has a number of specialist MBA executives retained to advise all types of ICT business and who are able to introduce clients to venture partners and funders. Our ICT team also includes lawyers specialising in intellectual property, IT, outsourcing, tax, employment, litigation and dispute resolution, media, e-commerce and commercial law as well, of course, as corporate finance and securities law.

Funders will require the entrepreneurs to 'put their money where his mouth is', by formally confirming those facts which they have presented to the funder. This formal confirmation is achieved by a contract (usually called a subscription agreement) including representations and warranties, often extending to many pages and minute detail. If the representations and warranties are untrue, the funder may claim damages against the entrepreneur. Lawyers will help to reduce the risk of a claim being brought.

The lawyers will also negotiate the terms of the various debt facility and investment agreements and 'disclosures' against the warranties. They will be familiar with the investor's proposed 'shareholders' agreement', 'subscription agreement' and other arrangements hidden in a shroud of jargon such as 'mezzanine finance'. Don't be frightened of the terminology, although they build to form a complex structure, the underlying concepts are relatively simple. Lawyers with appropriate experience will lead you through the process, help you anticipate the issues and save you time, money and hassle.

Our experience suggests that smaller advisers who help form the company and give it early intellectual property advice, are rarely best placed to help with negotiating funding arrangements involving sophisticated corporate finance structures.

Choose a firm with experience which enables it to add value to your business. Invest time with your advisers at the start of the fund raising process, get their advice on what is involved in raising funds and identify the issues which you will have to tackle.

Too many lawyers lose sight of the real issues – and fight personal crusades often based on academic arguments – when negotiating documentation. The entrepreneur and funder end up paying for these esoteric (often face saving) exercises. The best way of avoiding these lawyers is to take personal recommendations from others who have suffered the process before. To save time and costs, give clear and unequivocal instructions – defining the risks you are prepared to accept, those that you would be unwilling to concede and the real deal breakers. Encourage the other side keep their lawyers in check, too.

Experienced lawyers ease the process by identifying the commercially important points and not wasting time – and money – on irrelevant discussions. If the lawyers appear to waste time arguing, make sure you understand what is at issue. They may be arguing over a risk you are willing to accept, or in respect of which you can see a commercial compromise.

The continuing relationship between the business and its lawyers is an important one. The legal, regulatory and institutional frameworks in which ICT businesses operate are in a state of flux, and are constantly evolving. We find that by understanding our clients' businesses, and by keeping in touch with them, we are able to guide them through the complexities of developing regulation.

The best lawyers understand the business, its market and the problems it faces in a way which enables them to offer proactive commercial solutions – sometimes even spotting market opportunities for their clients. It is for just this reason that many of our clients use us as an informal sounding board to whom they present their business ideas.

Guidelines for success

The following guidelines will help convert the ICT opportunity into a business success:

- plan funding requirements, take care to manage cash resources and match demand to supply – prepare the funding facilities (so that cash is available) early so that you are not diverted from your core business by cash crises
- ensure you have a well defined and budgeted marketing strategy
- get the best advisers on your team, even if they charge a premium (many advisers, such as Berwin Leighton, will now accept contingent fee arrangements)
- communicate the objectives and results of the business throughout the management, investor and adviser teams – allow each of them to feel a part of the team – and, as the business grows, recognise the need to develop strategy and continue to maintain the information flows and consultation process
- be prepared – know what is going to be critical to the business as it moves through its various stages and keep funders and advisers informed: they are there to help you, and they don't like surprises
- a well developed set of business contacts is one of the keys to business success – these include customers, suppliers, trade associations, funders, government agencies and professional advisers. Each contact potentially opens the gate to a new network of opportunities
- the business plan represents the agreed route forward for the business, but other opportunities often arise with ICT – assess them, discuss them with your investors and pursue them if it makes sense for the business – adapt your business plan as your business develops and new opportunities are considered.

There is one final ingredient that will boost even the best businesses – good luck. We wish you lots of it.

Quentin Solt leads Berwin Leighton's Information and Communications Technology group

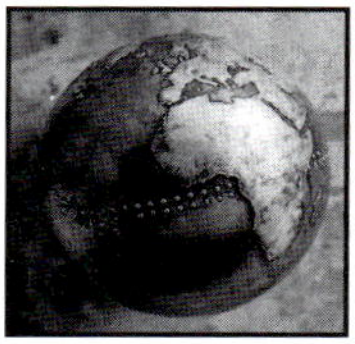

View from the editor

A view from the editor

It is perhaps the greatest irony of the digital age that a society which specialises in creating new and exciting names for things – and which has even created entire companies which subsist on such work – has signally failed to come up with a neat, pithy way to describe what is happening in the field of media, technology and communications. Convergence was the buzz-word of a few years ago, but merely described a trend. Few saw themselves as being in what could be described as the Convergent Industries. Digital media; digital mixed media; e-commerce; new media. All terms are pretty vague, but then so is the handle of most 'experts' on what happens next.

Law firms, traditionally slow to react to new trends in terms of how they manage and constitute their practices (and hence deliver the correct services to clients) are beginning to wake up to the fact that their entire world – based on the analysis of available information – is going digital, and that their clients' businesses – not just in obvious areas such as music, broadcasting and computer games – but in banking, insurance, retail and so on, are becoming irrevocably digital to some extent.

The law of this converging, emerging market is, principally, the law of commercial contract – business-to-business or business-to-consumer; it is the law of commercial agreements, of infringement, of exploitation of rights, of protection of rights. Most of it is nothing lawyers have not done before. It is just that the delivery mechanisms available, the speed of commercial adaptation possible and the disappearance of effective borders and hence legal controls in many areas means the law is a crucial component of digital life.

We have chosen the title Digital Media & E-Commerce to cover as broad a spectrum of definition as possible. Our aim is to serve those clients interested in the creation of digital assets, whether they be e-commerce systems or content; those interested in the protection both of digital assets and of the digital manifestation of more 'concrete' assets (such as trade marks on the Internet); those interested in how they may exploit the various delivery systems available to the best effect, and how they may best contract with the huge variety of other commercial entities also active.

This book is not a book about the law. It is a book about lawyers. It gives, in more depth than anything else in the market, an assessment of the capability, attitude and culture of all the relevant specialist firms active in the UK in this field. It is a book which unashamedly praises those firms which have taken what we believe are the correct steps to invest properly for the benefit of their clients. Not every law firm will suit every client, but we hope that during the course of this book, we have provided clients with some insight. We would welcome comments from those of you who have experiences to share on this matter. If you would like to become part of our ongoing research in this area and benefit further from the insights we have gained, please email m.brandon@ncm.uk.com or visit our website www.ncm.co.uk for more information.

Will things change?

But as e-commerce sets about revolutionising the way most of the commercial world will do business in the future, has it also seen a revolution in the way lawyers do business?

The research process for this guide has been the most exhaustive investigation to date into whether this is likely, and, unfortunately, the answer – for the moment – is 'no', or so it seems. (See also Charles Christian's article on page 11 for his own personal view on the matter!). Some firms still won't use email for regular correspondence, or won't respond quickly enough to the needs of the digital client. Too many still have the clock ticking from the moment the client walks in the door. Too many still rely or quoting the law, replete with heretofores and notwithstandings, rather than speaking the language of the new economy.

The following will come as no surprise to clients; lawyers will possibly dismiss it. But the most forward-thinking will hopefully seize upon it as an opportunity to take a serious lead. For, despite many positive comments about law firms, which we have mentioned here, there were a good number of negative ones. Clients were rarely unequivocally praiseworthy of law firms. There was a constant complaint of 'paying for the learning curve' and of 'sitting across the table from a bunch of associates who clearly have no idea how I run my business'. And they do not want to be billed for a lawyer's time spent in a cab getting to their office.

The comments of one in-house lawyer at a major international manufacturing company should strike home: 'Tailor yourself to the needs of the client, look at us very carefully, our culture and seek to serve that. Don't just sit in an intellectual palace – we want lawyers with commercial nous and a background in the area, not just legal technicians. We want people who are flexible and give credit for learning curves – we don't like paying for learning curves; appreciate our need for accessibility - give advice on the phone. And most importantly, don't treat us as a general file. Be willing to give us an hourly rate and a fully narrated bill. Without all of this, we're not interested.'

We couldn't have put it better ourselves.

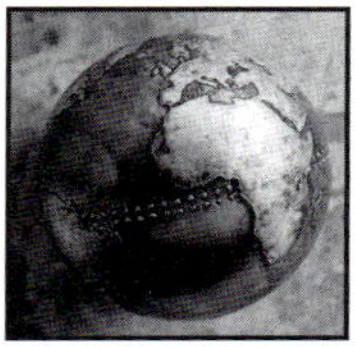

The research

by Neil Hambley of New City Media

The research

by Neil Hambley, New City Media

The background research for the guide was designed to address the legal implications of commercial activity on the web. This covered a broad spectrum, from the issues that concern these organisations, the legal consequences of their web presence to-date and the frameworks in place to deal with these. It was also designed to expand on perceptions of expertise among digital media legal advisors.

Given the extent to which the Internet has been embraced by major corporate bodies the research was focused towards the very top UK companies. As a result, the study was also aimed at examining the way in which these companies are adapting to the new regulatory environment and the extent to which this differs from the management of more mainstream legal affairs.

Sample

The sample comprised selected organisations from the FTSE index and top 1,000 UK companies. These were chosen on the basis that their business activities were compatible with the Internet, in as much that existing practices could to be easily adapted to the web. Particular emphasis was placed on the capacity to trade goods or services online, and as such, companies were drawn from relevant business sectors. Among others, these included retailers, financial services (such as insurance, banks), transport, media, computer services and software etc.

Over 500 companies were contacted, and a total of 149 responses were analysed.

Results – Web use

Our results certainly support existing evidence of the digital media boom. The vast majority of our respondents (91 per cent) use email on a daily basis, with almost all the remainder (7 per cent) expecting their organisation to provide the facility in the near future. Although slightly fewer had embraced the Internet, on average eight out every ten companies had established a web presence. Again, the vast majority of the remainder (a further 18 per cent) expected to go online in the near future.

Despite the variety of commercial interests among our sample there was considerable parity among the respective web strategies. Unsurprisingly, almost everyone recognised the marketing potential of the web, with over three quarters of respondents acknowledging the importance of the medium for promotional purposes. However, this was supplemented with a genuine commitment to interactivity. At the time of the research just under half of respondents with a website (43 per cent) were providing transactional services online, while a further 29 per cent expected to do so in the near future. For the most part, services were either based around the trade of information or, to a much greater extent, sales of existing product lines.

Legal implications

The legal consequences of corporate web activity have already been widely felt – often regardless of the purpose of the site. Nearly a third of respondents (31 per cent) indicated that they had already been involved in disputes, mostly related to intellectual property rights. With the odd exception, this was split between content issues such as trade mark or copyright infringement, and domain name disputes. In addition to this, 10 per cent had consulted law firms over the registration of their domain names.

Where transactional web services existed, legal recourse had been less common. With the exception of advice obtained in respect of setting up the facility (largely contractual), fewer than 10 per cent claimed to have encountered any significant issues since. Unfortunately, these respondents were often reluctant to expand on this due to confidentiality over ongoing proceedings.

In many ways, negligible legal activity in respect of e-commerce is unsurprising. Not only are many services relatively new, but they are often thinly-disguised pilot studies. It is quite apparent that many companies are experimenting with virtual trading to determine the role it might play in the future. As a result, current services are often rather limited.

This, however, did not mean that respondents are unconcerned about the legal impact of e-commerce – regardless of whether their employer is currently providing this service or not. Over two-thirds of the entire sample (67 per cent) indicated that they are worried about the potential legal consequences of online trading (as a general concept). More specifically, issues such as transactional security (58 per cent), hacking (54 per cent) and credit card fraud (46 per cent) were primary concerns, closely followed by compliance with the Data Protection Act (44 per cent). In many instances, respondents who openly refuted the legal consequences of e-commerce were from companies which already trade online. However, it is highly likely that this view is attributable (in part, at least) to minimal legal complications in respect of their e-commerce practice to-date.

Concern over the legal implications of e-commerce was only eclipsed by worries over the consequences of intellectual property infringement on the web. Perhaps only to be expected, given the number of respondents having already experienced disputes in relation to their IP, 70 per cent of the sample admitted their concern in this area. Whereas respondents had been roughly divided over the degree to which they were concerned about e-commerce, views on IP infringement were unequivocal; almost three times as many respondents claimed they were 'very', as opposed to 'quite' concerned.

Bearing in mind the reservations about corporate web activity – across all spheres – the measures outlined to address the legal consequences of this are surprising. This is true both in instances where digital media advice had already been sought, and where respondents described their intended course of action were such issues to arise. In short, relatively few respondents regard digital media as particularly distinct from any other legal matter. Almost two-thirds (62 per cent) revealed that any incident would be handled in exactly the same way as all other types of legal matter, regardless of the specialist and evolving nature of the law. Of the remainder, most were non-committal, claiming that it depended upon the matter concerned.

Use of in-house lawyers

Initially at least, this determination rested on the availability of in-house expertise. Lawyers were employed in almost two-thirds of organisations surveyed, with some respondents claiming in-house numbers in excess of 15 and, in one case, 40. However, while on average legal departments comprised around five lawyers, over half of respondents employed just one or two, with a solitary lawyer more common than not.

As a result, respondents often felt it necessary to have access to wider legal resources for issues of a more complex nature. As one commented; 'obviously we don't know everything in-house, but they are always the starting point – even if we have to pass it on', while another said: 'it depends what it is. We would look at it ourselves but if it was too risky we'd definitely go outside.'

In many cases, this involved close relations with one firm (or in some cases, a small number of firms) and in this respect, there is very little difference between companies with small-scale legal departents and those without. Respondents from both were often quick to defend arrangements whereby established links meant familiarity with external lawyers. This was also perceived to result in a greater understanding of the company's business and commercial goals.

Simply referring matters to a law firm in the expectation that it will have the necessary expertise, might be said to leave a lot to chance. Nevertheless, two-thirds indicated that such matters would be handled this way, either after initial consultation with in-house lawyers or not.

In all, 17 per cent of our companies handled legal issues in this field exclusively in-house.

Perceptions of expertise

Perhaps unsurprisingly, given that advice on digital media issues had only been obtained by a relatively small section of the base response, recognition of digital media legal expertise was low. Respondents were asked to identify the single law firm they believed to have the most outstanding digital media practice, or admit accordingly if they could not (see table for results). In a bid to minimise favoritism and bias from familiarity with existing firms (across any legal activity), respondents were questioned intensively as to their regular firm's digital media excellence in comparison to other sector players.

In total, 54 endorsements were accepted. Whereas respondents identified 29 different firms, only two stand apart from the rest. Bird & and Bird was the most frequently-cited firm with endorsements from eight respondents – many of whom were keen to extol the firm's virtues further; 'Bird & Bird have a dedicated practice in this area. They're a top firm', 'in this area many lawyers don't have a clue. We would only use Bird & Bird', 'there are external specialists in every area of law. We would choose Bird & Bird for this sort of work.'

Close behind Bird & Bird was Olswang, which received six endorsements; 'We would use Olswang because of their expertise in this sector', 'I don't employ Olswang but would do so if necessary.'

Described by one respondent as 'the best firm for litigation in this area', third placed Freshfields received three recommendations, which elevated it slightly from the remainder.

In conclusion

While commerce has been quick to embrace the potential of the Internet – and seems set to further integrate online trading into its commercial strategy – similar innovation and dynamism has failed to permeate the management of legal affairs.

Concern over the legal implications of digital media activity is rife. Yet, there is little evidence to suggest of any proactive intiatives to address this. Regardless of any recognition of the specialist nature or the unfolding regulations, buyers of legal services are still more likely to rely on existing advisors than seek additional expertise.

There may be many reasons for this: the importance placed on familarity was particularly apparent throughout the course of the research, for instance, both in terms of the commercial understanding that a law firm could develop and the working relationships built between respective parties; the general paucity of knowledge about the wider digital media legal arena; the reliance on in-house expertise.

It is to be hoped that the rest of this book will serve as guidance to clients seeking expert advice.

Law firms identified as having the 'most outstanding' practice in digital media and e-commerce (of 54 accepted endorsements)

1	Bird & Bird	(8)
2	Olswang	(6)
3	Freshfields	(3)
=4	Addleshaw Booth & Co	(2)
	Baker & McKenzie	(2)
	Bristows	(2)
	Cameron McKenna	(2)
	Clifford Chance	(2)
	Denton Hall	(2)
	Dibb Lupton Alsop	(2)
	Linklaters	(2)
	Lovell White Durrant	(2)
	Masons	(2)
	Pinsent Curtis	(2)
	Simmons & Simmons	(2)
	Theodore Goddard	(2)

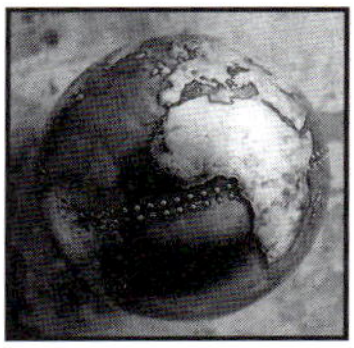

How the guide works

How the guide works

Each Insider's Guide publication – as with the other books in the series – is designed to enable buyers and referrers of work in the sector to access impartial and authoritative information about service providers. As detailed elsewhere, the information that forms the heart of the book is compiled from interviews with hundreds of senior individuals active in digital media and e-commerce work.

Our aim has been to include every firm and individual with a significant practice in the field. We have drawn our research as widely as possible and inclusion is largely predicated on recommendations from clients and fellow professionals. There are, as indicated, several practices of which we are aware which we would have preferred to include but which we were unable to do so; perhaps there are others still. If there are any particular lacunae which our readers notice, we would urge you to contact us so we can redress the balance in the next edition.

Market analysis

At the risk of stating the obvious, the market analysis contains our independent and impartial analysis of the firms and individuals which our research indicated had significant practices in the area. Inevitably much of the actual information has been supplied by the organisations themselves; however every effort has been made to verify that information independently. Although all references to specific cases and pieces of work have been cleared by the firms in order to ensure that there has been no breach of confidentiality, no organisation is offered copy approval or is allowed to review or comment on its editorial coverage.

To get the best out of the guide, we strongly recommend you to read the market analysis in full. Only by doing that will you be able to get a real overview of the whole market and an in-depth understanding of what each firm has to offer. Of course, we have in our star rating system offered you a precis of those firms or individuals which in our view have the strongest practices in different specific areas of expertise. However, each job will have its own demands and distinctions and the tables are designed to be the starting point for debate – not necessarily the definitive last word on the subject.

The independent editorial review

The independent editorial review is exactly that – without prejudice as to whether a firm has any commercial involvement in the guide. It is composed of six sections:

The firm: this is a basic description of the law firm and may include details we feel are relevant to your understanding of the firm as a whole

The group: this is a detailed review of the resources available to the firm in the area of digital media and e-commerce. This has been compiled using the cvs the firms submitted to us and as a result of the extensive face-to-face and telephone interviews conducted with the firms.

The work: this section contains examples of work undertaken by the firm in this area. This is compiled from the cvs submitted to us by the firms and has been taken largely on trust. Much of the work law firms conduct is, inevitably, highly confidential, and we have taken care to protect law firm clients where possible. Nonetheless, we have spoken to hundreds of clients during the process, which has acted, to some degree, as independent verification of these claims

Sample clients: these have in all cases been provided to us by the law firms and permission has been granted to use client names

This firm might suit: this is entirely our assessment of the firm's capability to serve clients in this area, a synthesis of all the information gathered on the firm – the cv, the telephone or face-to-face interviews and client interviews. It is, of course, entirely subjective: we cannot stress enough that chemistry is what is going to decide the instruction at the end of the day, and only the client can judge that. Hopefully, though, our analysis will point clients in the direction of those firms best able to suit their needs – this is a horses for courses market, and not every firm will suit every client.

Website: many clients, during the course of our interviews, suggested that it was preposterous for law firms to claim to be digital media experts without a decent website. Our reviews, once again, are entirely subjective. The reviews are not based upon a dedicated root-around in law firm websites. We have treated the subject as websites should be treated: how inviting is it? how easy is navigation? is there a search engine? etc. In every case, where a search engine exists, we have searched on 'digital media' and on 'e-commerce'. In virtually every cases where publications were available to order, we have ordered publications. It may be in some cases that we have missed a search engine or partner profiles or whatever. However, this will in all cases be down to the fact that said engine or profiles are so difficult to find or the site so unfriendly to navigate that we gave up. We make no apologies for this. For reference, websites were accessed via Microsoft Internet Explorer v3.0, ShockWave enabled, between June 7 and June 20 1999. Law firms may care to check whether their switchboard is properly briefed to give out website addresses when requested...

Where to find a lawyer

The basic listings – which are accorded to those firms which receive editorial coverage – are free of charge. We have endeavoured to ensure that all the address information is current and up to date; where a firm has more than one office we have selected the firm's head office for listing. Ditto the key contacts section.

However it should be pointed out that firms and individuals also have the option of taking an extended entry if there is information which they wish to impart directly to the marketplace. There is, of course, no correlation whatsoever between a firm's investment in any of the Insider's Guides and the editorial coverage that it may receive. Indeed there have been instances where firms or individuals have taken extended listings have not received any editorial coverage at all!

For more information on involvement in the Insider's Guides please contact Mark Brandon on 0171 440 7492 or by email at m.brandon@ncm.uk.com.

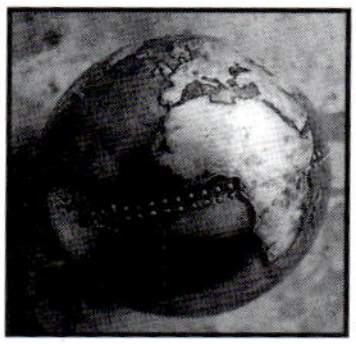

Market analysis...

All-round digital media & e-commerce firms
The digital dozen
New media start-ups
Delivery of services via digital media
US clients establishing in UK and Europe
Trade mark infringement
Advertising, marketing, promotions and sponsorship
Tax issues
E-commerce - system infrastructure and supplier contracts
Regulation
Data protection
Security and encryption
Corporate media
Online literary and information publishing
Interactive and digital TV
Music
Computer games
Mergers and acquisitions
Banking and financial services
IT
North of England,
Midlands and East Anglia
Scotland
South West and Wales
South of England and the Thames Valley

Looking for advice on...

ALL-ROUND DIGITAL MEDIA & E-COMMERCE FIRMS		
Bird & Bird	★★★★★	Has recognised its weaknesses and set about solving them; one of the closest to providing a 'full firm' solution to the new global economy – modest corporate practice and vestigial international presence still raise questions about the future, though
Clifford Chance	★★★★★	Pedigree and size give this global giant a top rating, although it has been keeping a low profile of late by all accounts; further development of its own digital services could take it out of reach of some of its competitors quite quickly
Denton Hall	★★★★★	Fantastic client list, too modest by half; needs to be careful to make sure the rest of the firm is in no doubts about how crucial the dm practice is to its future
Olswang	★★★★★	The original convergence firm continues to motor, but the future for Olswang is unclear – corporate media big-hitter or super-niche dominance? Needs to make sure all its clients are aware of its power in this sector
On their heels:		
Baker & McKenzie	★★★★	The importance of communications is vital to the digital revolution, and Baker & McKenzie has the pedigree and the personnel
Taylor Joynson Garrett	★★★★	Surging on the back of a top US client list – could quickly take the Internet top spot if investment levels are kept up and the partnership's embrace of its new strategy strengthens quickly
Ones to watch:		
Allen & Overy	★★★★	Steady, solid forward movement makes A&O one to be reckoned with for the Millennium, and its strength is broad and deep; firm needs to be more publicly in support of its initiatives in this area (website a case in point)
Freshfields	★★★	Huge investment in personnel should pay off for this blue chip giant
Kemp & Co	★★★	A different prospect to our other choices, but Richard Kemp remains one of, if not the best, digital media lawyers. The future is bright for Kemp & Co
Linklaters & Alliance	★★★	A little slow off the blocks, but never to be underestimated – will be interesting to see where the Alliance (its European network) takes it

Lovell White Durrant	★★★	Often underestimated, but some fine work and some fine individuals; the firm's portfolio of services is so broad, it is difficult to emphasise every area, and this may explain the fairly low profile to date
Osborne Clarke	★★★	Increasingly impressive all-round offering, but perhaps lacks a little focus – has come a long way in a short time
Simmons & Simmons	★★★	On the back of its carrier practice, Simmons continues to gain ground, and some impressive digital clients
Theodore Goddard	★★★	A dark horse, but impressive operators with good client feedback; not to be underestimated – the right merger could see it take the crown
Berwin Leighton	★★	Despite the recent loss of key mover Richard Lister, Berwin Leighton has the drive and energy to go places, particularly on the finance side
Nabarro Nathanson	★★	Good commercial perspective and some excellent work on the cv. The firm's industry sector focus may have resulted in a lower profile than competitors who have been quicker to market themselves in the area

Our recommendations for top digital media and e-commerce firms are based on research among over 150 clients, including extensive qualitative interviews. As explained in the overview, no firm can yet claim consistent strength across the wider sector – it is still very much 'horses for courses'. Please refer to the other tables and to the editorial section for independent recommendations to suit your own needs.

THE DIGITAL DOZEN – TOP INDIVIDUAL LAWYERS

Richard Kemp, ***Kemp & Co***	★★★★★	Kemp's own firm is thriving under the stewardship of this persuasive and quietly charismatic thinker
Christopher Millard, ***Clifford Chance***	★★★★★	Still maintaining guru status, Millard could be the one to herald the revolution in legal services
John Enser, ***Olswang***	★★★★	A star among stars at the entertainment-turned-new media firm
Mark Haftke, ***Bird & Bird***	★★★★	One of the new breed of new media all-rounders – excellent client feedback

Liam McNeive, ***McNeive***	★★★★	This sharp-minded sole practitioner has the AOL seal of approval
Graham Smith, ***Bird & Bird***	★★★★	Longstanding pedigree and boundless enthusiasm for the subject
Robbie Downing, ***Baker & McKenzie***	★★★	Difficult to choose a single person in the Baker & McKenzie team; the charismatic heir of a rich dynasty, we think
Christopher Grew, ***Brobeck Hale and Dorr***	★★★	Could take this partnership of powerful US firms to the top in the European dm firmament
Nick Gardner, ***Herbert Smith***	★★★	Clear-thinking, persuasive delivery, qualified solicitor advocate with experience in technology industries
Paul Gardner, ***Osborne Clarke***	★★★	Quiet, eminently sensible, respected by clients
Richard Lister, ***Freshfields***	★★★	Presents one of the most convincing commercial analyses around
Tom Wheadon, ***Simmons & Simmons***	★★★	A telecoms lawyer by background, Wheadon and partner Chris Watson have led the firm's communications practice to the top

And three rising stars...

Rafi Azim-Khan, ***Theodore Goddard***	Excellent client feedback and a sensible, commercial approach
Duncan Calow, ***Denton Hall***	Tipped for the top by close watchers of the industry
John Salmon, ***Masons***	Another rising star, this time north of the Border

This table represents those lawyers to whom we have spoken who possess the most cogent and persuasive analysis of where digital media law is and where it, and the growing e-business economy, is going. Some of them may be seen by the market as telecoms lawyers, some as entertainment lawyers, some as IT lawyers and some just as good commercial lawyers. We have not intentionally missed anyone out, nor included anyone on the basis of 'long service' or being a recognised 'guru'. These are our personal choices and should not be taken as anything but. Michael Chissick at Field Fisher Waterhouse was a candidate for our Digital Dozen, but refused to speak to us this year., so we were unable to analyse his practice in any depth.

Legal services

NEW MEDIA START-UPS		
Berwin Leighton	★★★	For a City firm, a refreshingly commercial perspective, and a firm which isn't going to get silly on fees; the choice of First Tuesday
Bird & Bird	★★★	Not averse to advising start-ups, but you need to be a serious commercial proposition to interest Bird & Bird
Brobeck Hale and Dorr	★★★	Experience acting for start-ups and significant US pedigree to bring to bear
Osborne Clarke	★★★	Solid all-round capability, and not too big in any office so as to intimidate the smaller client
Rakisons	★★★	Small City firm with the right attitude
Morgan Cole	★★	From Wales to London along the M4; well-placed for start-ups in Wales who prefer to deal in Welsh
Wiggin and Co	★★	Cheltenham-based firm with good, broad experience and excellent tax planning credentials

Although e-commerce is increasingly important to larger organisations, the new media industry is still bursting with new life. The firms above represent our top choices for start-ups who require understanding on bills, guiding through complex legal issues and the vagiaries of finance-raising, and, often, a quicker turnaround than larger companies. Caution: this is NOT an exhaustive list. Many law firms will be willing to consider acting for start-ups, but most require the business to be a viable concept in itself, and some will be more cautious than others.

Further copies of this publication are available at the RRP of £32.50 (plus £2.95 P&P) from New City Media, First Floor, 37-41 Bedford Row, London WC1R 4JH. Address your orders to Edward Bannell (phone 0171 440 7495; fax 0171 831 3171; email: e.bannell@ncm.uk.com)

DELIVERY OF SERVICES VIA DIGITAL MEDIA

Clifford Chance	★★★★	NextLaw paved the way for the delivery of information in digital format; CC is well-placed to change the face of legal practice
Linklaters & Alliance	★★★★	Linklaters flies the Blue Flag for the digital revolution with some success
Rowe & Maw	★	The firm's Fastrack service to Lloyd's market clients has proved that Rowe & Maw has potential in this area
Hammond Suddards	★	Hammonds Direct has revolutionised the way the firm does business in a particular area, and more is sure to follow
Briffa & Co	★	This tiny Islington firm brings online shopping to the legal market

Relatively few firms, even those at the forefront of digital media law, have made serious inroads into the delivery of legal services via digital media. There are many who posit that the legal profession simply will not be able to survive if it does not respond to the digital revolution and change the age-old practice of reinventing the wheel for every new client. Increasingly, clients may wish to download their own forms and contracts and fill in the blanks; certainly, many clients with in-house lawyers are already getting a taste for how law firms can become generic information providers, giving the client a base from which to work. Where the revolution will take lawyers is not yet clear, but change is in the air. Please note that we have NOT included here email systems, secure or otherwise, which many of our recommended firms have instituted in order to facilitate client contact and service.

US CLIENTS ESTABLISHING IN UK AND EUROPE

Baker & McKenzie	★★★★	Sheer breadth of European practice and decent-sized London office makes Baker & McKenzie our top choice
Sidley & Austin	★★★	Early into the telecoms sector here and still one of the leaders stateside
Taylor Joynson Garrett	★★★	Has gone looking for the business on the West Coast and has got it from some of the Internet's hottest rising stars
Weil Gotshal & Manges	★★★	Great finance practice and one of the most deeply established US firms in London
Brobeck Hale and Dorr	★★	Fantastic West Coast client base – one to watch over here
Shaw Pittman	★★	New investment means this firm is one to watch

US clients establishing in Europe need the best advice on a European basis; but they also need a friendly face and people who speak the same language. Our choices reflect the best of the US practices currently active in London. UK-based international firms (such as Clifford Chance and Allen & Overy) with offices in the US in particular, will be well equipped to help US clients with their needs and should not be ruled out. However, one UK firm stands out in its embrace of the new Internet culture, emanating mainly from the West Coast, and that is Taylor Joynson Garrett, although to date its activities will have escaped many of its major competitors here in the UK.

TRADE MARK INFRINGEMENT

Top choices:

Bird & Bird	★★★★★	Good strength in depth and excellent dm practice
Bristows	★★★★★	Some great individual practitioners grace this Lincoln's Inn firm
Eversheds	★★★★★	Isabel Davies is one of the best in the business and Eversheds has a good litigation pedigree
Lovell White Durrant	★★★★★	Heavyweight trade mark litigation expertise for household names coupled with good digital media practice
Taylor Joynson Garrett	★★★★★	One of the top names for IP work generally
Willoughby & Partners	★★★★★	Excellent fmcg client base in particular, blended rates and good case management skills make the firm a good port of call

Also recommended:

Baker & McKenzie	★★★★	Good practice with an international edge
Clifford Chance	★★★★	Huge registration practice and little experience on the contentious side
Herbert Smith	★★★★	Superlative litigation all-rounders
Simmons & Simmons	★★★★	Lower profile than the firm deserves, but a strong TM presence

Alternative choices:

Olswang	★★★	Trade mark work increasingly a strong suit at this top dm firm
Titmuss Sainer Dechert	★★★	Carving out a good reputation with some high profile work
Briffa & Co	★★	Smaller firm, personal touch – one of our personal favourites

Out of London:

Addleshaw Booth & Co	★★★	Exposure to high profile work has kept the firm on top in the North
Wragge & Co	★★	Solid IP operators in Birmingham

Make no mistake about it: a trade mark is a trade mark is a trade mark, whether your infringer is doing it on a website or in solid goods. Our choices represent the cream of the crop for trade mark work, though virtually every firm recommended in the editorial with an IP strength will be capable of handling infringement work. See also regional choices.

ADVERTISING, MARKETING, PROMOTIONS AND SPONSORSHIP

Ad agencies:

Firm	Rating	Comment
Edge Ellison	★★★★★	Of all the major advertising firms, the only one – so far – to have a serious handle on Internet too

General:

Firm	Rating	Comment
Theodore Goddard	★★★★	For general advice in this area, TG is our top choice – Rafi Azim-Khan had more positive feedback than any other individual lawyer in our client research
Lawrence Graham	★★★	Longstanding practice in the area

TAX ISSUES

Top choices:

Firm	Rating	Comment
Freshfields	★★★★★	Resurgence of IP practice should give the firm's tax people new challenges
Linklaters	★★★★★	Strength in depth, now backed by significant European depth
Slaughter and May	★★★★★	The best in the business according to many; replete with stars and strength in depth

Alternative choices:

Firm	Rating	Comment
Berwin Leighton	★★	Ex-Customs expertise gives Berwin Leighton an edge on VAT issues in particular
Field Fisher Waterhouse	★★	Good tax practitioners, excellent dm firm

Most of our recommended firms will have at least one tax practitioner (you don't need many), but for the really thorny problems, our top choices have the most experience and the greatest credentials. Although expensive, it is worth considering that any investment may be offset by good advice.

E-COMMERCE - SYSTEM INFRASTRUCTURE AND SUPPLIER CONTRACTS		
Allen & Overy	★★★★	Banking practice has meant A&O has had early exposure to the beating heart of e-commerce
Bird & Bird	★★★★	Broad and deep skillset for a wide range of e-commerce issues
Clifford Chance	★★★★	Pedigree ensures CC is on the list
Denton Hall	★★★★	One of the best cvs of any firm
Olswang	★★★★	Coming to e-commerce from a different direction, but recent investment has strengthened the firm's position
Simmons & Simmons	★★★★	Increasing exposure on the back of its excellent carrier practice
Taylor Joynson Garrett	★★★★	Blasting onto the e-commerce scene with a mission – a rising star
Ashurst Morris Crisp	★★★	Some recent losses have rather dimmed Ashursts' star, but this City firm is unlikely to just sit there
Baker & McKenzie	★★★	Communications practice is the keystone to success here
Freshfields	★★★	Currently cresting a wave of new investment and a surge of work
Linklaters	★★★	Can field over 70 lawyers in its communications and IP/technology practices and the corporate department provides excellent feed
Lovell White Durrant	★★★	Key client Barclays has exposed Lovells to some of the highest-profile work around
Masons	★★★	Active in online financial services
Nabarro Nathanson	★★★	Some interesting recent work for good clients makes this firm one to watch for the future in this area
Theodore Goddard	★★★	TG's skill-matrix covers the bases and impresses clients
Berwin Leighton	★★	One of the most impressive visions of e-commerce we were exposed to – not to be underestimated
Bristows	★★	Clients rate Bristows' commercial acumen highly
Eversheds	★★	Eversheds is now firmly on the map in e-commerce work
Hobson Audley Hopkins & Wood	★★	Developing out of its games niche into insurance, among other things

Kemp & Co	★★	No danger of overstaffing here: but the Kemp approach will not suit those seeking a full-service firm
Osborne Clarke	★★	Fast building a credible practice in e-commerce
Rowe & Maw	★★	Decent all-rounders and good back-up
Slaughter and May	★★	Quietly ambitious and the corporate heart of the firm should provide raw material
Charles Russell	★	Modest firm, but with a good, broad range of skills and decent potential

All the firms mentioned in this guide will, to a greater or lesser extent, have had some experience with the fabric of e-commerce; it is important to read this table in conjunction with our editorial assessments in the case of each firm, and to refer also to the industry-specialisation tables hereafter for a better indication of those firms with experience to suit particular industries

REGULATION (EU DIRECTIVES, UK GOVERNMENT REGULATION)

Lovell White Durrant	★★★★★	Superb Brussels office and oodles of experience in London makes Lovells a good choice
Clifford Chance	★★★★★	Christopher Millard is still one of the top names on regulatory work
Denton Hall	★★★★★	Has the confidence of Government on dm issues
Olswang	★★★★	Arrival of Colin Long should enhance Olswang's offering
Simmons & Simmons	★★★★	Exposure to telecoms regulatory regimes has given Simmons valuable experience

DATA PROTECTION

Top choices:

Firm	Rating	Comment
Clifford Chance	★★★★★	Christopher Millard is an acknowledged guru in this area
Masons	★★★★	Shelagh Gaskill is the other leading light on data protection work
Allen & Overy	★★	Strong on data protection work for banking clients
Dibb Lupton Alsop	★★	The firm's Data Protection Taskforce aims to focus the firm's resource
Freshfields	★★	A number of substantial clients and an increasing resource
Herbert Smith	★★	Superb litigation experience
Garretts	★	Experience on database mergers
Hamiltons	★	Sole practitioner Angus Hamilton can lay claim to a place in this niche
Osborne Clarke	★	Strong technical interest, with authorship credentials
Taylor Joynson Garrett	★	Experience on database mergers same as Garretts... stacks very boldly!

Legal services

SECURITY AND ENCRYPTION

Baker & McKenzie	Contact: Harry Small or Robbie Downing
Bird & Bird	Contact: Graham Smith
Clifford Chance	Contact: Christopher Millard
Denton Hall	Contact: John Worthy
Lovell White Durrant	Contact: Conor Ward
Norton Rose	Contact: Richard Barratt or Alex Hamilton
Olswang	Contact: Victor Timon
Sidley & Austin	Contact: John Edwards
Simmons & Simmons	Contact: Tom Wheadon
Taylor Joynson Garrett	Contact: Glyn Morgan

Confidentiality makes it difficult to research this area properly, but these seem to be the firms with most experience on their cvs, although many of the firms in our editorial will have undertaken encryption work. The Guide was not abe to rate firms in this area in any detail, but the list above includes names with experience of this work.

CORPORATE MEDIA

Allen & Overy	★★★★	Client list is studded with the media mega-corps
Denton Hall	★★★★	Closer to bridging the gap between City and West End than any other City firm
Olswang	★★★★	Rising corporate stars allied to major dm practice
Weil, Gotshal & Manges	★★★★	Huge investment in the London office of this US firm has brought impressive corporate and finance work its way
Taylor Joynson Garrett	★★★	You could be forgiven for overlooking TJG as its corporate dept hides its light under a bushel somewhat. A good choice, somewhat less expensive than the City's elite top five

Alternatively...

Manches & Co	★★	Smaller corporate firm but has proved it can deliver
Rowe & Maw	★★	Good solid corporate all-rounders

Virtually any firm of any size will have a corporate department capable of handling media deals; our recommendations are based upon a range of factors, including client commentary.

ONLINE LITERARY AND INFORMATION PUBLISHING		
Denton Hall	★★★★★	Key client Bertelsmann has set its stall out as one of the major players in the future of digital services
Bird & Bird	★★★★	Good client feedback propels Bird & Bird to the heights in this field
Biddle	★★★	A traditional publishing practice which has embraced the digital revolution with conviction
Hobson Audley Hopkins & Wood	★★★	Traditional publishing practice coupled to a fine dm stable
DJ Freeman	★★	Anglo-Dutch publishing giant Reed Elsevier turns here for dm advice
Manches & Co	★★	Excellent publishing heritage and fine IP lawyers

Budget choice:

Linnells	★	This Oxford firm is likely to present lower bills than London counterparts and has had exposure to the right kind of issues

The technological revolution has hit traditional publishing hard. After the industry's chequered experience with CD-ROM, publishers are struggling with the new business models presented by the Internet.

Legal services

INTERACTIVE AND DIGITAL TV

Firm	Rating	Comment
Olswang	★★★★★	Client list reads like a TV guide, while practitioners like David Zeffman, Selina Potter and John Enser are among the best in the business
Denton Hall	★★★★	Thorough pedigree across the range of media issues
Simmons & Simmons	★★★★	Ex Videotron and General Cable lawyers are at the heart of Simmons' oft-unsung TV practice
Clifford Chance	★★★	Daniel Sandelson in particular has an excellent name
Field Fisher Waterhouse	★★★	The merger with Allison & Humphreys has brought fresh expertise into the FFW stable
Weil, Gotshal & Manges	★★★	The corporate side of the converging communications sector has fuelled expansion at Weil, Gotshal
Wiggin and Co	★★★	Expert service using City-trained lawyers at out of London prices makes Wiggin a sound choice for digital TV
Marriott Harrison	★★	A more traditional choice for the broadcast industry
Morgan Cole	★	Cardiff office has been advising on digital TV in Wales, including some interesting distribution issues
Rakisons	★	Some good individual practitioners here

The jury is still out on whether the consumer actually wants 200 channels and whether there is enough advertising or subscription revenue to pay for it; one thing is certain, that the focus on TV currently is on carriage and access as much as content, with telecoms companies heavily involved. Our top choices reflect this bias. Traditional broadcast issues, film and broadcast finance, are beyond the scope of this guide.

MUSIC

Firm	Rating	Comment
Theodore Goddard	★★★★★	Unique blend of City firm, dm practice and traditional music lawyers makes this a top choice for the industry
Harbottle & Lewis	★★★★	Music practice and dm practice makes this firm a good choice for music megastars
Paisner & Co	★★	MCPS/PRS alliance has brightened Paisner's star in music
Davenport Lyons	★★	James Ware embraces the digital revolution for this well-respected West End player

Many of the capital's traditional music practices remain in the Dark Ages as far as technology goes, and few are thinking about how the Internet is revolutionising the music industry. Some firms are thinking seriously, and have the pedigree to back their efforts. Our choices reflect those which are successfully marrying knowledge of the music industry with expertise on dm issues.

COMPUTER GAMES		
Osborne Clarke	★★★★★	Paul Gardner and team continue to forge ahead on the games front
Harbottle & Lewis	★★★★	A good client list and some high profile work
Hobson Audley Hopkins & Wood	★★★★	Robert Bond has the pedigree and the clients to put this small City player on the map in this field
Bristows	★★★	Paul Cooke and team are building a real name for themselves
Field Fisher Waterhouse	★★★	Major console experience in particular
Herbert Smith	★★★	Mark Turner gives the top ten firm computer games cred
Lawrence Graham	★★★	Acting for Sony Computer Entertainment has given this firm an insight into all the major games deals
Manches & Co	★★★	Experience for Eidos has given Manches exposure to the entertainment industry's new stars
Taylor Joynson Garrett	★★★	Simon Walker's move to TJG has brought the corporate side of the games market into the firm's grasp
Theodore Goddard	★★★	Arnold Segal is one of the old hands of the games market
Bird & Bird	★★	The appointment of ex-Sega in-houser Howard Rubin gives B&B a foot in the console door
Marriott Harrison	★★	Small, friendly, West End practice helping Mindscape out
Bird Semple	★	Red Lemon has thrust this Scottish firm into the limelight
Masons	★	Ex-Bird Semple practitioners should mean a bright future for the Scottish arm of Masons

Before dismissing computer games out of hand, it is worth remembering that the European computer games market is worth more than the European cinema industry. With new and seductive product to offer, delivery system (PC) prices coming down and the wave of home delivery digital product about to crest, those firms in the forefront now have the potential to seize the future. Never underestimate the power of the game...

MERGERS AND ACQUISITIONS

Top choices:

Firm	Rating	Comment
Freshfields	★★★★★	Renewed vigour on the IP side should bring new skills to this excellent corporate firm's M&A activities
Linklaters	★★★★★	No light between Linklaters and Slaughter and May some say; we can't disagree, and Linklaters has the upper hand on dm work to date
Slaughter and May	★★★★★	The ultimate, the City's choice; currently underpartnered on dm work though
Clifford Chance	★★★★	Less involvement on the huge deals as the top three here, but its dm practice should give it a distinctive edge
Allen & Overy	★★★★	Corporate lives in the shadow of finance at A&O, but can match the best

Alternative choices:

Firm	Rating	Comment
Olswang	★★★	The original convergence firm has not had the exposure it might on the corporate side, but steady investment should bring rewards
Simmons & Simmons	★★★	Communications practice continues to prove that this City firm can punch its weight in the sector
Taylor Joynson Garrett	★★★	Robust if rather low profile corporate department, but with some determined individuals on the dm side

BANKING AND FINANCIAL SERVICES

Top choices:

Firm	Rating	Comment
Allen & Overy	★★★★★	Mondex gave A&O an early insight into the ins and outs of e-commerce
Clifford Chance	★★★★★	Possibly the top banking firm in the UK – though A&O might disagree
Freshfields	★★★★	Not just the Bank of England knocking on Freshfields' door; a raft of investment banks turn to Freshfields for advice
Lovell White Durrant	★★★★	Barclays is the key client, and also one of the first UK clearers to embrace digital life

Also recommended:

Firm	Rating	Comment
Denton Hall	★★★	Good combination of traditional banking practice, good digital media skills and hard IT practitioners
Simmons & Simmons	★★★	Banking is one of several favoured suits at this City firm
Berwin Leighton	★★	NatWest work has broadened horizons at the corporate-to-property firm
Norton Rose	★★	Well-respected banking firm but has not yet had the exposure to e-commerce of some of its major rivals

The Internet is already revolutionising the way banks do business; our choices represent a selection of firms with decent experience in e-banking and financial services. Please note that those looking for advice on business-to-business e-commerce should consult the table above.

Legal services

IT		
Baker & McKenzie	★★★★	Good, solid IT practice, with some of the best individual lawyers in the business
Bird & Bird	★★★★	Government outsourcing has given Bird & Bird a particular insight here
Nabarro Nathanson	★★★★	The firm's IT pedigree is excellent and it has been quietly amassing an impressive e-cv
Bristows	★★★	Technology a strong suit at this Lincoln's Inn firm
Clifford Chance	★★★	Outsourcing expertise coupled with major digital media practice
Denton Hall	★★★	Perhaps less identified as a hard IT firm, but some good work on the cv
Linklaters	★★★	Not to be underestimated – a fine cv
Masons	★★★	IT litigation expertise in great quantity
Taylor Joynson Garrett	★★★	Glyn Morgan heads TJG's charge impressively
Dibb Lupton Alsop	★★	A loss of key personnel has dimmed Dibbs' star somewhat, but the firm is regrouping with speed
Tarlo Lyons	★★	Quietly building decent strength in depth
Rakisons	★	Quiet operator, but some fine work

Our forthcoming guide to IT & Telecoms will contain more specific recommendations for those in technology industries; for the moment, though, these firms represent our main choices for those approaching digital media from an IT angle

NORTH OF ENGLAND

Top choices:

Firm	Rating	Comment
Addleshaw Booth & Co	★★★	Probably the premier Northern firm – a sound choice
Dibb Lupton Alsop	★★★	Still struggling to cohere properly in this field, but a good breadth of expertise
Eversheds	★★★	Able to draw upon first class expertise in the rest of the firm
Hammond Suddards	★★★	Some interesting developments at Hammonds – one to watch
Walker Morris	★★	Patrick Cantrill is a good operator
Dickinson Dees	★★	Newcastle's top choice

Worth a look:

Firm	Rating	Comment
Cobbetts	★★	One of Manchester's leading firms
Keeble Hawson Moorhouse	★	Jonathan Armstrong is a good proponent of the Internet revolution
Oxley & Coward	★	John Yates is more of an IT man, but the firm is definitely worth a look

MIDLANDS AND EAST ANGLIA

Top choices:

Firm	Rating	Comment
Wragge & Co	★★★★	One of the finest firms outside London; best choice in the Midlands, and not a bad choice for the client elsewhere looking for top quality friendly lawyers at non-London prices
Eversheds	★★★	Powerful in both regions, able to draw on excellent resource elsewhere

Worth a look:

Firm	Rating	Comment
Mills & Reeve	★★	Cambridge has had good exposure to the rise of the new technology industries
Taylor Vinters	★	Smaller than main Cambridge rival Mills & Reeve, but worth a look for local advice

SCOTLAND

Top choices:

Maclay Murray & Spens	★★★★	Good IT/IP pedigree
MacRoberts	★★★	A shortlist must for any client with dm issues North of the Border

Worth a look:

Bird Semple	★★	Recent losses have hit the firm hard, but efforts are being made to regroup with vigour
Masons	★★	New blood makes Masons the one to watch in Scotland
Ledingham Chalmers	★	The only Scottish firm outside the central belt taking dm issues in hand

SOUTH WEST AND WALES

Top choices:

Osborne Clarke	★★★★	Very good all-round practice with the advantage of a good London office

Worth a look:

Bevan Ashford	★★	Competent commercial advice with a sprinkling of dm experience
Morgan Cole	★★	Cardiff office counts this as a strong suit

SOUTH OF ENGLAND AND THE THAMES VALLEY

Top choices:

Firm	Rating	Comment
Manches & Co	★★★★	Oxford office is home to the firm's Internet services group
Osborne Clarke	★★★★	Thames Valley office is relatively new, but can offer access to an impressive team

Worth a look:

Firm	Rating	Comment
Donne Mileham & Haddock	★★	Decent choice for the Internet client in particular
Morgan Cole	★★	Oxford office remains one of the region's premier law firms
Nabarro Nathanson	★★	Reading office is the hub of activity for Nabarros' IT practice
Thomas Eggar Church Adams	★	Website is a good indication of the firm's down to earth attitude to business
Clark Holt	★	More of an IT practice, but some good client feedback for this Cheltenham firm
Linnells	★	Oxford firm offering a good commercial service

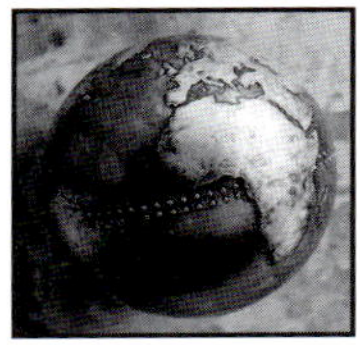

Market analysis...

An independent assessment of the practices of nearly 100 law firms in the United Kingdom

Addleshaw Booth & Co ☎

One of the leading firms in the North of England, now with an office in London. Addleshaw Booth & Co can offer a wide range of commercial services, principally from its strongholds in Leeds and Manchester: in each city it can lay claim to being one of the, if not the, leading firm, although its London office is too new to challenge its major rivals. That said, Addleshaws is hoping to market itself as a national firm, drawing in clients from a wide geographical base.

The group: The information technology unit at Addleshaw Booth & Co, a component of the firm's intellectual property group, is staffed by five partners, and a total of 13 other fee-earners. Jointly headed by Richard Kempner and Robert Stoker, realistically speaking the focus of the group is away from digital media and on IP generally, with a generous helping of IT.

The work: The firm has seen an increasing amount of Internet-related work over the last 12 months, and has advised on a range of issues for clients from a variety of industries. Work has included advising in relation to a proposed online shopping mall, in relation to an Internet catalogue service – the client here being e-business service provider Tradezone – and acting for Interactive Media Services, which sells advertising space on its website through third parties.

In addition to these types of Internet agreements, the unit has, perhaps not surprisingly given its expertise in the area (Addleshaw Booth & Co was ranked top firm in the North-West by this publication's sister volume, *The Legal Insider's Guide to Brands*) been advising on IP issues for a number of clients. As an example, the firm has advised supermarket giant Asda on third party trade mark infringement and passing-off using the Internet as the medium. The firm has also advised flight operator Airtours on similar issues.

In the computer games field, the firm has advised on licensing issues, clients in that domain including Games Workshop plc.

Key contacts: Richard Kempner, Ian Sampson, Robert Stoker

Sample clients: Airtours, Asda, Games Workshop, Interactive Media Services, Tradezone

This firm might suit: As mentioned before, Addleshaw Booth & Co is one of the premier providers of legal services in the North of England, and the digital media practice holds its own in both Manchester and Leeds. The combination of a sizeable and strong banking and finance practice, and an adequate digital media practice makes this firm an automatic shortlist choice for any client looking for a firm in the North. The firm evidently takes costs very seriously. One client commented that the firm 'achieved our objectives with minimal costs', which can't be bad.

Website: www.addleshaw-booth.co.uk An elegant-looking website overall, with a decent publications ordering service (although with nowhere near the range of freebies available from some firms). Unlike many sites, Addleshaw Booth & Co mentions clients on its site and provides maps to its various offices. However, there are few partner profiles (only group heads), no search facility, and a client wanting information on the firm's prowess in this area will have to guess at where to look (hint: it's in commercial services, and there's not a great deal of it). As with many websites, a triumph of style over substance. ★★

For more information see pages 77

Allen & Overy ☎

Allen & Overy is one of the world's leading finance law firms and is in the top five of UK law firms. It has an extensive international network and can offer a complete spread of services to the largest clients.

The group: The communications group at Allen & Overy is composed of some 23 fee-earners, including four partners – two principally known for intellectual property (Laurence Jacobs and Colleen Keck) and two telecoms (Iain Ferguson and Clare Wright). Recent recruits include ex-Garretts senior assistant Andrew White.

The work: The firm's prowess in all things banking has, inevitably, given rise to a good deal of work in this area, both intra-bank e-commerce and electronic trading work and retail bank work. Banking clients include HSBC, NatWest Group and Mondex (where six years of experience has given the firm a particular insight into the setup of consumer-focused operations). Otherwise, the firm has been active advising Ericsson on the joint venture with Nokia, Psion and Motorola to develop EPOC software for the famous PDA; advising IQ Port on the establishment of a major online information service; and acting for a number of large media clients on the development of their e-commerce and general Internet activities (including News Group, United News & Media and Channel 4).

Key contacts: Iain Ferguson, Laurence Jacobs, Colleen Keck, Clare Wright

Sample clients: Channel 4, Ericsson, HSBC, IQ Port, KPN Multimedia, Mondex, Motorola, NatWest Group, News Group, News International, Pfizer, Twentieth Century Fox, United News & Media

This firm might suit: The claims that the firm places this area of work at the centre of its being seem hard to sustain if one visits the website (see below) where the scant information available is hidden deep in the 'Litigation' and 'Corporate' practice areas (under intellectual property and the communications group variously). However, it is clear that the need to be at the centre of all things e-commerce is gaining currency in the firm, with, helpfully, strong advocates in the banking department (as well, obviously, from the communications group itself).

Indeed, thanks to its superlative reputation in finance, Allen & Overy would be one of our top choices for banks and financial institutions involved either in their own web strategy or e-commerce and trading. Its international telecoms practice, particularly on the finance side again, is such that the firm has been exposed to a wide range of regulatory issues. Its corporate department, though not matching that of a Linklaters or a Freshfields in volume terms, is highly experienced and of the best quality, and its performance on large commercial matters (company set-up, joint ventures, etc) will be excellent.

We would not tend to recommend the firm for the smaller client (for whom it would seem extremely expensive) or developers/producers/artists on the content side of the converging industries, although large media clients should consider the firm's expertise in all kinds of infrastructure projects.

In our view, Allen & Overy is one to watch in this area as e-commerce takes hold of the global economy.

Website: www.allenovery.com
Looks slick, but suffers from often unhelpful navigation. Clients will be hard-pressed to find anything immediately on the website about this area of work (try looking in Litigation or Corporate) and a search on the word 'e-commerce' returns nothing, though 'digital media' will be more profitable. The site says nothing specific about the work the firm does in the area. Design is clean and clear, and download times are fine, but the 'Press Office' and 'Press Release' archive are a mess and intimidating to a casual viewer. Impressive list of publications, though.
★★★

For more information see pages 59, 66, 68, 70, 74, 75

☕	**Face to face interview**
☎	**Telephone interview**

Ashurst Morris Crisp ☎

One of the City's leading firms, with a particular reputation for management buy-out work.

The group: The communications, media and technology group at Ashursts (currently composed of seven partners and 43 other fee-earning solicitors) has not grown immensely of late, and in fact has lost a couple of its high-fliers. However, there is a growing feeling of

Legal services

confidence among partners in the group that things may be changing.

One sign of the development is the installation of Chris Ashworth as overall head of the group. His position is merely titular, as he is a corporate lawyer by trade, but his position may be an indication of the increasing seriousness with which the firm is taking new media. Another indication could be the structure of the CMT group, which includes corporate M&A lawyers specialising in technology transactions, as well as drawing in banking and financial services specialists when appropriate.

The work: As one might expect from a City firm of Ashursts' size, the practice is relatively diverse, and includes some major clients – both nationally and internationally. On Internet matters the firm has advised a number of the larger UK and European ISPs, including Virgin Net. Issues advised on include content and trade mark issues, regulatory issues, network access arrangements, and terms and conditions of service.

On the e-commerce front, again the client list is not unimpressive. Clients include HMV Media, Cyberlife technology, and two major UK publishers. Ashursts has also been advising the companies behind two imminent online projects, one in the insurance market, and the other in financial services.

Although the digital television market is still relatively embryonic in this country, the firm has also advised several clients in relation to their services in that area. Kingston Communications is one such client, with Ashursts advising on the roll out of high speed interactive ASDL services. Further afield, @Entertainment used Ashursts as legal counsel on all aspects relating to the launch of its multi-channel platform in Poland in September of last year, with ongoing work since then. Leading this area is partner Tony Ghee, widely regarded as a leading light in the communications and media fields.

Key contacts: Chris Coulter, Tony Ghee, Mark Lubbock

Sample clients: @Entertainment, Cyberlife Technology, Elmsdale, HMV Media, Kingston Communications, Virgin Net

This firm might suit: Despite its image as a corporate firm, Ashurst Morris Crisp has a decent digital media practice. Undoubtedly, the attraction of choosing a firm like Ashurst Morris Crisp is the level of corporate expertise in addition to the new media practice. However, although its individual practitioners are well respected in the area, we have a lingering suspicion that dm work is not top of the pile at Ashursts, and that despite a significant resource, the firm has failed to capitalise on an early lead over its rival City firms. Significant departures from the communications practice are also a possible indication of a less than ideal practice set-up, although the firm's resources are such that the loss of partners Stewart White and James Nimmo will come as less of a setback than they would at a smaller practice.

Ashursts is a firm equipped to act for major corporate clients, but there is some evidence of a more entrepreneurial streak within the group which would probably lend itself to newer companies in this field.

Website: www.ashursts.co.uk
Crisp, if staid-looking. One nice feature are the 'trees' which drop down from the static subject bar at the top. Relatively up-to-date publications to order, but only organised in chronological order and non-searchable (can you really be bothered to look through them all?). Mercifully, look under Practice Areas and you actually see the word 'e-commerce' with its own description of how the firm organises itself to do this kind of work (unlike many law firms), but there is no site search facility, so be prepared to rummage around. Not bad, but not wonderful. ★★

Baker & McKenzie

One of the largest law firms in the world, with 55 offices in 34 countries. The London office is modest by City standards, but highly focused on technology and intellectual property issues.

The group: The firm can field a wide range of lawyers in this area, from amiable 'techie' Harry Small to the charming, understated Peter Strivens, but unlike some of its competitors, every lawyer will tend to have had exposure to the full range of a matter (ie from non-contentious to contentious work). This somewhat cross-disciplinary approach, the firm feels, gives a more rounded quality of advice.

It is worth noting also that because of its unparalleled international network of offices, Baker & McKenzie lawyers tend to have access to a wide spread of expertise in different jurisdictions – this is particularly relevant with regard to digital media work, given the facility of email and the firm's use of a knowledge-sharing intranet.

There have been a couple of recent departures from the team worth noting, namely the move of partner Stephanie Liston to US firm McDermott, Will & Emery and the move of Graham Allan in-house to client Cisco Systems. Although both lawyers had a name, neither departure will significantly affect the team's ability in this area.

The work: The firm's client base in this area, traditionally, has been supplier-led, both in IT (Oracle, Lotus, 3Com) and telecoms (Orange, NTL, Racal Network Services), but a user-base has developed off the back of this, including household names such as Kellogg and Bank of Scotland, as well as a major packaging supplier.

Recent work includes advising NTL on the launch of digital interactive cable channels; advising on the set-up of the groundbreaking Bolero electronic trading system and advising Kellogg on the implementation of its global email system.

The firm is quite hot on what it calls 'Client Connectivity', through BakerNet (the firm uses Lotus cc:mail), allowing desktop-to-desktop access to its lawyers, a system it has operated for some time.

Key contacts: Robbie Downing, Michael Hart, Don Jerrard, Harry Small, Nigel Stamp, Peter Strivens

Sample clients: 3Com, Bank of Scotland, Kellogg, Lotus, NTL, Oracle, Orange, Racal Network Services

This firm might suit: Baker & McKenzie will be of interest to any international client, particularly those involved in IT, telecoms or related industries, where the firm has a thorough pedigree.

Although coming at convergence from an IT/telecoms angle, its growing exposure to digital media issues means large clients involved in e-commerce would do well to consider it.

Perhaps because of the international nature of the firm, Baker & McKenzie lawyers are less reserved than many of their kind and can lay genuine claim to being a friendly, enthusiastic – and knowledgeable – bunch.

Website: www.bakerinfo.com
Animated intro sequence leads to a clear, clean homepage for the global firm. Navigation is easy, with plenty of links and IP/IT/Communications is well flagged everywhere. Beyond that, however, it's pretty thin. There is no press release archive, nothing on specific pieces of work undertaken, aside from the usual description of kinds of work undertaken and no global search facility. All Baker & McKenzie lawyers are listed, though only partners have profiles (as is standard on law firm sites). ★★

For more information see pages 59, 61, 63, 64, 66, 69, 76, 220, 246, 247

☕	**Face to face interview**
☎	**Telephone interview**

Berwin Leighton ☕

Berwin Leighton is a medium-sized City firm, particularly renowned for property work, but with an energetic practice in a number of other areas including all things new media. The firm's corporate and finance practice is also well-regarded.

The group: The firm's practice for the convergent industries combines lawyers from the media and communications department with their counterparts in other commercial and corporate departments, such as tax and competition. The information & communications technology group (ICT), as it is known, is staffed by three full-time and ten part-time partners, and a further 20 assistants. Corporate partner Quentin Solt has recently taken stewardship of the group, following the move of partner Richard Lister to Freshfields.

Coincidentally, Berwin Leighton has just appointed two solicitors (one from Customs & Excise) and a barrister who will be active in the group.

The work: Berwin Leighton has, in particular, concentrated on areas such as finance raising in the technology sector, and claims close ties with many of the leading venture capitalists in the UK.

The ICT group acts for a range of large institutions both hi-tech and on the user side. In the latter category, Berwin Leighton has advised several of NatWest's ventures, including NatWest Global Financial Markets (on the procurement of Public Key Infrastructure), and Platform 7.

Interestingly, the firm has recently been chosen to advise First Tuesday, the Internet interpreneur network.

Key contacts: Lloyd Evans, David Grossman, Amanda Lewis, Quentin Solt, Andrew Somper

Sample clients: Platform 7, NatWest Global Financial Markets, Telematix Ltd, Premium Credit

This firm might suit: Berwin Leighton is not your average City firm, being rather more commercial and entrepreneurial in spirit than many of its rivals – one client described them as 'a half-City firm', for instance, citing the expertise of 'a City firm with a less City attitude'. The firm's digital media lawyers are a pretty polished bunch, which is what you might expect from a firm which attributes great value to an MBA, and is evidence of the deal of thought which has gone into its pitch to the new media community (other clients describe the service as 'very professional – very focused and with a good commercial understanding', and are appreciative of the firm having 'taken the time to understand the technology and business that we are dealing in').

The firm has good business links, and has a clear strategy for how to get the high-profile, high-income work which should propel it to the forefront of the hi-tech legal market.

Website: www.berwinleighton.com
A colourful, even flashy site with some good features. The search engine brings up three instances for 'digital media' although nothing for 'e-commerce'. Publications are a bit thin on the ground compared to some firms and partner profiles are not exceptionally forthcoming. On the plus side, the firm does list some key clients, although the practice areas are once again listed from the supplier (ie law firm) point of view rather than from the purchaser's. The

firm was in the process of deciding exactly how to proceed with the next generation of its site as the guide went to press. ★★★

For more information see pages 60, 62, 65, 66, 75, 227, 246

Bevan Ashford ☎

Known above all else for its expertise in healthcare advice, Bevan Ashford has offices in Bristol, Cardiff, Exeter, Plymouth, Taunton and Tiverton, and is one of the top firms in the South West.

The group: The intellectual property/ information technology group at Bevan Ashford, headed by Gareth Jones consists of four partners and seven assistants – not a bad tally by any standards – and the total number of 'fee-earners' is 13. Jones is a member of the CBI's IP forum, while fellow partner and recent recruit Stuart Whitfield is a member of the same organisation's working group on the draft EU e-commerce directive.

The work: Much of the work from the last 12 months has been IP-related, with the firm advising on trade mark and copyright issues arising from the use of domain names, hypertext links, frames, and online advertising. The group has advised a number of clients on their online ventures; among these can be found an online bookstore, an online fantasy basketball competition, and numerous cases where Bevan Ashford has advised on Internet trading in general. Issues covered include formation of contracts, liability, consumer trade law, and online advertising.

Key contacts: Gareth Jones, Stuart Whitfield

Sample clients: withheld

This firm might suit: A solid commercial firm with a broadly-based IP team, Bevan Ashford would suit any client determined to instruct locally in the South-West. Its particular expertise in health matters means medical insurers and health authorities nationally should also consider it where relevant.

Website: www.bevanashford.co.uk
Coolly-modern brochure site with some nice features and some irritating ones, chief of which is the annoying horizontal navigation applied throughout the text, which forces the user to click an arrow to pass from one pretty generic piece of blurb to the next. There is a nice links section, a publications section (still relatively rare among regional firms) and press releases (not ordered and dreadfully presented), but no profiles of the firm's 50 partners. ★★

For more information see pages 78

Biddle ☎

A small commercially-minded firm, Biddle is primarily known for its media and entertainment practice, acting for a number of large media players, generally from the world of publishing, such as the Press Association and Associated Press.

The group: Led by partner Kim Walker, Biddle's media and publishing department comprises nine lawyers, with Walker heading the non-contentious side of the practice. Litigation is led by Martin Soames, and David Hooper, whose main area of specialism is defamation. Brian Palmer leads the IT litigation practice.

The work: Biddle's digital media practice has developed largely on the back of its media and publishing practice. In this area the firm advises many media companies. Typical clients include The Press Association and ITN, for whom Biddle has advised on matters relating to its web presence and strategy. The latter client is one of the department's most active clients, owning vast amounts of content on its own archive, and the Reuters TV and Film archive. ITN also runs the ITV website, and handles the website of Euronews, a European satellite broadcaster owned by ITN.

One major piece of work during the last 12 months has been the advice given to Dawson Holdings plc for its Private Finance Initiative bid for the contract to digitise the holdings and catalogue of the British Library.

Key contact: Kim Walker

Sample clients: PA, ITN, ITV Website (owned by ITN), Dawson Holdings plc

This firm might suit: Clients from media backgrounds, or clients moving into online media coverage could shortlist this firm, acting as it does for so many media companies now crossing over into new media. The firm has a becalming atmosphere about it, and partner Kim Walker is a quietly spoken but reassuring head for the media and publishing department.

Website: www.biddle.co.uk
Stylish but spartan site, with no publications or articles to download (and no search engine); however, there is editorial about how the firm does business and partner profiles with pictures. Overall, functional but definitely web-lite. ★★

For more information see pages 71, 186, 250

Bindman & Partners ☎

Bindman & Partners is a niche civil liberties and libel practice based along Gray's Inn road, within walking distance from King's Cross, but also a stone's throw from legal centres, Gray's Inn and Lincoln's Inn.

The group: Specialising in civil liberties,

the firm does not genuinely have a digital media department, although where online defamation is concerned, Nick Braithwaite should be a point of contact.

The work: Bindman & Partners is not, and probably never will be, a firm generally associated with digital media. Its place in this guide, however, is through partner Nick Braithwaite's involvement in an ongoing libel case brought against Demon Internet by Braithwaite's client, Dr Laurence Godfrey.

At the time of going to press, Bindmans had secured an interlocutory ruling from the High Court stating that for libel purposes, ISPs are publishers, a somewhat crucial point.

Although it will be some time before the case is heard in full, it is already provoking stronger opinions on both sides than any Internet case before it. All ISPs should take note of the decision when it comes, as it may place them in a position of responsibility they have hitherto tried to avoid.

Key contact: Nick Braithwaite

Sample clients: Dr Laurence Godfrey (*Godfrey v Demon Internet*)

This firm might suit: Nick Braithwaite has modestly assured New City Media that he is just one of many competent libel lawyers. However, it should be noted that he is currently advising his client with great success in a case which could prove potentially crucial for the Internet community.

Website: No website, according to the firm's switchboard.

For more information see page 216

Bird & Bird

Relatively modest-sized City commercial firm, situated just off Holborn Circus. Regarded by its peers and clients alike as one of the leading firms for technology and communications law.

The group: Whereas many firms approach digital media from the point of view of seeing which of their existing services has a digital media angle, the Bird & Bird philosophy has led to the concept of digital media pervading the relevant areas of the firm. Thus, whereas many firms have digital media lawyers or indeed departments, Bird & Bird is on the road to becoming an e-commerce firm. This is driven by a group (headed by the breathlessly enthusiastic Graham Smith) with a genuine understanding of convergence, and capitalises on a seeming will within the greater part of the firm to accept the osmosis of dm issues. A perceived weakness on the media side (from which many other players in digital media, such as Olswang and Harbottle & Lewis, for instance, have approached the area) has resulted in a focus on bolstering the firm's content practice, most notably with the relatively recent addition of Mark Haftke (ex of music firm Russells) and Howard Rubin (ex of entertainment firm Sheridans, via a post in-house at Sega Europe), both of whom display the easy charm of lawyers used to dealing in entertainment circles (and in contrast to Bird & Bird's historically rather more reserved image). The arrival of another ex-Sheridans litigator, Petra Williams, further illustrates the determination of Bird & Bird to bolster its strength in the media arena.

Otherwise, the group can call on expertise across the key sectors of telecoms (David Kerr being a doyen of the field, backed up by quality through the ranks – new partner Graham DeFries is highly rated by clients, for instance), intellectual property (a host of names including Morag MacDonald, David Harriss and Trevor Cook) and IT (Roger Bickerstaff and Graham Smith, for instance). The breadth of collected expertise puts Bird & Bird in the front ranks of those firms able to offer a service right across the converging industries.

The work: Recent work includes acting for Datastream on its global data network deal with Equant; for EMAP and Amazon on content sharing and traffic generation deals; for Lloyds TSB on its Internet banking product; for Planet Online in its deal with Freeserve; for IMVS on a variety of e-commerce deals and for a host of media companies on various dm deals, as well as traditional IP and publishing issues. Corporate work (particularly finance-raising) is also in evidence in the firm's dm cv.

Key contacts: Graham DeFries, Mark Haftke, Morag Macdonald, Howard Rubin, Graham Smith, Trystan Tether, Justin Walkey

Sample clients: Carlton Online, Datastream, Demon Internet, Electronic Telegraph, the Football Association, Lloyds TSB, Planet Online

This firm might suit: Bird & Bird is a good choice for most clients seeking specialist e-commerce advice, with experience of a wide range of work and the capacity to innovate where needed, to cope with new technologies and ideas. The pervasiveness of the new media ethic throughout the firm is genuinely rare among UK law firms, so where Bird & Bird cannot match some of its larger City rivals on, say, corporate or property resource, this is compensated for to a degree by the likelihood of a deeper understanding of the industry issues involved.

While it is difficult to generalise, Bird & Bird lawyers do have a reputation for being quite picky, but this is perhaps a reflection as much of their potential for coming up with new points with which to challenge the opposition as it is of obsessive perfectionism (although its competitors would doubtless disagree!). Nonetheless, this sometimes leads to a degree of nervousness among clients: 'they can get bogged down in detail – sometimes it's more important for us to get something done within the next half an hour than wait until tomorrow'.

Where the firm has a distance still to go is on bolstering its media practice – it is still some way off the likes of Olswang and Denton Hall, particularly on broadcast matters – but developments in this direction are encouraging. It has also yet to establish a defined e-commerce core, but this will come with time (indeed, we would caution clients to beware of firms which do claim 100 per cent devotion in their digital media (or equivalent) groups). Looking forward, it will be interesting to see to what extent Bird & Bird becomes involved in larger corporate deals and joint ventures on the e-commerce frontier. Certainly the capacity is there, but its larger rivals have more extensive corporate client bases to depend upon as this kind of work develops.

Probably more than the major international firms such as Clifford Chance and Baker & McKenzie, Bird & Bird is able to offer the genuinely small, entrepreneurial client a favourable hearing and a flexibility when it comes to talking money, although the firm's burgeoning client list is unlikely to put it in the frame for 'taking a gamble' on a small client in the hope that the work will give it profile or exposure: it needs neither. Only genuinely commercial prospects need apply.

In our judgement, Bird & Bird remains one of the finest examples of legal service providers in this area, described as 'clear, consistent and responsive' by effusive clients. One commented: 'In this area, many lawyers don't have a clue – we would only use Bird & Bird' while another described them as 'a top firm'. Mark Haftke, in particular, comes in for significant praise, regularly described as 'excellent'.

The firm's steady commitment to identifying and filling any gaps in its practice has seen it lever itself out of the relatively narrow 'hard' IT/telecoms niche in which it found itself to become a genuinely broad practice. Recommended.

Website: www.twobirds.com

Bird & Bird's Office On The Web is the stated 'home of digital media, telecommunications, intellectual property and information technology lawyers' (just don't try saying it while drinking a glass of water). The site is organised, as one might expect, as a virtual office, although much graphical allusion to this is (disappointingly) missing, and the overall feel is quite dated. Digital media is easy to find, with links to partner profiles (but no pictures), although a search on 'e-commerce' finds nothing. There is a selection of key legal developments, in the News Room, but there is no detail on specific pieces of work undertaken or specific clients. The Lunch Room promises to introduce us to

B&B partners, but is just (disappointingly) a link to the partner profiles again, while the Library gives access to articles and books and the Seminar Room lists forthcoming conferences and seminars as well as slides from selected talks given by B&B lawyers. Design is looking tired, but this is made up for by good functionality (search engine on the first page is particularly welcome). ★★★

For more information see pages 59, 60, 61, 62, 64, 66, 69, 71, 73, 76, 187

Bird Semple ☎

Scottish firm Bird Semple has gone further than most law firms in taking a sector approach to business; while one sector focus is on property and related matters, the other - branded as Techmedia - aims to encompass new technology industries in their broadest sense.

The group: Headed by Norman Oliver, Techmedia currently consists of two partners and six assistants. The group has had a year of fluctuating fortunes, including the departure of rising star John Salmon – one of the architects and most charismatic proponent of Techmedia – to the Glasgow office of construction and IT specialists Masons, but the firm is keen to stress that staffing levels remain constant (Lisa Forsyth was recently recruited from Norton Rose, for instance).

The work: All Techmedia's clients are drawn from the technology sector, giving the group an unrivalled number of clients from the sector. Among others, the group has advised in a computer trade mark infringement case, which the firm successfully resolved on behalf of its client. The firm's early accent on smaller clients is also paying off: Glasgow-based games developer Red Lemon's game 'Braveheart' has been one of the hits of 1999.

Having advised many clients on deals and agreements with venture capitalists, the next move for Techmedia is in advising the venture capitalists themselves. Yet to really launch into this area, it will be interesting to see how the phenomenally successful – to date – Techmedia group will fare on the other side of the funding fence.

Key contact: Norman Oliver

Sample client: Red Lemon Studios

This firm might suit: Almost every law firm one comes across will describe itself as friendly, but few manage the transition to what the man in the street (as opposed to other lawyers) would genuinely regard as friendly. At Bird Semple, this tendency is a fusion of good humour, practicality and honest-to-goodness enthusiasm for the work it does. The result is one of the friendliest and least pretentious firms a client could hope to instruct. The firm's commitment to the sector is undoubted, even if its rather daring approach to marketing (once again, daring from a lawyer's perspective) has ruffled feathers among its competitors. Its recent losses to Masons are to be regretted (although not for Masons!).

Website: www.birdsemple.co.uk
Professional-looking, easy to navigate and rather more client-focused than many competitor sites. There are plenty of articles which are of interest to the digital client and the helpful Business Guides raise flags for the client to further explore. Case studies provide examples of Bird Semple in action for its clients. The lack of a global search engine means the information is to be discovered rather than got at straight away. One nice feature is the Enquiry area, where clients can post general enquiries to the firm. All in all, a well thought-out, elegant site. ★★★★

For more information see pages 73, 78, 188

Briffa & Co

Established by Margaret Briffa, who trained at Clifford Chance. Briffa & Co can be found inside the Business Design Centre in Islington, North London.

The group: It would be inaccurate to talk of a digital media group or department within the six-lawyer (including five solicitors and one barrister) firm, as Briffa & Co focuses exclusively on intellecutual property issues.

The work: The workload is exclusively focused on IP, and among the firm's clients, many are new media companies, ranging from small web developers to a large multinational (Briffa & Co has recently been awarded a contract with this latter client to advise on its UK and European liabilities and responsibilities in respect of its Internet strategy). Although the small clients perhaps make up the majority of the client base, the firm is now at a stage in its life where it is looking to get work from more and more sizeable clients.

Key contact: Margaret Briffa

Sample clients: Withheld

This firm might suit: Anyone who can't stand the thought of crusty old law firms or wandering around lost amid the imposing grey slabs of the Square Mile would be well-advised to travel to Islington to meet this friendliest of firms. Margaret Briffa is often mentioned by her peers as someone who 'knows her stuff', and the firm's open, quiet offices would seem to reflect an attitude not normally associated with commercial law firms.

Website: www.briffa.com
Something else which sets Briffa & Co apart is its website. The firm is one of few to currently offer online legal

services, with a series of standard form documents which you can order online for a modest sum (and is certainly the only firm to offer a 'shop' in which to buy them). The site is elegant, well-designed and simple to navigate. Articles are short and to the point and everything encourages the client to contact the firm. Disappointingly, there are no proper lawyer profiles and no pictures, which takes a human edge from proceedings, and no search engine, although the firm is focused enough for this not to be a problem. Overall, one of the more promising sites we visited. ★★★

For more information see page 64

Bristows

Medium-sized London firm with a market-leading reputation for intellectual property work. Bristows has long been seen as the specialist IP and technology choice for many blue-chip corporates and household names. Although it has suffered from a rather stuffy image, the shedding of its construction department and shortening of its name (from Bristows Cooke & Carpmael) has proved a catalyst to shaking off its old image as well. Confirming this, its traditional-looking Lincoln's Inn frontage now gives way to an office replete with stylishly understated furniture and some 'challenging' pieces of art...

The group: The inevitably cross-disciplinary group can field some eight partners and 14 other fee-earners, although none of the firm's lawyers spends 100 per cent of their time on dm issues.

The work: Bristows has a growing practice in computer games with highlights including acting for flight simulation developers Digital Image Design (Paul Cooke advised on the recent sale to Infogrames), acting for Revolution Software in corporate and IP matters and acting variously for industry players such as Ian Hetherington (Psygnosis) and Fergus McGovern's HotGen Studios. One new client is Trillion Telecom, for which Bristows has been active advising on the company's patentable Internet telephony product. On the more heavyweight corporate side, recent work includes acting for Panasonic on its digital interactive satellite joint venture and for MTV Networks on a range of contractual and regulatory issues.

Key contacts: Paul Cooke, Lisa Roberts, Matthew Warren, Philip Westmacott

Sample clients: Digital Image Design, Revolution Software, Panasonic UK, MTV Networks, Psygnosis, HotGen Studios, Trillion Telecom

This firm might suit: Bristows' IP practice was founded on heavyweight patent and trade mark work for household name clients, and as a result the firm probably has a greater percentage of technically-qualified lawyers than any other, particularly relevant here as relates to technology and electronics. As a result, Bristows can field serious expertise where IT and other technology-related clients are concerned (its telecoms practice has grown out of acting for mobile handset manufacturers, for instance).

By nature, the firm is an understated one. Its lawyers, perhaps because of their science/technology backgrounds, come across as very down-to-earth, practical, and, when you get to know them, very friendly, although they are perhaps initially more reserved than many of their peers.

In our view, the Bristows approach will have particular appeal to the technology client seeking a reassurance that their lawyer genuinely understands the business they are in and will speak the same language. For those clients with serious brands to protect, Bristows' has serious litigation expertise, especially with regard to the Patents County Court.

Although it has come at convergence from a different angle to, say, Olswang or Denton Hall, its experience in the 'content' side of practice is growing, particularly with regard to computer games, where Paul Cooke, head of the corporate practice, has a refreshingly commercial perspective (and is described as 'the best in the business' by one games client – his colleague, solicitor Lisa Roberts also comes highly recommended). However, it is less well-equipped to deal with straightforward general media matters and the heavyweight regulatory side of telecoms, although has had limited exposure in both cases.

Clients are happy with the approach generally: 'with Bristows, I don't feel I'm paying for the learning curve, as you are with so many lawyers' was a typical comment. Although described as 'quite expensive', clients feel they get value for money with the firm: 'it's a false economy to use cheap lawyers', says one Bristows user.

Website: www.bristows.com
A graphically stylish site, but light on content. There is some good legal update material and an impressive back catalogue of publications is available but that's about it (aside from a Japanese version, which is obviously of particular interest to some clients). A search on 'e-commerce' brings up nothing (aside from some juddering of the screen), ditto 'digital media' (although stick a comma in and you get 21 documents). The lack of any press release database, partner profiles and client or work details leave the site with a slightly sterile feel. ★★

For more information see pages 64, 66, 73, 76, 189

Face to face interview

Telephone interview

Brobeck Hale and Dorr

Established at the beginning of the decade, Brobeck Hale and Dorr is the result of a joint venture between US firms Brobeck Phleger & Harrison LLP and Hale and Dorr LLP. The firm's main thrust is in advising hi-tech clients on a range of corporate and commercial issues, including IPOs, cross-border M&A, and licensing and intellectual property. The recent addition, from City firm Norton Rose of dual-qualified (England and Canada) Pierre-Andre Dubois illustrates the firm's intentions for growth, and expansion.

The group: Pierre Andre Dubois heads the firm's IP and IT practice, with Chris Grew the other partner in the group. In truth, however, the digital media practice is spread through the firm; Grew is a partner in the corporate finance department, while other partners in the corporate department also spend a significant amount of time on digital media related issues. In short, the firm is focused on the hi-tech, with most partners involved to some extent in that sector.

The work: Rather than specialising in niche practice areas such as IP or IT, as delineated by UK law firms, Brobeck Hale and Dorr's practice in this area consists of advice on general business, trade, and commercial matters, but delivered to a specific client-set. Clients such as Eyretel Ltd – publishers of voice recording software and Internet applications – and ECsoft plc, an English IT consulting services company have made use of the Brobeck's experience of stock market flotations.

The firm advises many start-up companies, and so has wide-ranging contacts with both merchant banks and venture capitalists both in the UK and in America. In many instances, the firm has been instructed by these companies in deals, rather than the company to be floated. Brobeck's advised on the IPO of data storage specialists iXOS Software AG (Germany), as counsel to the underwriters in the first listing, and then as advisors to the company itself on a secondary offering of the same company.

Key contacts: Julia Bracewell, Pierre-Andre Dubois, Christopher Grew

Sample clients: FortuneCity.com – IPO on the Neuer Markt, European Venture Partners, Eyretel Ltd, ECsoft plc

This firm might suit: US technology sector clients looking to float on one of the European markets would be well advised to consider this joint London operation, which client commentary rates as 'very good'. The firm's partners have experience of many European indices, while also having a good grasp of US issues, and an 'attitude which generally differs from their UK counterparts', according to one client. The firm believes strongly in taking the lead with clients rather than waiting to receive instructions before making decisions or creating ideas. If you want your lawyers to know your business as well as they know their own, then Brobeck may meet your requirements.

Website: www.bhd.com
Simply serves as a link page to the two founding firms' websites (www.brobeck.com and www.haledorr.com). Anyone in any doubt about the firms' calibre or client bases should visit either related site: Brobeck's in particular is very client-focused (the list of sample IT clients is quite astonishing), while the more stylish Hale & Dorr site is more run-of-the-mill in content terms. (No rating)

For more information see pages 61, 62, 63

Cameron McKenna

Formed from the merger between Cameron Markby Hewitt and McKenna & Co, the former featuring a well-reputed insurance and financial services practice as well as a fledgling IT practice – led by current head of IT John Armstrong – while the latter brought to the newly conjoined firm skills in energy, property and mainstream intellectual property work, among others.

The group: Led by John Armstrong, the group of lawyers active in digital media work is still relatively small. Armstrong is the sole partner responsible for the digital media practice, although the information technology and telecoms department is staffed by a total of five partners (four in London and one in Budapest), all of whom have digital media experience.

The work: Not having a particularly sizeable department has not, however, prevented the firm from advising several impressive clients on a range of commercial and IP matters (its McKenna & Co roots have been important on the IP side, for instance).

The firm's strong client base of financial institutions means it should be in a good position in relation to business to business e-commerce, being able to apply existing business models (as far as is practicable) to the new carriage mode, but resources are slim compared to most of its rivals.

Key contacts: John Armstrong, Jeremy Newton

Sample clients: withheld

This firm might suit: Digital media is not an area of focus at Cameron McKenna, but the firm's exposure to a wide range of banking and financial services work will have given it an insight into commercial principles applicable to e-commerce. Although direct resource is pretty thin, the firm is broadly-based and has some strength in conventional IP work, so clients need not feel uncomfortable or that they are 'taking a chance' on

Cameron McKenna. Armstrong's relaxed air and clear vision will also reassure.

Website: www.mckenna.co.uk
Extremely professional-looking site, which effectively makes the point that Cameron McKenna is an international firm (partner search keyed to location, for instance). Annoyingly, however, searching for an expert in anything brings up nothing unless you know the name you are looking for. There is no global search facility – clients in this sector search in commercial services under the usual suspects (intellectual property, information technology). Partner profiles are very detailed, though. Publications are replaced by the firm's LawNow email update service, which is easy to register for. The Client Focus section tantalises, but it might have been more convincing if the clients had been responding to the firm's value statements. Nonetheless, among the finest-looking sites. ★★★

Charles Russell

One of relatively few firms in this guide still to operate a private client practice, Charles Russell is an unassuming practice based near Fleet Street, with 76 partners and a total of 203 fee-earners. Digital media is one of around four or five core competencies the firm will advise in; namely charities, media and communications, commercial property, insurance and reinsurance, and the aforementioned private client practice.

The group: The computer law, IT and Internet interest group is a subset of the firm's overall media and communications practice, with David Berry at the head of the former, and Mark Moncrieffe occupying the same position in the latter. The computer law group itself consists of three partners (Robin Bynoe and Tim Bamford complete Berry's team) and seven assistants, following a relatively recent recruitment drive. Rather than treat digital media as a discrete area within IP, telecoms and media, these lawyers all devote their entire practice to legal matters covered by that umbrella area.

The work: From a commercial agreement perspective, the group has advised on several impressive deals in the last 12 months. Notable among these has been the establishment of a global trading exchange. Using the Internet as the technological backbone for the dealing floor, initially IT products will be traded. Also established in this same period was LONAP, a new trade organisation for UK Internet Service Providers. Other technology companies the firm has advised include Wam!Net and Cerbernet Ltd.

The communications side of the practice, which should not be discounted, has been active in several new ventures, notably for a major telecommunications company. Charles Russell's role has been to advise on documentation relating to a new e-

Legal services

ssment independent editorial assessment independent editorial assessment independent editorial assessment independent edito commerce service operated by this client.

The firm also offers a domain name registration service, which has close ties with the firm's intellectual property practice. One of the aims, quite apart from avoiding domain name disputes, is to encourage clients to reconsider the way they see their brands.

Key contacts: David Berry, Robin Bynoe, Ellen Cooper-de-Groote, Mark Moncreiffe

Sample clients: LONAP, Wam!Net, Cerbernet Ltd

This firm might suit: A naturally modest firm, Charles Russell is not among the elite digital media practices, and the partners in the computer law group would not deny that. Although there is a real ambition at the firm to become more prominent in this area, Charles Russell is sensibly playing to its strengths rather than overstretching into untenable territory, and has some good individual lawyers to field. Whether or not the firm can discover the depth of expertise to realise its dream remains to be seen, but certainly to a certain type of client the combination of sound and unfussy legal advice and a slightly old-fashioned – although certainly not quaint – atmosphere could be very attractive.

Website: www.charlesrussell.co.uk or www.cr-law.co.uk
Brochure site, marred by rather disorganised construction, particularly noticeable in details such as the lack of theming in the publications section and the lack of interlinks within the site (the out-Links page had no links at all!). Downloadable Acrobat files are promised, although none were highlighted, and the Navigation bar is a mess. There are no partner profiles, no search engine (check out Media & Communications and IP/IT) and nothing about how the firm does business, although the firm's online magazine is a welcome bright spark. ★

For more information see pages 67

Clark Holt ☎

Formed from City firm Charles Russell, Clark Holt is an independent firm, but one which still retains strong links with its City ancestor. Based in Swindon, the firm's location gives it excellent access to the London market, and a practice with few local competitors.

The group: The computer law group at Clark Holt consists of partner and head of group Jeremy Holt, and Martin Bazen, an assistant solicitor. A little over half of the group's work is taken up by digital media issues, the remainder being IT-based.

The work: Clients of the department include several computer security companies, which have instructed Clark Holt on issues relating to the development of security policies, and a number of web developers and companies looking to raise their profile through having a presence on the world wide web or looking to trade using the same medium.

In addition to this client work, the firm has also been asked by the Department of Trade and Industry to advise and lecture to the business community on the legal aspects of the Internet.

Key contacts: Martin Bazen, Jeremy Holt

Sample clients: British Computer Society, DTI

This firm might suit: It is worth noting that Clark Holt is considerably cheaper than most London firms, which may be a relevant factor to clients. The Thames Valley is a flourishing area for technology companies, and these are the mainstay of the firm's practice, although London clients also feature, possibly attracted by the 'can-do' attitude which head of department Jeremy Holt hopes to project towards potential clients. Feedback from existing clients is good (as evidenced by the website – see below – and the interviews undertaken during the research process for the guide), particularly citing a 'high standard of service and personal attention – very responsive'. It has also been noted that you 'don't necessarily have to go to London to get the best legal advice'.

Website: www.clarkholt.co.uk
Impressive site, largely marked out by its extensive range of client testimonials and information on charge-out rates. The site is well-organised, although primarily a marketing tool, so legal information is largely absent. Highly effective. ★★★

For more information see pages 79

Clifford Chance

One of the largest law firms in the world, and certainly the largest by some margin in the UK, Clifford Chance is a general-service corporate law firm with a particular reputation for banking and finance, among other things. Within the legal profession, it is perceived as one of the most akin to a corporate (as opposed to partnership) style of management, which has meant that despite its size, the firm has been relatively fleet of foot in its approach to the changing nature of legal service provision. As the guide went to press, Clifford Chance was in the process of merging with US firm Rogers & Wells and awaiting the result of a vote on a further extension to that merger, with German firm Pünder,Volhard, Weber & Axster.

The group: Of all the large City firms, Clifford Chance has, since before its inception some ten years ago, had a genuine commitment to the area of

Legal services

ssment independent editorial assessment independent editorial assessment independent editorial assessment independent edito technology in all its guises. Head of the practice, Christopher Millard, is regarded as one of the true 'gurus' in digital media law, although his regular appearance at conferences attracts catty comments from some other lawyers in the field. The firm lists seven other partners in its media, computer and communications group, all of them acknowledged experts in their respective areas – Elizabeth Hiester and Tim Schwarz (IT and telecoms), David Griffiths (IT, with particular renown for outsourcing work), Raj Parkash (commercial/competition), Vanessa Marsland (IP), Michael Smyth (media/defamation) and Daniel Sandelson (TV/broadcast media). As the guide went to press, we learned of the arrival of John Angel, formerly a consultant at TheodoreGoddard, a move which will enhance Clifford Chance's e-commerce capability.

The work: Clifford Chance's work on dm issues has taken it far and wide, from advising its traditional banking and finance client base on issues such as Internet banking and electronic commodity exchanges, to the wider spread of commercial and regulatory work increasingly associated with the area of practice. Key among its achievements is the successful launch of a pioneering electronic delivery system for legal updates across 30 jurisdictions, NextLaw. Although the take-up has largely been from major corporates (who can afford its £2,000 per jurisdiction per year pricetag), the firm is also concentrating on how it can expand its online offerings to appeal to different client markets. One achievement it is understandably proud of is the fact that it can offer clients a one-stop global data protection compliance service.

Key contacts: John Angel, David Griffiths, Elizabeth Hiester, Vanessa Marsland, Christopher Millard, Raj Parkash, Daniel Sandelson

Sample clients: Not available

This firm might suit: From the outside, Clifford Chance may seem like an expensive choice. However, the quality of service and sheer breadth and depth of the practice makes any premium worth the while, in the estimation of clients (who routinely describe the firm's service as 'very good' or 'expert'). In fact, its knowledge systems are such that the firm is able to deliver cutting-edge solutions quickly and easily, and the continued development of 'commoditised' legal services, such as the firm's NextLaw service, will increasingly mean that clients can access Clifford Chance at a number of different price levels.

In our view, any international business which did not at least consider Clifford Chance for its shortlist would be making a mistake, and its virtually unparalleled expertise in banking makes it an ideal choice for financial institutions and the like. On a more specialist note, Christopher Millard is one of only a few acknowledged experts on data protection law.

While CC has had a headstart over the other major City firms in this area, its lead in the UK has all but evaporated now (although the mergers mentioned above may open new avenues of exploration). Constant innovation is the key, something which the firm (happily) recognises. Recommended, but cannot afford to rest on its laurels.

Website: www.cliffordchance.com
Probably the only law firm site available in 17 languages. The site is comprehensive, easy to navigate, and the search function is good: 'e-commerce' brings up a number of starred links to other relevant parts of the site, and information on digital media lawyers and loads of legal information. Perhaps a fraction dull, and the publication-ordering system is very irritating (would be improved by use of a shopping basket...) but otherwise one of the most comprehensive law firm sites. ★★★

For more information see pages 59, 60, 63, 64, 66, 67, 68, 69, 72, 74, 75, 76

Cobbetts ☎

Cobbetts is one of Manchester's, and indeed the North-West's, best known and most respected commercial law firms.

The group: Within the firm's commercial deparment is the IT unit, headed by partner Graham Wood. The unit also comprises three further partners and two assistants.

The work: Over the course of the last few months, the group has seen a significant shift towards e-commerce work, through recently established links with web developers, but despite this move digital media still represents the minority of work undertaken by the firm's IT unit.

Much of the work is derived from Cobbetts' existing clients, mainly clients of the IT unit. The firm has been advising across a range of industry sectors, acting for clients such as Music On-line and Datel Computing Ltd.

One area of significant interest for Cobbetts has been venture capital, with the firm identifying the key fund owners in the North of England. In doing this, the firm hopes to be able to bring together IT companies who need capital investment, and the individuals who can supply that much-needed injection.

Key contacts: Philip Atkinson, Mike Grierson, Robert Roper, Graham Wood

Sample clients: Music On-line, Datel Computing Ltd

This firm might suit: Cobbetts' digital media practice still plays second fiddle to its big brother, the IT practice: the firm takes the approach that it is best to combine closely the disciplines, rather than identifying two distinct niche areas of practice, which makes it difficult to assess the independent scope of the digital media practice. Clients seem pleased with the approach, though. One typical comment: 'some [lawyers] know what they're doing, but it seems to me that some are just bluffing to get by. However, Cobbetts always seem to have their finger on the pulse'.

Clients looking for a more IT-focused practice, therefore, but one with the ability also to advise on digital media and e-commerce issues should shortlist Cobbetts. In addition to the knowledge that the firm can provide a high-level of IT advice, clients can be reassured that the corporate and commercial services offered by the firm are among the best in the North of England.

Website: No website.

For more information see pages 77

Face to face interview

Telephone interview

Davenport Lyons

Davenport Lyons is one of a small number of respected media firms in the West End of London. Having traditionally advised clients from the worlds of film and television, the firm is now joining in the chase for the new breed of media clients. In addition to the media practice, corporate and commercial departments exist at Davenport Lyons.

The group: The most significant addition to the firm's digital media practice, and possibly the start of a genuine digital media practice focusing on media entrants to the digital world, has been the recruitment of IP partner and head of the firm's new media practice Stephen Digby. Formerly head of intellectual property at City firm Withers, Digby has extensive experience of IP issues and is an important addition to the firm. In addition to Digby a number of experienced media lawyers are also part of the digital media practice, such as James Ware, who heads the firm's music group. The importance of recent technological developments in this field has not been lost on the firm, and Ware is one of several lawyers learning to adapt to the music industry revolution.

The work: As one might expect from a firm which has previously specialised in media work, the firm's core practice is content-driven. Although much of the work can be categorised as general commercial work, and has not substantially changed in the last 12 months, Davenport Lyons, like other firms in this area, is feeling the gradual creep of new work deriving from the impact of technology on business. Distribution is a key function of several of the firm's major clients, drawn from the recording, publishing, and broadcasting industries.

Clients the firm has advised on digital media issues include new media consultants Razorfish and OCC Group, The Mersey Television Company, Ginger Media Group, and Mirror Group Newspapers Ltd.

Key contacts: Stephen Digby, Melanie Haddad, Leon Morgan, James Ware

Sample clients: Ginger Media Group, Mirror Group Newspapers, OCC Group, Razorfish, The Mersey Television Company

This firm might suit: Although Davenport Lyons is breaking into the digital media market, by the firm's own admission it is still only a relatively small part of the overall workload. This situation may suit the needs of media companies who themselves are now adjusting to the changes ahead, and who need a firm who understand more their majority interest with a developing knowledge of future ambitions.

Website: www.davenportlyons.com
In a very lawyerly move, the homepage forces the browser to read the firm's disclaimer before accessing the rest of the (quite stylish – some nice Shockwave animations) site. Overall, though, the site suffers from a lack of human interest, although there is quite a lot of cv-type detail for certain areas of practice. There is a small amount of legal update and publication information available, although no search engine and clients will find it difficult to find much of substance on digital media issues. ★★

For more information see pages 72

Davies Arnold Cooper

Having ditched its non-contentious corporate practice, the firm is now looking to centre work around areas such as dispute resolution, including digital risk, banking and property and insurance. More recently, the firm suffered the loss of a number of lawyers from its IP and digital media team.

The group: Now led by Keith Mathieson, the three-partner digital risk team will concentrate on a mixture of defamation and intellectual property, with a focus on mediarelated work, having lost Catrin Turner who acted for the department's retail clients. The group is not heavily into e-commerce, at least not yet, but straddles a number of departments namely IP and media, corporate, professional indemnity inurance, and property insurance.

The work: The loss of Catrin Turner and her team will affect the firm in a number of ways, although it does not mean the loss of an entire practice area. Although losing retail clients will be a blow to Davies Arnold Cooper, it will mean that there is potential to focus on the insurance side of the digital media practice. This will mean advising both large corporate insurers also an involvement in the Lloyd's of London market. This will take the form of advising insurers on selling their product online, and also advising on claims which have arisen in relation to online activities, or use of email.

Key contacts: Keith Mathieson, Maddie Mogford, Kirsty Watt

Sample clients: withheld

This firm might suit: An obvious choice for this firm would be insurers, many of whom already look to Davies Arnold Cooper for advice relating to digital media. Insurers concerned with either their own liability through exposure to new technologies, or with potential liabilities of their clients have already consulted Davies Arnold Cooper.

Having recently lost a significant number of lawyers, and a significant part of its digital media practice, the firm will need to focus on its remaining strengths.

Website: No website

Denton Hall

Denton Hall is a medium-sized City firm, led more than others by its niches, principally media and technology, energy and property. The firm has had a somewhat turbulent recent history, having been the instigator of two failed tri-partite law firm mergers. Evidence suggests, however, that it is now business as usual at the bottom of Chancery Lane, and the firm has been concerned of late with reinforcing its growing international network of associations, Denton International.

The group: Nicholas Higham and Alan Williams lead the media & technology department at the firm, while Higham is also head of Denton International's newly-constituted global communications group. Broadly, the group can field some 40 lawyers in this area, 20 of them from the media and technology disciplines.

The firm's history has led many competitors to regard it as a jumped-up media or publishing firm, but in fact recent developments have tended to favour rather 'harder' disciplines such as telecoms (under Higham) and IT (Catherine Bingham and John Worthy), putting some distance between Denton Hall and its West End rivals. The firm will also be able to draw upon expansion in the firm's banking and insurance groups in support of Higham's stance that the future of e-commerce law lies in business-to-business transactions rather than at the consumer interface.

One lawyer who should not go unmentioned is Duncan Calow, who is busy carving out quite a reputation for himself among close watchers of the growing web industry.

The work: Denton Hall's digital media cv is among the finest the research team encountered, particularly in its spread of work. As might be expected, Denton Hall has serious experience at the top end of media work, for instance advising Bertelsmann on its joint venture with AOL and on the UK launch of its Tripod ISP service (a jv with Lycos), and advising British Digital Broadcasting/OnDigital and Teletext on the launch of their respective digital TV services.

On the Internet side, the firm continues to act for Springboard (the BT, News International and United News & Media jv) and on a wide range of web matters for a user base including BUPA, British Gas, Cartoon Network and the English Cricket Board. Its regulatory experience has seen it acting for the DTi and Home Office on Internet content regulation. The FA Premier League, media companies and a major retailer have turned to Denton Hall on domain name disputes.

On a broader, e-commerce stage, experience includes acting for United News & Media on the establishment of the European Repo Exchange; for Bertelsmann on its online book service, BOL; a major insurance broker on establishing its online insurance broking services and for a major commodity exchange on its online subscriber and price feed agreements.

Its computer games experience has been relatively limited to date, but has included acting for Revolution Software and on licensing issues for the Premier League and English Cricket Board and for leading music score software company Sibelius Software.

Key contacts: Catherine Bingham, Duncan Calow, Suzanne Garben, Nicholas Higham, Simon Levine, Nicholas West, Alan Williams, John Worthy

Sample clients: Bertelsmann, Bertelsmann BOL, British Digital Broadcasting/ OnDigital, British Gas, BUPA, Cartoon Network, DTi and Home Office, the English Cricket Board, FA Premier League, Revolution Software, Sibelius Software, Springboard, Teletext, United News & Media

This firm might suit: Denton Hall is not ideally suited to the smaller client, such as artists, developers etc. Although its fees will tend to be in the mid-range, and thus relatively affordable, its experience and corporate weight are with large organisations. Its ability to offer a broad international service has been heightened of late and it has an edge over many of its competitors on the regulatory side, both through acting for some of the largest players in the market and for government on Internet regulation. Although it is not in the same league as, say, Linklaters or Freshfields on mergers & acquisition work, it is capable of handling large deals, and its specialist knowledge may give it the edge on crucial IP transfer and regulatory issues surrounding a deal in this area.

Its digital broadcasting practice, meanwhile, is the equal of any in the field. We would also recommend it for deals involving broadcasting and sport, particularly with the addition of Mark Gay (ex Herbert Smith) to its sports team.

Clients should not be unduly concerned with the firm's recent turbulence, although Denton Hall's competitors may make merry. In our view, this has not resulted in a diminution of the firm's service, particularly in this area. Any future merger is unlikely to take place where it does not favour such an important part of the practice, so continuity, equally, should not be an issue in that event. Recommended.

Website: www.dentonhall.com or www.dentonhall.co.uk
A decent site search facility (helpfully available on the first screen) brings up 44 hits on 'digital media' and four on 'e-commerce', so clients do not have too far to root for information. There is a legal update section in 'What's New' and 'Publications' (with a few articles relating to digital media) as well as press releases in a searchable archive and the usual partner profiles. ★★★

For more information see pages 59, 61, 66, 67, 69, 70, 71, 72, 75, 76, 191, 227, 254

Dibb Lupton Alsop

A major national firm with offices in all the key centres of UK commercial life. Dibb Lupton Alsop has a reputation for commerciality above all. As one might expect, given this most unlawyerly characteristic, the firm has come in for constant flak from most of its competitors, whose outlook on the development of legal practice is more conservative.

The group: It is fair to say that Dibbs' reputation in IT and telecoms work, from where the group has historically come at convergence, has suffered terribly in recent times, thanks to defections of many key players (principally to US firms).

The addition of the IP strength of Alsop Wilkinson, the firm's most recent merger partner, has added a slightly different skillset to Dibbs' offering.

The firm's e-commerce group, which forms the centrepiece of the IP and IT practices, is currently 22-strong, of whom seven are partners. This cross-departmental department is headed by Sheffield corporate lawyer Andrew Darwin, and draws in partners from the firm's corporate department (David Glover), tax department (Trevor James), IT litigation (Julian Stait), financial regulatory group (Ioannis Alexopoulos), communications and technology (Paul Pattison), and the national heads of IT and IP (Danelle Dinsdale and George Godar respectively).

The work: With the firm's lawyers having a wide variety of backgrounds, Dibb Lupton Alsop has been able to advise in a wide range of matters. The department's impressive client list includes Cable & Wireless Communications, Cybersource International, Demon Internet (Dibbs is one of several firms advising this client), and a major magazine publishing house. The firm has also been involved in the public sector, advising the DSS and MoD.

Key contacts: Simon Deane-Johns, Danelle Dinsdale, Julian Stait

Sample clients: Cable & Wireless Communications, COLT, Cybersource International, Demon Internet, JBA Holdings, MCI WorldCom Ltd, NTL, Reed Business Information

This firm might suit: The firm's strategy at the moment appears to be to cast as wide a net as possible in the hope of catching as much work as possible, regardless of niche specialisms the work may fall into. Although there is much to be said for niche practices, or firms which concetrate on a small number of key areas within digital media – these firms are often the ones which often receive the highest rankings – there are a number of positive points to be said about Dibb's approach. At a time when no-one can be genuinely sure of future market developments, a wide net is more likely to encompass any direction the market is likely to choose, and additionally, looking at a shorter-term perspective, the firm should be presently capable of advising any particular client on more diverse issues than many of its competitors. This coupled with Dibbs' national reach could prove a powerful tool. The problem the firm has to overcome first is in gaining recognition for the work it does, as although it covers many bases, the practice does not currently stand out from the crowd in any of them.

Website: www.dibbluptonalsop.co.uk or www.dla-law.co.uk
The latter address was not working on the day we tried, but we managed to get in on the former, although our attempts to access the Flash version were sadly fruitless. The result when you do get in is one of the most instantly impressive sites we visited. Design is modern and e-commerce has its own button on the navigation bar (Shock! Horror!). Links lead from that button to a wealth of good basic information on e-commerce issues. Publications are available to order (but we tried twice, failed and gave up). The search engine was not working properly on the day we tried, and the various technical glitches marred the overall effect. Nonetheless, what we were able to access represents, in presentation and content, one of the best UK law firm websites currently in existence for the digital media client. ★★★★

For more information see pages 68, 76, 77

Dickinson Dees ☎

Dickinson Dees is by far and away the top firm in Newcastle, and hence the North of England. Its membership of the national Legal Resources Group has tended to localise its work perhaps more than the firm deserves, given its reputation, but it seems content with being King of Newcastle.

The group: The firm's IT group is a cross-departmental group, taking in lawyers from the company commercial department, litigation, and property groups. A team of 12 lawyers, of whom three are partners, is led by Nigel Bellis. 'Hard' IT takes up most of their time, with each lawyer concentrating around 10 per cent of their time on digital media issues.

The work: Reflecting the pattern of the firm as a whole, the IT group's clients are not particularly disparately located, although due to the nature of the industry, clients from further afield have approached the Dickinson Dees, often after visiting the firm's website (see below for a review of the site).

Key contacts: Nigel Bellis, Jamie Pass, James Wilders

Sample clients: withheld

This firm might suit: Quite simply, any client whose nearest major city is Newcastle would be mad to ignore Dickinson Dees if they wanted to consider the best legal advice available. Newcastle is still a relatively discrete, and small market, and Dickinson Dees' IT practice is certainly well advanced of any other in that region. Rather than attempt to compete with the major players in London, Dickinson Dees is once again concentrating its resources in having up to the minute knowledge of the legal and commercial issues faced by clients in its own neck of the woods.

Website: www.dickinson-dees.com Certainly the most amusing homepage we saw – 'If it's legal, we'll do it'. An attractive site, with thought given to making it relatively client-friendly. The search engine came up blank on 'digital media' and on 'e-commerce', and even going for intellectual property or information technology gives little clue as to the firm's experience in the area, and there are few articles available to shed any further light. One excellent feature is the inclusion of hourly rates and methods of charging, for which the firm should be commended. ★★

☕	**Face to face interview**
☎	**Telephone interview**

DJ Freeman ☕

DJ Freeman is a medium-sized City

firm, with 57 partners. At the turn of the decade, the firm made a policy decision to concentrate on several specific areas, in order to provide a more competitive service to a smaller range of clients. Broadly speaking, the firm's focus areas are; property, insurance, litigation, and media & communications.

The group: Despite currently being the firm's smallest practice group, the media and communications group should have a growing role to play in DJ Freeman's future. As with many other firms, it is becoming apparent to lawyers of other departments that they need to understand and appreciate the application of new media technologies to old industry sectors.

The group is headed by Tony Leifer, with Clive Davies heading the department's IT practice alongside him. One of many City lawyers with industry experience, he was at ICL until his move to DJ Freeman in 1990.

The firm's IT practice is perhaps the forerunner of its new media practice, so although DJ Freeman does act for a couple of media companies, the firm's approach into digital media has a definite IT slant. In order to provide a service to fully converged industries, the firm is currently looking to recruit, or has recently recruited, in areas such as telecoms.

The work: Clients vary from IT suppliers such as Bull Information Systems, to content owners such as Channel 4. DJ Freeman advised this last client in relation to legal issues arising from the content of its website, including content issues and advertising issues. Considering the relatively small size of the department, it has advised on a large range of issues, from the commercial use of websites to the legality of online lotteries.

Key contacts: Clive Davies, Tony Leifer

Sample clients: Bull Information Systems, Channel 4, Reed Elsevier, The Post Office

This firm might suit: DJ Freeman is an IT-conscious firm, which is often ahead of its larger rivals in embracing information technology as part of the make-up of the modern law firm. It may therefore appeal to clients who like their law firms to be not only proclaiming a knowledge of their business but also employing the tools of that business to enhance its own.

Another area of strength in coming years could be the firm's BrandSecure service, a limited company set up by the firm to support clients by offering brand valuation, protection and licensing services. If harnessed in conjunction with an online practice, DJ Freeman could become an excellent alternative choice for clients wishing to protect their IP rights online.

Website: www.djfreeman.co.uk
Hint – press the red button to enter. Overall, not a bad site – partner pics revolve to become business cards in one

nice touch, for instance, and clicking on the firm's trade mark quill anywhere on the site returns you home – and it succeeds in making its content look more than it is. Searching on digital media brought up two files and e-commerce returned nothing. The News section is somewhat hidden (not accessible from the homepage) but has some interesting stuff once you get there. ★★★

For more information see pages 71, 218

Donne Mileham & Haddock ☎

One of the leading firms on the South Coast.

The group: Donne Mileham & Haddock's recently formed and renamed innovation and media group comprises nine fee-earning lawyers, of whom four are partners. The group is headed by Tim Aspinall, the firm's managing partner. It is relatively unusual to find that the managing partner is also the head of a firm's digital media practice, and this may be an indication of the importance placed by this firm in this area of work. The group is a subset of the firm's overall commercial department, although partner Dennis Edmonds is drawn from the firm's corporate practice. Two of the partners, Tim Ashdown and Tim Aspinall, are members of the firm's commercial litigation practice.

The work: With clients drawn mainly from Sussex, Kent and Hampshire, Donne Mileham & Haddock is one of few digital media firms operating in that catchment area. As a result the firm acts for many of the area's up and coming new media and Internet businesses. Among these clients are software producers, such as Enterprise Software Systems and Computer Experts (UK) Ltd, and website design and hosting companies.

The firm also acts for a number of companies involved in e-commerce and interactive online services. One such client is e-buy, a company which produces online shopping software. Showing the breadth of the practice is the presence of another client of the firm, brokerserver.com, an e-trade broker.

The next move for Donne Mileham & Haddock is to extend the reach of the client base into London, and indeed the firm already acts for a number of clients based in the capital – clients you may normally expect to be instructing London firms.

Key contacts: Tim Ashdown, Tim Aspinall, Justin Ellis

Sample clients: brokerserver.com, Computer Experts (UK) Ltd, e-buy, Enterprise Software Systems Ltd

This firm might suit: This is a firm which comes highly recommended by its clients on a number of counts - notably an ability to find relevant contacts in the US, and a proficiency in networking. Donne Mileham & Haddock appears to have what it takes to be a relatively small firm outside London practising successfully in digital media law.

Anyone in the South of England should consider Donne Mileham & Haddock for digital media legal advice, knowing that the firm in addition will be able to offer legal advice in a range of commercial and corporate matters. Clients further afield could also do a lot worse.

Website: www.dmh.co.uk
Legal advice on Internet issues is actually the first thing you come across on Donne Mileham & Haddock's website, with an Internet tip (no, you have to visit it yourself to find out what it is!). One of the most visually appealing sites we visited, with client quotes and case studies used to best advantage. There is a 'Hot Topic' discussion thread, a competition and a good selection of articles, although partner profiles are a bit difficult to find and there is no search engine. Overall, though, a fine and functional site. ★★★

For more information see pages 79, 221

Edge Ellison

Edge Ellison is one of the UK's largest par-regional firms, with offices in Birmingham, Leicester and London. Recent years have seen a focus on the London office, including a recent merger and a number of high-level hires. The firm recently underwent a major rebranding exercise which included dropping the '&' from the middle of its name and the adoption of what for a law firm is quite a radical brand image.

The group: The firm's marketing and media unit consists of three partners and an equivalent number of assistant solicitors.

The work: Edge Ellison comes at this area from a rare direction, that of advertising. The firm points out that the Internet was recognised as an advertising medium before it became a transactional medium for e-commerce, and that it has been active for advertising clients from the word go – for instance advising Ogilvy and Mather on the implementation of Guinness' 'dancing man' website, from which 100,000 people downloaded a screensaver. It was also involved in one of the first pieces of domain name legislation, for Aspect Internet Marketing in relation to a dispute over registration of the 'Scrabble' domain name.

Current advertising clients include Ogilvy and Mather, Bartle Bogle Hegarty and J Walter Thompson.

The firm has also become active for website design and production clients, such as Mindshare Digital, Clever Media and Sygyzy, mainly off the advertising base once again. It has also acted for 'users', including a major high-street retailer in relation to the setting up of its home shopping operation.

One of the highlights of 1998 for the practice was the establishment of WebVet, a fixed fee (£650 at time of going to press) website vetting service.

Key contacts: Nick Mason, Robert Wegenek

Sample clients: Aspect Internet Marketing, Bartle Bogle Hegarty, Clever Media, J Walter Thompson, Mindshare Digital, Ogilvy & Mather, Sygyzy

This firm might suit: Edge Ellison needs no introduction to the advertising industry client from this guide: it has more than proved its mettle in that demanding arena. Its recent experience, however, has shown that the skills it has honed may also be of value to 'user' clients (such as retailers) as well as those in the wider marketing field (such as PR agency Hill & Knowlton, another client). Clients who have not used the firm before will appreciate a certain practical edge (pardon the pun) and a focus on speedy response which comes from its longstanding dealings with clients who absolutely, positively MUST have things done by yesterday at the latest... 'He's got nous – he's never afraid to come forward with tactical advice on a deal,' says a client of Wegenek, who is also described as 'approachable' and 'user-friendly'. It is also worth pointing out that the unit, although relatively modest in size, does have the back-up of solid departments in other areas of the firm, particularly notable in employment and property, for instance, as well as access to other specialist practitioners in related fields (such as sport).

Website: www.edge.co.uk
Quite a snazzy-looking site, with plenty of animation (which, mercifully, does not affect speed). However, digital media is seemingly absent from the firm's interests (although there was an ad for a websites and e-commerce seminar in the News section), and the lack of a search facility does not help, while the site map merely underlines the lack of client-specific information available. There is no legal update section and there are no partner profiles, making the site, for all its colour, curiously chilly. ★

For more information see pages 65, 235, 252

Eversheds

National firm Eversheds is spread across a complement of 13 offices in England and Wales. The firm offers a broad range of commercial and corporate legal services.

The group: Eversheds' digital media practice, an inseparable component of its IT work, is a national club, with separate practices in different offices. Led by national IT head Michael Arnold from the firm's Birmingham office, a total of 30

lawyers nationwide advise on digital media issues.

Aside from Arnold in Birmingham, there are currently six other offices operating digital media practices, under the auspices of the IT practice. Imminent growth of the department is expected, to produce a more manageable workload for an already deluged practice.

The work: Although the practice is overshadowed by the strength of the firm's IT practice, this has not stopped Eversheds from gaining notable clients in this area. Among these is one of the most successful of the growing breed of online brokerages, and represents an impresive feather in Eversheds' cap, having very high market capitalisation.

Other clients include a major building society , which Michael Arnold has been advising on an online banking service, and Mitsubishi, with Eversheds advising on ISP documentation.

It would be unfair to concentrate on the Birmingham practice, though, as a great deal of work takes place in other offices. In the East England office, David Woods has been advising Eastern Newspapers, and heads a practice mainly advising service providers on content provision issues, while in Leeds, regional head Neil Brown has been advising on aspects of Internet service provision for the telecommunications industry.

Key contacts: Michael Arnold, Joanna Berry, Michael Burden, Charles Drayson, Suzanne Mercer, Rex Parry, Paul Sampson, David Woods

Sample clients: Eastern Newspapers, Mitsubishi

This firm might suit: Eversheds' national reach must be an attractive feature for any clients seeking the comfort of a universal brand across a variety of regions and disciplines. However, in a shrinking hi-tech world, this advantage has to be constantly reinforced if it is to remain a selling point.

If you believe in the national law firm, then Eversheds, having more offices than any other firm, as the most national of them all would have to be a definite shortlist candidate. Doubts over the firm's true expertise are slowly withering away as more and more impressive deals are announced, and the firm asserts its national strength. Eversheds' may appear to fall victim to the theory of a chain being only as strong as its weakest link, but in reality this is rarely tested. Effectively, the weigh-up for the client is between national reach and depth, and fears about consistency, and the true level of expertise in any one office.

However, it is clear that the firm has to raise its profile if it wants more work in this area. One regular client commented: 'I don't know of any digital media specialists at all, but our group lawyers, Eversheds, would be asked first... they would be able to recommend an appropriate firm.'

Website: www.eversheds.co.uk
A nice-looking site which makes a real feature of graduate recruitment (which is rather difficult for the careless wanderer to get out of!). The information available on the firm's services is depressingly basic for such a large and comprehensive firm, although the addition of an enquiry feature is an excellent idea (common to few other sites). A search on 'digital media' brought up four returns, while e-commerce returned 20, most of them links to practice areas, although entering the firm's newsletters online meant we still had to scan through pages of text to find the references we wanted. ★★

For more information see pages 64, 66, 77

Field Fisher Waterhouse

A modestly-sized City firm with a general practice, Field Fisher Waterhouse has concentrated in recent years upon building its profile in intellectual property and information technology.

The group: Michael Chissick, a highly-regarded individual lawyer, is the key player in the firm's practice, and the recent hiring of Nigel Wildish from Osborne Clarke (he was previously with Nabarro Nathanson) will certainly strengthen the firm's hard IT practice; its intellectual property practice is already well-known. Although the firm refused to co-operate in the research process for the guide, it would be foolish to compile a text covering this area which did not recommend Chissick in particular as an expert in the field.

The work: No information available.

Key contacts: Michael Chissick, Nick Rose, Nigel Wildish

Sample clients: No information available.

This firm might suit: While the *Insider's Guide* has no current information upon which to base its own recommendation, our view is that if a client receives a personal recommendation from another source to talk to Field Fisher Waterhouse, they should be assured that the firm does indeed have a recognised practice in the field and is certainly worth talking to.

Website: www.ffwlaw.com
A search on digital media was fruitless, but e-commerce found 19 documents, most of them press releases. The design is basic to say the least and navigation is made difficult by a lack of a static menu bar. There were no partner profiles but a little information on how the firm does business (which some sites lack) and some pdf downloads. ★

For more information see pages 65, 72, 73

Face to face interview

Telephone interview

Freshfields

Top five City firm with an impressive international network, not least its extensive Asia practice. Freshfields has a strong reputation in particular for corporate and project finance work, but can boast strength in most areas, providing a full service to major corporate clients in the UK and internationally.

The group: Just a few years ago, Freshfields' intellectual property department (where digital media is centred) was among the weakest of the top London firms. Its realisation and subsequent investment has in fact put it in the forefront of the larger firms in this area, although it is still playing catch-up to the likes of Clifford Chance and Allen & Overy. The two major recent investments were in Avril Martindale, formerly head of non-contentious IP at Bristows and now departmental managing partner, and Dinah Nissen, formerly head of IP at West End media-to-aviation practice Harbottle & Lewis. In Martindale and Nissen, Freshfields has bagged two energetic, focused individuals who display none of the boffinish qualities of many traditional IP lawyers (as well as bags of charm!). The result has been a transformation in the practice area at the firm. With management support, the two are driving a new culture of positivity towards what was hitherto seen simply as corporate support work.

As the guide went to press, partner Richard Lister – one of our Digital Dozen (see page 60) – moved from Berwin Leighton to Freshfields, a move which promises much.

The work: Freshfields' superlative corporate client base has, in common with many of its City rivals, given rise to great opportunities for digital media work. Financial sector clients, such as the Bank of England and Nomura, among a host of others, have turned to the firm for advice on electronic banking and trading systems, and the firm has advised on the development of a cross-industry utility platform for the electronic transfer of commercial trade information. Mainstream corporate media/telecoms work has seen the firm in action for several media companies on the rollout of digital TV services and on regulatory issues and ownership of digital TV channels. On IP work, the firm acted for Microsoft on the other side of the Rocky the Dog case (see also Bird Semple), successfully working with Scottish law firm Maclay Murray & Spens defending an application for an interlocutory injunction and in a number of domain name enforcement cases, including one for AstraZeneca, as well as for Virgin on licensing its brand electronically. Nissen was also involved in the landmark *One In A Million* case while at Harbottle & Lewis.

Key contacts: Richard Lister, Avril Martindale, Dinah Nissen

Sample clients: AstraZeneca, Bank of England, Microsoft, Nomura, Virgin

This firm might suit: As with other City firms, Freshfields is not a good choice for small, entrepreneurial clients – the firm will generally be too expensive and not geared appropriately.

For the large corporate or banking client, however, our view is that Freshfields is clearly worth consideration on dm issues. Perception will always lag behind the reality of any situation, and the reality seems to be that the firm has significantly strengthened its capability in this area, something its steady recruitment can only continue. On the 'supplier' side, its telecoms practice and experience in infrastructure projects has given it the kind of exposure to regulatory and competition issues that the largest clients require.

More generally, its tax, employment and pensions practices are among the finest in the City. Freshfields' international network is also an added advantage over smaller or niche players (the firm can boast some 50 lawyers worldwide with direct experience in/interest in this area).

As its practice in this area continues to broaden and strengthen, the difference between Freshfields and its City rivals can only be one of culture. Nissen and Martindale in particular have brought a breath of fresh air to what might easily have been seen as a blue-chip/blue blood environment, and this change in culture is sure to bed in further as time goes on. A rising star. Recommended.

Website: www.freshfields.com
The Insider's Guide was able to sneak a look at Freshfields' (then) unlaunched new site prior to publication. The site is a significant improvement on its earlier incarnation but remains pretty standard law firm 'marketing brochure' fare: publications, partner profiles and a know how bank with some good legal update articles. The feel is fairly fresh (no pun intended), helped by the significant amount of news content on the site when we visited, which it would be good to see the firm continue as time goes on. One neat feature is a well-flagged '60 Second Guide' to the firm. The search engine was not working when we visited, but those in search of e-commerce or digital media law would be advised to head for IP/IT. ★★★

For more information see pages 59, 61, 65, 66, 68, 74, 75, 193

Garretts

City-based law firm Garretts was the first to be set up in the recent wave of accountants moving into the legal fray. Since then, fortunes have fluctuated at the firm, which has lost many of its founder partners. However, with the support of its sister accountancy practice Arthur Andersen, there can be little doubt that Garretts is here to stay.

The group: Across the UK Andersen's legal network, the number of digital media lawyers is around 20, with as much effort as possible to pool resources. Through Andersens, the firm hopes to be able to interact with clients at a much earlier stage than most other firms could manage. The loss of key digital media partners Richard Kemp and Mark Turner, however, have set Garretts back somewhat in recent times.

The work: Garretts is a broadly-based commercial firm, and although much of its work is corporate-related (the firm recently advised a computer games company on a significant acquisition, for instance), it does not get access to the kind of corporate work the major City firms can boast. Consequently, much of the work of its digital media department does not take the form of corporate support work. A range of issues are dealt with, for a wide range of clients. Eschewing seemingly passé areas of work such as multimedia publishing and web development agreements, Garretts claims to be concentrating on more lucrative areas of work, advising on the electronic initiatives of several well-established clients.

Clients include a major computer industry player, and a prestigious car manufacturer. Garretts has also been advising on the risks associated with running a closed electronic network, and on agreements with a cable provider.

A combination of the old and the new can be found in the practice, with Garretts advising paper-based publishers, but also on issues relating to Internet access through mobile phones.

Key contact: Mark Crichard

Sample clients: withheld

This firm might suit: Garretts can field competent commercial lawyers at a reasonable price, but some clients do not like to think that their law firms are associated with their accountants. However, it may be that rubbing shoulders with accountants leads to a better appreciation of business factors and a move away from the more academic discipline of law. There is some evidence of the former at Garretts: where digital media is concerned, there seems to be an air of calm confidence, organisation and slickness. However, it is clear that Garretts has yet to regain the high-flying status in this area it had two years ago.

Website: www.arthurandersen.com
There is a little information on this associated site with regard to Garretts

(UK services), but nothing approaching any of the other law firms reviewed here. (No rating)

For more information see page 68

Hamiltons ☎

Single partner firm in Hackney, London.

The group: Partner Angus Hamilton and assistant David Campbell form the firm, which deals primarily with criminal law, but does an increasing amount of data protection work.

The work: Hamilton has become something of a name in data protection circles, and now spends approximately 25 per cent of his time on this work, although mainly due to the size of the firm and frantic workload, obviously has somewhat of a lower profile than the larger firms with marketing muscle. He has been commissioned by legal publisher Sweet & Maxwell to write its guide to the Data Protection Act 1998 and writes regularly for *PC Pro* magazine on Internet and computer law.

Key contact: Angus Hamilton

Sample clients: not available

This firm might suit: Hamiltons will offer the client a completely different perspective from the City firms (as well as significantly lower costs) on data protection work, and comes highly recommended. He presents a good example of how significant intellectual resource can be concentrated in a small group (in this case, one individual) for this kind of work.

Website: www.btInternet.com/~hamiltons/ Simple, functional brochure-site with a wealth of articles on data protection and Internet and computer law. ★★

For more information see page 68

Hammond Suddards ☎

Based in Manchester, Leeds, Bradford, and London, Hammond Suddards' main strength is in corporate finance. Having outgrown its Yorkshire roots, the firm now operates a national practice, with an additional office in Brussels advising on EC law.

The group: Based in London, the firm's e-commerce group comprises 12 of the firm's partners, and a further eight assistant solicitors, with the redoubtable Larry Cohen at the helm. This cross-departmental group comprises five partners from the firm's IP/media group, two from both financial services and corporate finance, and a partner each from insolvency, commercial dispute resolution, and a team which advises Lloyds syndicates. The eight assistants are similarly drawn from these departments. The IP / media group itself comprises 33 lawyers, led by Cohen, and advises on all aspects of IP except applications work.

The work: Hammond Suddards' digital media client base is relatively wide-ranging, taking in companies from both the user and supplier side of the market. Industry areas of focus include banking and finance, although the firm is hoping to be able to advise on a broader range of clients.

Recent highlights for the digital media practice include advising Visual on rights clearances for a CD-ROM game, and Burberry on online trading. A whole host of clients remain confidential, but they include a major online personal finance company, a major mobile telecoms company – which the firm has advised on customer contracts – and one of the UK's most active investors in the information technology sector.

Recent corporate work includes acting for Planetfootball.com on its £24m sale to Sports Internet Group plc, believed to be the first sale of an Internet content provider in the UK.

The group's contentious work has included several Internet disputes, including online defamation allegations, and a domain name dispute – in which the firm advised General Housewares on the protection of the Oxo.com URL.

Key contacts: Michael Mahoney, Stephen York

Sample clients: Affinity Internet Holdings, Burberry, General Housewares, Visual

This firm might suit: Hammond Suddards is pinning its hopes on the breadth of its practice (cf Dibb Lupton Alsop).

One finance client noted that 'few lawyers in this area provide good value for money and not all seem to know what they are doing. Some really shine, and Hammond Suddards is one of those'.

The firm's cross-departmental approach is therefore very important to this strategy, and it is encouraging to see that the firm draws in lawyers from many departments. This is expected to continue and develop further in future months.

One way in which the firm hopes to offer a superior service to its clients is through Alternative Dispute Resolution (ADR). Stephen York, a partner in the e-commerce group, is a leading light in this discipline, and the firm hopes through York, and his colleagues, that it can attract clients reluctant to pursue full-blown litigation, in favour of practical, negotiated solutions.

Another interesting aspect to Hammond Suddards' offering is the firm's experimentation with digital delivery of services. Investment and interest comes from the highest levels of the firm and the most successful fruits of the decision yet to appear relate to Hammonds Direct, the legal support provider to financial institutions and mortgage lenders, based on the firm's Bradford site (website at www.hammondsdirect.co.uk). The firm is using the lessons learned from the direct provision element of Hammonds Direct in its development of a wider range of direct services. One to watch.

Website: www.hammondsuddards.co.uk Among the better brochure sites offered by law firms, although the site search facility returned nothing on either digital media or e-commerce. Looking under IP in the legal updates section returned one e-zine with four articles in it, all relating to more general IP matters. Interestingly, there is a section limited to client access, providing the firm with a platform for the digital delivery of legal services as time goes on. Another good feature is the inclusion of the firm's annual review. Assuming the firm continues to develop its client base and services to this sector, the relevance of the site to the digital media client will increase, although for the moment it does the job in terms of providing reassurance to the more general corporate client. ★★★

For more information see pages 63, 77

☕	**Face to face interview**
☎	**Telephone interview**

Harbottle & Lewis ☕

Harbottle & Lewis is a West End firm which wants to stay that way. Its organic growth over the last few years has seen the firm's size rise in the firm to its present complement of 15 partners, four consultants and 55 other lawyers – still small by London standards. The firm is very keen to promote itself as distinct from City firms, and is keen to distinguish its culture and attitude to lawyering from that of its Square Mile counterparts.

The group: One of the firm's main practice areas is covered by its new media and interactive entertainment group. Consisting of six partners and three assistants, the group, led by Mark Phillips, acts for a range of online and interactive entertainment clients, including many computer games publishers and developers. Recruiting generally from City firms, Harbottles aims to bring in impressive recent qualifiers who can adapt to the firm's culture and ethos, and learn a more 'commercial' way of dealing with clients. Sebastian Belcher, who was recruited from Slaughter and May three years ago, is one example of a young solicitor moulded into the Harbottles' way.

The work: Four main focus areas can be identified in the practice; online services, electronic publishing, computer games, and IT. Of these, historically the computer games practice has been the best known, with Mark Phillips' team advising a number of up and coming industry players, and a number of established companies in the sector.

Recent work in the interactive entertainment field has included advising GT Interactive on a range of issues, including development agreements with the Bitmap Brothers, an ownership dispute over Discworld Noir – another game based on Terry Pratchett's popular books – and on publishing and development agreements for the same product.

Perhaps the biggest coup has been the group's work for Sci in relation to its computer games, Carmageddon and Carmageddon 2. Having beaten off the BBFC over its attempt to ban the original game, Harbottles once again challenged over the subsequent refusal by the BBFC to grant a certificate to the game's sequel. To date Harbottles is the only firm to have taken on the BBFC on behalf of a client in this way.

In other areas, Harbottles has been advising clients ranging from MSN (in relation to online libel liability) to The Spice Girls (advising in the One-in-a-Million domain name suit).

Key contacts: Melanie Allen, Sebastian Belcher, Mark Phillips

Sample clients: GT Interactive, MSN, Sci, Take Two Interactive, The Spice Girls

This firm might suit: Despite not being in the City, this firm prides itself on the quality of its lawyers, many of whom have experience of both City and West End life, and know and appreciate the differences. Do not confuse the presence of NME and Q magazine in the reception with a lack of professionalism in this firm's lawyers – the suits may not be as sharp as in the City, but the lawyers' minds certainly are. This is borne out by client commentary: 'they're the experts', says one. This expertise – 'very useful where releases are time-driven' – can also sometimes mean that if it is Mark Philips you're after, you may have to wait as his extensive list of clients can sometimes bog him down.

Harbottles prides itself on its appeal to the smaller client as well as its relaxed atmosphere and 'not the City' approach. For anyone young, keen and gifted, it represents an experienced and inexpensive source of legal advice, with a good track record in publishing, IP, media and new media.

However, the firm's corporate department lacks the clout of its more serious competitors (and has to watch that it does not get out of its depth), and the firm on the whole has a UK-centric outlook, meaning that larger international clients may find better pickings elsewhere.

Of all the major media firms, Harbottles is in a good position to take advantage of the new media revolution, and will come out of it stronger than the majority of entertainment and media practices, as a result of its foray into computer games and online advice. However, the firm is still a long way from offering a completely rounded convergence practice.

Website: www.harbottle.co.uk
Less slick-looking than many other law firm websites and lacking many of the sophisticated features of competitor sites. Information about the firm is presented in an unfriendly way and there are no partner profiles or examples of work undertaken. Not the easiest site to navigate either, but the firm's New Media newsletter is available online, which is a minor plus. ★

For more information see pages 72, 73, 240

Henry Hepworth ☎

Henry Hepworth is a niche media and IP firm based in Holborn, London, originally established in 1997, and recently bolstered by the arrival of several former members of Davies Arnold Cooper's IP practice.

The group: Broadly speaking the practice breaks down into three areas, with Catrin Turner (who led the Davies Arnold Cooper exodus) heading the IP litigation practice, Michael Henry leading the transactional and commercial practice, and Jason McCue running the media litigation practice. In total, there will be five partners, and eight assistants at the firm working, to a greater or lesser extent, in digital media.

The work: It is difficult to estimate the scope of the firm's digital media practice, as the new members have only very recently joined the firm. Established work, though, includes acting for David Trimble in his ongoing libel litigation against Amazon, a landmark case, as the publisher is being sued for the simple act of publishing (as distinct from the *Godfrey v Demon Internet*, see page 91)

In IP litigation, the firm's major client is a leading UK Internet Service Provider. However, Catrin Turner has in the past acted for a number of retail clients, building up a specialism in the area, and a number of these clients can be expected to continue to instruct her at Henry Hepworth.

Key contacts: Michael Henry, Jason McCue, Catrin Turner

Sample client: David Trimble

This firm might suit: Selling itself on a mandate of clarity and succinctness, Henry Hepworth is in a strong position now to act as a niche media, IP, and IT practice. The arrival of Catrin Turner and her team from Davies Arnold Cooper will bring experience and, perhaps more importantly, clients to the practice. Also significant is the David Trimble libel action case, which if handled successfully could establish a further niche for the firm.

Website: No website

Herbert Smith

A top ten, international City-based practice, Herbert Smith is particularly renowned for its litigation prowess (it has over 50 litigation partners, the largest department in any UK law firm), but it also claims to be the first firm to have become seriously interested in intellectual property.

The group: Mark Turner and Nick Gardner are the pivotal players in Herbert Smith's digital media practice, which is run out of the intellectual property and technology group (which can boast six partners in total). That team is headed by the redoubtable IP lawyer Bill Moodie. Gardner and Turner are both highly likeable, down-to-earth lawyers who, while retaining a reassuring technical knowledge, are both practical and plainspeaking, a refreshing change from some of the more technocratic City practices.

The work: Recent work includes advising Network Solutions Inc on English law; US toy manufacturer Mattel Inc on website and Internet sales issues and acting for longstanding major client BSkyB on the British Interactive Broadcasting project in particular. The firm also advised WH Smith on its agreement with Microsoft to set-up the stationer's portal WH Smith Online. On the games side, the firm acts for Broderbund (of Myst fame), Sony's Psygnosis offshoot and leading multimedia publisher Dorling Kindersley

Key contacts: Nick Gardner, Bill Moodie, Mark Turner

Sample clients: Broderbund, BSkyB, Dorling Kindersley, Mattel Inc, Network Solutions Inc, Psygnosis, WH Smith

This firm might suit: Herbert Smith has long been seen as the best choice for those with a difficult dispute to resolve, and we would certainly recommend it in this regard. It is highly likely that, with over 50 partners specialising in contentious work, both in the courtroom and in the subtler delights of arbitration and mediation, there will be a case that someone at Herbert Smith has had close experience of. This has ensured that Herbert Smith's client base has remained of the best quality, which in turn has exposed its digital media practitioners to some excellent and cutting edge work. More than anything, though, and at odds with its 'hard' image, a client can expect to be working with likeable, practical lawyers. Price bracket is near the top of the range, but as ever, clients with clout will be able to strike a good deal, and quality will never be an issue to worry over.

Website: www.herbertsmith.com
A visually appealing site, with thought clearly having gone into enticing the browser further through the site (though a number of broken links and glitches rather spoiled the effect on the day we accessed it). A search for 'digital media'

brought up 39 instances, including partner profiles and publications in various sections, plus a further ten instances of 'e-commerce' when that was searched. Publications can be ordered from the site (with pithy case summaries and legal updates to read while online) and partners are profiled. Altogether, one of the more pleasant law firm sites to visit. ★★★

For more information see pages 61, 64, 68, 194

Hobson Audley Hopkins & Wood

Small commercial firm based in the City of London. Has formed a joint venture – Faegre Benson Hobson Audley – with US firm Faegre & Benson.

The group: More by accident than design, Hobson Audley Hopkins & Wood is now a firm driven by its core technology practice, allowing it to offer the expertise of a niche firm with a reasonable back-up in the form of property and corporate services.

The work: Although the main driver for the practice has been the software side (with computer games being a particularly 'sexy' angle), the firm has followed client demand and developed accordingly. One recent highlight has been a growing practice for insurance industry users. Notable digital media clients include, Compaq Computer, Eastgate Group, Maris Multimedia and National Magazine

Jewel in the crown of HAH&W's digital media practice has to be its computer games practice. Kicked off by Robert Bond, one of the first specialist games lawyers in the country, the firm's main client continues to be industry giant Electronic Arts. Another headline client is Eidos Interactive/Core Design (ultra-famous for the Tomb Raider series), but Eutechnyx, Ubisoft and 3DO also use the firm. Back-up is also there: Claire Poll is described as 'very good indeed' by satisfied clients.

Key contacts: Robert Bond, Alan Hawley, Claire Poll, Iain Stansfield

Sample clients: 3DO, Compaq Computers, Core Design, Eastgate Group, Eidos Interactive/Core Design, Electronic Arts, Eutechnyx, Symantec, Ubisoft

This firm might suit: HAH&W is well-placed to serve both the suppliers and users of software, both on digital media issues and more standard software contract work (where Alan Hawley has a good name). Both publishers and increasingly developers in the computer games industry would do well to consider Robert Bond on their shortlist, as would a more general run of publishers, to see whether chemistry develops. In the words of one client, 'thorough legal knowledge tempered with good business sense', will make HAH&W a good choice for those wanting a City service at a more attractive price, although it cannot realistically compete with the big City firms where larger deals are in the offing.

Website: www.hobsonaudley.co.uk
How to find the firm is the first order of the day on Hobson Audley Online (including a map). The site is well organised, with a registration form to access articles (password operated), a links page to related organisations (heavy with information technology companies) and the usual partner profiles (unusually with colour pictures...). The library of articles is positively overflowing with good, basic information on a wide range of subjects. A search for 'e-commerce' brought up eight articles, while 'digital media' found a staggering 58. ★★★

For more information see pages 66, 71, 73

Keeble Hawson Moorhouse ☎

Keeble Hawson Moorhouse is one of several law firms in the North offering digital media advice. The firm has existed under its present name since May 1998, when Sheffield firm Keeble Hawson merged with Leeds firm R. C. Moorhouse & Co, and since then has retained the existing profile in IT law while growing an ever improving digital media practice.

The group: Comprising four partners and two assistants, the firm's IP and IT group is headed by Jonathan Armstrong. Among the lawyers in the department it is Armstrong who spends the most time advising on digital media issues, although even he only concentrates around one-third of his time in this area. This is a common feature of many firms with smaller practices in this area, however, and the focus on digital media at Keeble Hawson Moorhouse is comparable to that found at the majority of similar firms.

The work: Broadly speaking, the firm's expertise lies mainly within the intellectual property field, covering e-commerce as well. Recent activity on the part of the IP / IT unit has included advice in respect of ISP liability, audit work on the delayed Data Protection Act, a copyright dispute centring on the underlying script in a website.

Unfortunately it is the firm's policy not to discuss specific clients and work undertaken, although it is known that the firm does advise some fairly significant companies and organisations both in and around the North and East of England.

Key contacts Jonathan Armstrong

Sample clients: withheld

This firm might suit: Certainly anyone looking for digital media or intellectual property legal advice in Yorkshire should consider Keeble Hawson Moorhouse. The firm has a strong regional practice, and a good reputation for this kind of work. In its head of department, Jonathan Armstrong, the firm has found itself someone willing to lead very much from the front, and he can regularly be seen in the media, either writing for legal or industry publications, or appearing on radio or television.

Website: www.keeblehawson.co.uk
Basic-looking, but highly functional website. Internet law is dealt with specifically, including examples of work done. An email update on relevant issues is available from the firm. ★★

For more information see pages 77

Kemp & Co

Small, niche City practice established in 1998, marketing itself as 'a law firm for the .com world'

The group: The eponymous Richard Kemp is widely-regarded as one of the finest, if not the finest, lawyer of his kind; eschewing the rather academic air possessed by some of the 'gurus' in the field, the affable Kemp is resolutely practical and convincing.

To say the firm is open is something of an understatement. Its brochure reveals annualised billings by quarter as well as 'tombstone' information on work undertaken and testimonials from clients. 75 per cent of work is now undertaken by email, with some clients using email exclusively. As the guide went to press, Kemp's younger partner Ashley Winton announced his move to Osborne Clarke. Kemp & Co had previously announced two new lateral hires including Jonathon Little from Bird & Bird.

The work: The Kemp & Co approach is one which has won it favours with some blue-chip clients, both on the supplier side (Microsoft, Intuit) and the 'acquirer' side (Volkswagen Financial Services, Tomkins). The firm recognises that for large, often multinational organisations, it is not going to be first port of call for major corporate finance deals, for instance; rather it trades on its expertise in the field, effectively 'partnering' general counsel one-on-one where needs be (ie where digital media work is a small part of the client's concern) and allowing its larger City brethren to 'throw lawyers' at the more general work.

Examples of key work include acting for Microsoft on the launch of its Expedia travel service; acting for Digital River on the establishment of its UK and European operations and for FTSE International on its agreement with Amsterdam Exchanges for the establishment of Eurotop Indices.

Its exposure to media clients, while not matching those of some of its niche rivals (who have largely come up through the entertainment route, thus giving them access to a ready client base as traditional content providers turn digital), was given a boost with its involvement for Phonographic Performance Ltd in joint venture negotiations with MCPS and BPI.

Key contacts: Richard Kemp, Jonathon Little, Kenneth Mullen, Lucy Vernall

Sample clients: Digital River, FTSE International, Intuit, Microsoft, Netlife AG, PPL, Tektronix, Volkswagen Financial Services

This firm might suit: No client should consider itself too large for Kemp & Co – the firm is equally at home partnering general counsel on digital media issues as it is acting for the suppliers in the converging industries. While the firm's near-City costs may be too much for the very small client to consider, the firm is still below the major City firms in its charging and its one-on-one approach avoids meetings packed with associates, a situation which tends to rack up the fees. We would recommend the firm highly for the smaller client who is far-sighted enough to see that taking good legal advice can be an investment rather than a burden.

Richard Kemp himself comes in for some of the highest personal praise from clients: 'excellent advice, interpretation and practical application – it would take a lot to beat Richard's personal service'; 'very, very client-focused'; 'very pragmatic, very responsive and happy to give advice or guidance over the phone, unlike many lawyers'.

Solicitor Lucy Vernall ('excellent, very bright') is also particularly recommended. Resource is clearly an issue for the firm as time goes on, as Ashley Winton's departure illustrates. Kemp & Co clearly cannot provide the full-service commercial offering of rival City firms, but many clients find its offering to that liking.

Kemp & Co's key strengths, in IT and financial services particularly, have been bolstered by recent experience in 'sector-specific' areas (such as travel, for Microsoft's Expedia), although media and telecoms remain sectors to which the firm has not had great exposure, historically. Although recognising the need to grow with the sector, Kemp & Co is more realistic than many of its competitors about its abilities, and any client can be sure of getting an honest assessment of whether its needs can be properly serviced. A number of clients currently use Kemp & Co exclusively via email, which means the firm is well-versed in the quick turnaround encouraged by the medium. Recommended.

Website: www.comlegal.com
A stylish, functional and appealing site which never deviates from its prime purpose. The firm profiles all its lawyers (including trainees) and sets out clearly what it offers, telling clients not just about the service, but about the level of

technology the practice has invested in, and its business practices. The site mentions clients the firm has acted for, including links to client sites. There is no legal content, either in update form or articles, and no publications are available. Despite this, one of the most professional, client-focused law firm sites. ★★★

For more information see pages 59, 60, 67, 195, 231, 239

Lawrence Graham

A medium-sized London law firm with a reputation for property, litigation and private client work, among other things.

The group: Digital media work is undertaken as part of Lawrence Graham's intellectual property group, into which the firm has recently merged its not inconsiderable practice in advertising, marketing, direct sales and sponsorship. Head of the group is Jonathan Riley, whose experience stems from the broadcasting and publishing side of the content spectrum. A number of other partners, including highly-respected competition expert Anthony Woolich, add a distinctive, if content-focused, edge to the practice.

The work: Lawrence Graham has approached convergence from the content side, its practice driven by intellectual property (mainly copyright and trade mark) work and to a certain extent, media and broadcast (BBC Worldwide is a major client). Commercial work undertaken on the online side is broad, if not exactly headline; examples include international joint venture and data provider agreements for Interactive Investor International; acting for domain name onseller NetNames International in agreements with MSN and IBM; and advising on the merger of the Electronic Commerce Association and the Article Number Association to form the E Centre.

On the 'pure' content side, meanwhile, acting for Sony Computer Entertainment Europe has tended to conflict the firm out of advising the rest of the industry, but has given it unique exposure to the core of the games industry (eg the Tomb Raider series).

Key contacts: Wendy Batchelor, Jonathan Riley

Sample clients: E Centre, Interactive Investor International, Magnetic Storm Inc, NetNames International, Pure Entertainment Games, Sony Computer Entertainment Europe, Sony Electronic Publishing

This firm might suit: Lawrence Graham's skillset and experience in this area would be of particular interest to those organisations wanting to engage in a broad spread of commercial activity on the Net, where advertising, marketing and sponsorship are key to the deal. Although its computer games experience is broad and deep, acting for Sony Computer Entertainment Europe, as noted above, precludes it from acting for most of the rest of the industry (although developers who do not intend to seek PlayStation licensing would be well-advised to talk to Lawrence Graham as a first port of call). Lawrence Graham is also a good choice for major brand owners and for contentious matters, clients would be hard-pressed to find a more sensible litigator than LG's head of litigation, Andrew Dobson.

The firm's practice in local government is probably second to none, so it should be considered by any public body (including housing associations and health trusts) to whose needs it will be particularly sensitive.

Website: www.lawgram.com
A functional, if slightly bland site, containing a vast, often bewildering amount of information about the firm and its services (though little specifically about the work and clients). Those searching for digital media or e-commerce can go for the usual 'IT and Communications' or 'Intellectual Property' or search on 'What's On This Website', where the search engine is hidden. 'Digital media' brings up a single entry, 'e-commerce' nothing. Publications are available (a selection online, the rest to order). ★★

For more information see pages 65, 73

☕	**Face to face interview**
☎	**Telephone interview**

Ledingham Chalmers ☎

Based in Aberdeen, but with international offices in Azerbaijan, Baku, Istanbul, and the Falkland Islands, Ledingham Chalmers was formed in 1990 from the merger of two other Aberdeen firms. The new firm covers all manner of legal advice, from residential conveyancing to corporate advice. Ledingham Chalmers is also a member of a trans-European alliance of firms, covering over 20 European jurisdictions.

The group: As with most Scottish firms, IP and IT have traditionally sat together at Ledingham Chalmers, although this a situation the firm is now actively looking to address. Appreciating the potential of marketing the two areas separately, the firm is currently examining how best to do this.

The work: Being based in Aberdeen, one of the firm's major client industries is, of course, the oil and gas industry. Ledingham Chalmers is one of a select band of firms with large oil and gas corporate clients, and is one of very few not based in London. In addition to corporate matters, the firm has advised clients in these industries on a range of IP and IT issues, from Y2K to a planned web-based database of critical information for the industry.

However, it would be unfair to only recommend this firm to clients involved in oil or gas, as clients in other sectors have been advised by Ledingham Chalmers. In a project similar to the web-based database mentioned above, the firm is currently advising on the creation of a 'holiday finder' database which suggests holidays and accommodation based on user information, for instance. Additionally, the firm has been advising on a range of electronic sports training products, designed to replace the chalk and blackboard diagrams of the changing room.

Key contact: Robin Fletcher

Sample clients: withheld

This firm might suit: Clearly for oil & gas clients, or those with substantial value relating to that sector, Ledingham Chalmers is be an ideal firm if you are looking for lawyers with industry focus, experience, and understanding.

However, there is more to the practice than that. The firm's breadth of practice could see it lending itself well to any technology boom in the North-East of Scotland, and could potentially advise for clients ranging from the very small or entrepreneurial, to major international energy companies.

Certainly cheaper than London, and possibly on average cheaper than the Scottish Central Belt, a partner-led approach with ideas for the future is how this firm sells itself.

Website: www.ledingham-chalmers.co.uk A rather wordy site, design a bit dated, speaking of another generation of Internet life. Some intriguing bits and bobs, though, including a history of the firm and a statement of core values which endearingly includes the firm's 'moral duty' to have fair dealings with the community. ★

For more information see page 78

Linklaters & Alliance

One of the 'big five' law firms in the UK, Linklaters – formerly known as Linklaters & Paines – is part of a Europe-wide association of firms, which together are known as Linklaters & Alliance. The firm has long been known as one of the very best for corporate work, and in particular its corporate institutional clients.

The group: The combined resource of the communications group and the intellectual property and technology practice is impressive. With five partners and 12 solicitors in the former, and seven partners and 33 solicitors in the latter division, and a further 15 lawyers between the two groups, the total number of lawyers advising in digital media issues currently stands at 72. Reflecting the firm's overall focus, many of these practitioners are drawn from the firm's corporate group, and Linklaters strength in this area is being translated into an ever-expanding digital media practice.

The work: It should come as no surprise that Linklaters has been advising on some big ticket work in this area. With the corporate department supplying an almost inexhaustible supply of blue chip clients, the firm's new media lawyers are never short of impressive deals to be involved with.

As a flavour of some of the major clients represented by Linklaters in the last 12 months, the firm has advised the BBC on a range of major projects. Among these are advice on the ever more important world of digital TV, and the contract with the European Commission for the provision of Schoolnet Websites.

International work is also a feature of the practice, with work including a draft e-commerce law for the Government of Bermuda, and, also in e-commerce, Linklaters has acted on behalf of a major European client.

Key contacts: John Crozier, Robyn Durie, Robin Whaite

Sample clients: BBC, Government of Bermuda

This firm might suit: Of course, corporate support work is all well and good, and a firm in Linklaters' position should be expected to have developed a strong support practice in this area, as an inevitable consequence of the adoption, by blue chip clients, of new technologies. However, Linklaters is keen to demonstrate a commitment towards stand-alone high quality digital media work.

Although Linklaters is not a firm we would recommend to the smallest clients, it is beginning to position itself to take on more entrepreneurial clients. Provided you have a solid business plan and a saleable idea, the firm could happily take you on board. And, if you are looking for a firm which can really handle the big deals, on national and international bases, then Linklaters is a very worthy choice.

Linklaters is also one of few firms to operate any sort of digital legal services. The firm has shown great commitment to its Blue Flag scheme, and is preparing to expand its services in this area.

Website: www.linklaters.com
More illuminated than illuminating, this is a fine-looking, if limited, 'advanced brochure' site. The offering is rather basic: no search engine, no publications to download, no articles to read. There are partner profiles, with some pics, and an explanation of the Blue Flag service,

which contains sample advice but nothing on price. ★★

For more information see pages 59, 63, 65, 66, 76, 196, 221, 252

Linnells ☎

Oxford firm Linnells is one of the biggest players in the Thames Valley market, with a particular reputation locally for its general commercial expertise.

The group: Rather than operating a discrete digital media practice, Linnells is one of many firms advising in this area on the back of practices in IP and IT. Consisting of four partners and two assistants, the scope of the firm's IP and IT unit covers a range of IP issues relevant to various indstry sectors. The firm has litigation expertise, and, although Edward Lee is leaving the firm, this will continue under the jurisdiction of Jonathan Lloyd Jones, the firm's senior general litigator.

The work: The firm's main areas of focus in digital media largely fall into line with the sort of institutions and industries in the Oxford and Thames Valley area; a long-standing involvement with Oxford University goes hand in hand with specialism in charity law. Charities are increasingly appreciating the value of the Internet as a revenue gathering tool, and they form a unique class of client to which relatively few firms promote their expertise.

Also historically relevant to the firm has been advice for clients in the world of publishing. Linnells' major client in this area has been Blackwells, which the firm has advised on a number of separate projects. Blackwell Science, looking to publish an extensive range of scientific journals on the world wide web instructed the firm on licensing and back-office functions in relation to that project, while the online bookshop operated by Blackwells also called upon Linnells for advice on e-commerce issues.

Key contacts: John Deech, Jonathon Lloyd Jones, Edward Lee, Joss Saunders

Sample clients: Blackwells, Blackwell Science, Digitext plc, Dun and Bradstreet, OXFAM

This firm might suit: Although for the most part clients of this firm, and most regional firms in general, are drawn from the geographical area in which the firm can be found, some clients have found Linnells to be a welcome alternative to London firms. One area other than digital media which has seen this transition is construction law, with the firm advising several London based clients.

Other than the potential reduction in overall cost, there could be a number of reasons for choosing to instruct out of the capital if you are based in London. If you are in the Thames Valley, Linnell's should be one of the firm's on your shortlist for advice in this area, particularly if you have charitable status.

Website: www.linnells.co.uk
Under construction.

For more information see pages 71, 79

Lovell White Durrant

Major international City-based corporate law firm in the UK's top ten by size.

The group: In common with many of the larger firms, Lovell White Durrant operates a cross-disciplinary approach to this kind of work. The computer, communications and media group is headed by Quentin Archer, and now boasts some 21 lawyers including five partners, although it is fair to say that despite a significant amount of work and backing within the firm, the group has not to date perhaps had the profile its calibre of work and lawyers deserves. However, the emergence of such personalities as Lindy Golding and Conor Ward (along with the ebullient Heather Rowe) will doubtless result in a raising of that profile as time goes on.

The work: The group has the advantage of access to Lovells' considerable corporate client base, not to mention the support of probably the finest Brussels office of any UK law firm and a dedicated parliamentary lobbying function. This has combined to give the firm a particular strength on the regulatory and lobbying side.

The firm's cv includes acting for Barclays Bank plc on the setup of the Endorse smart card-based digital signature service; for the same client in relation to the Global Trust Organisation and for encryption software manufacturers (the firm has a strong practice in this area).

Key contacts: Quentin Archer, Lindy Golding, Heather Rowe, Conor Ward

Sample clients: Barclays Bank, Mirror Group

This firm might suit: To a certain extent, Lovells' reputation as a quality firm covering all the bases does not do its digital media practitioners justice. In fact, its lawyers are both focused and approachable, and lend an easy enthusiasm to the work at hand giving the client the impression that they are unlikely to be either equivocal or evasive (both qualities all too common among many lawyers).

Lovells is probably too expensive a choice for the smaller client, but is worthy of consideration by an offshoot of a major player, for instance, where capital growth is likely to be large and thus City-type fees less of a problem after a short while.

Given the firm's enormous banking

Legal services

expertise, it is a worthy choice for any financial services or insurance-related e-commerce work, and its regulatory and competition expertise across the board is such that it is well-suited both to report on developments and to help clients lobby for change. This is borne out by the comment of a key financial services client, which commented that Lovells showed the 'complete understanding' of the issues of online trading which only comes with 'specialist knowledge'.

We would also recommend it for major brand owners thinking about possible infringement – the firm is one of the few City firms which has kept intellectual property in the forefront of its commercial practice through thick and thin, a feat not to be underestimated.

Website: www.lovellwhitedurrant.com
A conservatively-styled, but nonetheless easy on the eye site, where navigation is relatively straightforward. The lack of any interest, either design or photographic (no partners to be seen), however, gets a little wearing after a while. However, there is a great deal of information available, both online and to order, although digital media returned nothing on the search engine (there were three documents mentioning e-commerce). Overall, dull but very worthy. ★★★

For more information see pages 60, 64, 66, 67, 69, 75, 197, 225, 244

Maclay Murray & Spens ☎

One of Scotland's top firms, Maclay Murray & Spens has a broad base of legal expertise, with particularly strong practices in trusts, personal tax, shipping and intellectual property.

The group: The firm's intellectual property group is led by the highly-rated Fiona Nicolson, and comprises a further three partners and a total of 16 fee-earners, although most lawyers at the firm are involved in IP issues to some extent. Contentious work is handled by Gill Grassie, while the other partners concentrate on the non-contentious practice. Within this group is the firm's IT and Internet team, which handles the bulk of Maclays' digital media work, both contentious and non-contentious. Having been the first firm to establish a dedicated IP practice in Scotland, the firm believes it has reached another milestone in the creation of a specialist fraud unit, which operates to look at computer and Internet fraud. Maclays' recent growth has been reflected in the growth of the IP practice, which has grown to its current total from only three lawyers five years ago.

The work: Maclay Murray & Spens has been very active of late in respect of domain names, and operates a range of services in that area. The firm's Domain Name Alert service – in conjunction with NetSearchers International – aims to provide initial clearance searching, coupled with legal information on protecting brands and reputations online. Maclays' has been involved in a series of domain name disputes in Scotland, advising Nominet – for which the firm acts as Scottish counsel – in most cases.

Aside from domain names, the firm has clients ranging from the very big and well-established – such as Microsoft and Adobe Systems Europe, for whom the firm acts as Scottish counsel – to smaller more media-based clients such as Scottish Screen. Continuing to advise 3i, among other investment companies, Maclay Murray & Spens has reinforced its position as a leading corporate finance firm in Scotland, and has been involved in investments into Red Lemon, Kymata, and Kingston SCL, the latter representing the largest investment to date in a Scottish technology company.

Key contacts: Gillian Cameron, Gill Grassie, Fiona Nicolson, Alistair Orr

Sample clients: Scottish Screen, 3I, Microsoft, Adobe Systems Europe, Nominet

This firm might suit: Maclays does seem to operate a greater range of value-added services than its local competition; in addition to the domain name search, the firm offers its innovation help line and 'innovation group' as a way of demonstrating close pastoral care for its clients.

There is no doubting the level of experience this firm has in its IP practice – experience which backs up highly recommended corporate and commercial divisions. If you are looking for legal advice in Scotland, in the areas of IP, IT, or digital media, then Maclays is a good choice.

Website: www.maclaymurrayspens.co.uk Encouraging and attractive site, quite sensitively written and even light-hearted in places. Nicely, there are full profiles and pictures of associates, not just partners. There is no search engine, however, and press releases are organised chronologically, which is a bit of a pain. The Know How section, though, presents a very good selection of articles to read and questions to be asking oneself. ★★★

For more information see page 78

MacRoberts ☎

One of a select band of premier providers of IT and IP legal advice in Scotland – an area which has sprouted small specialist groups at several of the top Scottish firms – MacRoberts is small in size compared to many firms south of the border, but when it comes to IP and IT, the dedicated department advises some of Scotland's major players.

The group: Headed by David Flint, the eight-strong intellectual property and

Legal services

technology law group boasts both non-contentious expertise and the knowledge of the firm's IP litigation practice. Flint is a recognised expert in this area, and has many years of experience behind him. The other partners in the department, Joanna Boag-Thomson and Richard Barrie – one of the firm's litigators – supply able support.

Both Flint and Boag-Thomson have been accredited by the Law Society of Scotland as Intellectual Property specialists, and MacRoberts is one of only two Scottish firms which can boast this of more than one practitioner.

The work: With experience of IP and the technology sector running through all parts of the firm, and a recognition of the need to provide all-round corporate and commercial advice MacRoberts has begun to assert itself strongly in this area.

MacRoberts has been advising a major Scottish company on cyberpiracy. Other clients include a Scottish-based ISP, and several IT developers, also based in Scotland. As with most firms advising in this area, MacRoberts' clients are drawn from far and wide, including a number from the US.

In addition to client work, the firm has been active in providing consultation documents on a range of digital media issues, most recently on the UK government's proposed e-commerce legislation.

Key contacts: Richard Barrie, Joanna Boag-Thomson, David Flint

Sample clients: withheld

This firm might suit: An open billing policy operates at the firm, designed to make the firm more approachable for the smaller client. With the belief that an honest appraisal of the likely cost of legal advice on a particular issue will benefit clients in the long-run, MacRoberts hopes to be able to take on clients who have a good awareness of their likely bill, and will be able to meet that commitment.

The firm should certainly be shortlisted by almost any client looking to instruct a firm in Scotland on new media issues.

Website: www.macroberts.co.uk
The accent is on utility in this rather stern-looking but nonetheless useful site. The site is full of information in the way of articles, many of them on dm-relevant issues (the search on digital media brought up 14 positives, although e-commerce returned nothing), although the firm is clearly moving away from producing newsletters, judging by how out of date the ones available were. There are the usual partner profiles, a deals section (under construction when we visited) plus a good links section. ★★★

For more information see pages 78, 215, 223

Manches & Co

Manches is a mid-sized firm with a London presence, advising on a broad range of commercial matters. The firm's Oxford office, established in 1982, was strengthened last year when it subsumed the niche practice of Morrel Peel & Gamlin. One of the traditional strengths of the firm's practice has been publishing, where Manches has a long and distinguished history.

The group: Manches Media is the umbrella title covering both traditional media forms such as print, film and television, as well as new media like the Internet. The practice in London is led by Peter Stevens, while the Oxford office comprises 12 fee-earning solicitors, of whom Christine Reid, Chris Shelley, Steven Maier, David Tighe and Cathleen Blackburn are partners. Christine Reid is nominally head in Oxford. In the Oxford office, the group's work is split roughly into two camps, with the client bases of the respective offices remaining largely independent of one another.

The work: In London, traditional media is to the fore; the addition of partner Paul Woolf has added clout to the firm's film financing practice. Clients in the capital also include a number of notable publishing conglomerates – Conde Nast for instance. One of the most significant clients of the department is computer games star Eidos.

The client base in the Oxford office differs from its London counterpart as you might expect, given its location. Clients include several publishers of business software, ranging from providers of large-scale infrastructures to developers of single unit products. Manches is also on a general retainer to advise Nominet, the UK domain name registrar – which controls the registration of the world's third most popular domain name extension – '.co.uk'. In all cases relating to domain name disputes, Manches has advised Nominet as a third party relating to the case.

Key contacts:
London: Bernard Nyman, John Rubinstein, Peter Stevens, Paul Woolf, Ian Yonge
Oxford: Cathleen Blackburn, Steven Maier, Christine Reid, Chris Shelley, David Tighe

Sample clients: Eidos, Conde Nast, Nominet

This firm might suit: Software producers looking for a no-nonsense, calm and unfussy approach to their legal work could do a lot worse than approach a firm which, housed inside unassuming but attractive offices on the Strand, has a broad media practice which, although it has not yet translated into a fully-developed digital media practice, certainly gives Manches a more substantial feel than many of the other traditional 'media' firms also entering the digital media race. The Oxford office also

Legal services

adds weight to the practice, and advising Nominet is no small coup. The firm's commitment to smaller clients has been demonstrated by its work in the creation of ISOC England, the recently established chapter of the global Internet Society.

Website: www.manches.co.uk
Those with Shockwave Flash 3.0 installed will benefit from the impressive animated sequence introducing the browser to Manches' attractive, easy-to-navigate website. Beyond that, the site is of the standard law firm offering: partner profiles, a list of services (look under IT/IP/Media for dm services where Internet has its own sub-category), press releases, and a small selection of publications, although there is no search engine. One welcome bonus is a client list. ★★

For more information see pages 70 71, 79, 241, 247

Marriott Harrison ☎

Marriott Harrison has one of the best known media, film and television practices in the country, and, despite its relatively small size, has consistently maintained an impressive client list in these areas, especially in film financing.

The group: Led by Tony Morris, the Media department is staffed by two partners, Morris on the non-contentious side, with David Hinde, a recent arrival from Schilling & Lom, providing litigation expertise. Roughly half Morris's workload is digital media related, the rest being traditional media work, Hinde spends just over a quarter of his time in this area.

The work: During a year which has seen a substantial increase in the size and scope of the firm's digital media practice, Marriott Harrison has kept quite a low profile, while continuing to act for several notable clients.

On the computer software side, the area on which Tony Morris has built the digital media practice, the firm continues to act for noted games company Mindscape and The Learning Company on commercial, contractual, and intellectual property matters. The firm also advised the second of these clients on a substantial e-commerce agreement with a well-known telecoms company.

Much of the increase in the department's work this year has been Internet-related, and has included advice in relation to broadband e-commerce services, terms and conditions for websites, music streaming, and corporate finance for technology ventures.

Key contacts: David Hinde, Tony Morris

Sample clients: Asset Control, Global Recall, Mindscape, The Learning Company,

This firm might suit: Priding itself on its commercial approach to problem solving, Marriott Harrison is a firm not known for self-promotion. In its own quiet way, however, the firm has established an impressive digital media practice in its areas of specialism, namely computer games and media related spin-offs. The strength in advising on film packages to a host of major companies in that field could be a good springboard into similar online services, given the firm's knowledge and experience of the issues involved. One client commented that 'they have a good handle on the new media technologies... a big vision of Internet law and its possibilities'.

For a traditional media firm, Marriott Harrison is ahead of many of its direct rivals for digital media work, and the personable, laconic Tony Morris has developed a good sideline in computer games, making this firm a good and relatively inexpensive choice for a client looking to better rates than the City.

Website: www.marriottharrison.com Currently under construction, though as a temporary measure has an email enquiry form, which is a good thought. ★

For more information see pages 72, 73, 238

☕	**Face to face interview**
☎	**Telephone interview**

Masons ☕

Although Masons is a City firm, you will not be able to see its modern offices from the Bank of England, situated as it is in the heart of trendy Clerkenwell. The firm is generally associated with two areas of practice: construction and information technology. Working on the principle that the development of construction contracts is similar to the drafting of IT contracts, Masons has built up a very strong reputation in both fields. In IT especially it is generally regarded as having an excellent practice. In both areas the firm has a strong litigation reputation.

The group: A large team of lawyers is active in this area, consisting of nine partners and 19 solicitors, backed up by the help of two outside consultants. It is fair to say, however, that digital media is not the mainstay of the practice, which for the most part is focused on IT and telecommunications. That said, a number of the lawyers spend the majority of their time on digital media work, such as partner Shelagh Gaskill, and three assistants.

Recently, the firm's Glasgow office achieved something of a coup by taking on two of Bird Semple's Techmedia team as lateral hires, John Salmon and John MacKenzie.

The work: Recent work has included non-contentious work and dispute resolution for a number of high profile clients. Masons has been advising a well known ISP on its legal liabilities across the board,

Legal services

from content agreements and acquisitions, to data protection.

Although the world is alive with the buzz of online commerce and auctions, relatively few disputes have arisen in the area. Masons is one of a select band of firms to have advised on a dispute over online auctioning, having advised the supplier of the technology for an online auction system after its client, a subsidiary of Mercedes-Benz argued an alleged real-time systems failure.

An area not generally associated with Masons is the provision of financial services. However, the firm has advised a number of clients on issues relating to online banking and services, including the problem of establishing an online and offshore banking service. Having already advised one client on outsourcing matters, Masons was asked to produce a report on the global issues arising from such a service.

Key contacts: Shelagh Gaskill, Robert McCallough, Iain Monaghan, Clive Seddon

Sample clients: withheld

This firm might suit: Masons' excellent IT practice, its construction experience – a related field, if not directly relevant – and its projects group form an impressive triumvirate. The expectation within the firm is that these practices areas, and in particular the IT and project practice – with the cross over of PFI work – can lead the firm forward.

Clients who themselves are focused on IT or digital media and expect their law firm to be of a similar disposition might reasonably shortlist Masons. The firm's lawyers exude a not unreasonable confidence in their abilities, and in dispute resolution and litigation the firm is a fierce ally.

Website: www.masons.com
Slightly dated-looking site, but packed with information about the firm's services and a great links section. Content is a little overwhelming and certain passages are unacceptably wordy. Intriguingly, the site contains Masons' views about the Internet as a delivery medium for legal services, which is well worth a read, and although the site itself does not quite deliver on the grand theories (yet) it does have a huge wealth of content on legal issues, consistent with the firm's vision of the changing model of legal service provision. Searching for 'digital media' found five items and 'e-commerce' 14. The firm is currently working on a next generation version, so watch this space, but currently among the best law firm offerings. ★★★★

For more information see pages 61, 66, 68, 73, 76, 78, 199, 225, 236

McNeive

Liam McNeive left City firm Masons in 1997 to set up his own practice, to advise on media, communications and Internet law.

The group: Until recently McNeive operated on his own, but he has since recruited an assistant solicitor, Natasha Doman, from Masons to ease the intense workload.

The work: McNeive's most recognisable clients are the two large service providers AOL and Compuserve. AOL UK and AOL Europe have been clients for three years, and after AOL's acquisition of Compuserve the latter company also became a client of McNeive. McNeive advises these clients across the board, with issues relating to content acquisition, data protection, linking deals, online advertising, and competition rules. These clients have the largest data transmission needs in Europe, so it is not just straightforward commercial agreements and intellectual property advice that McNeive is called upon for. In fact he is almost in the position of external general counsel.

McNeive's clients tend to be leaders in their fields. Aside from AOL and Compuserve, he advises QXL – the recently listed European online auction house – on the many issues which arise from running the service. Real Media Solutions – an Internet marketing company – is another client of McNeive's, and is also a highly successful business.

McNeive also advises Good Technologies, one of the few surviving major independent web development agencies, which itself has a host of impressive clients, and Crunch Music, a recently launched online MP3 distributor.

Key contacts: Natasha Doman, Liam McNeive

Sample clients: AOL Europe, AOL UK, CompuServe Europe, CompuServe UK, Crunch Music, Good Technologies, QXL, Real Media UK, Rosetta Stone Consultancy

This firm might suit: Entrepreneurs with sound business plans and exciting products would be well served by McNeive, as would anyone frustrated by instructing larger firms or departments and who is looking for something a bit more personal and informal. McNeive's offices are reassuringly busy looking without being intimidating, and McNeive himself is one of the most approachable lawyers on the circuit. The fact that he has been retained by AOL for so long is surely an indication of his ability to handle crucial issues for major players, so if you are happy getting your corporate advice elsewhere (and you should be), McNeive would be an excellent choice.

Website: www.mcneive.com
A simple, stylish marketing-brochure website, with information about McNeive's services and list of credentials (although no client names or specifics about projects undertaken). ★

For more information see page 61

Mills & Reeve ☎

Mills & Reeve has offices in Cambridge and Norwich, the main focus being on agriculture and on corporate work, with healthy sidelines in insurance, universities and charities, property, and private client work.

The group: Headed by Alisdair Poore, who is overall head of the intellectual property department, the team dealing with digital media and e-commerce. Poore is one of three partners active in digital media work – the other two being Isabel Napper and Nick Fischl. Gillian Thomas and James Hunter, both assistant solicitors, make up the remainder of the team.

The work: The practice has certainly developed of late from traditional IP into a more online based one, and Mills & Reeve has taken advantage of its geographical location to combine the IP practice with the its clients in academia. This has resulted in the firm advising on website disclaimers among other issues for universities.

Domain name disputes are also still very much part of the practice, as companies begin to consider Internet domain names as proprietary interests. Other IP rights work has involved advice on the patentability of Internet software.

Key contacts Alisdair Poore

Sample clients: withheld

This firm might suit: Silicon Fen has traditionally been seen as a hotbed for technology development – think Apple, think UUNet – so it is not surprising to find that a modestly forward-thinking firm in the area is comfortable dealing with the demands of hi-tech clients. Many of the lawyers have a technology background, which is another factor that differentiates the firm from some local rivals.

Website: www.mills-reeve.com
Not a bad-looking website, with some decent content – information about the firm's services, articles and suchlike. Not the easiest site to navigate, however, and the lack of a search engine means hunting around for the firm's credentials and experience in this area. ★★

For more information see page 77

Morgan Cole ☎

Formed last year from the merger between Welsh firm Morgan Bruce and Thames Valley practice Cole & Cole – more recently the firm has also merged with Fishburn Boxer, an insurance niche firm – Morgan Cole is now spread across a wide swathe of the South of England – Swansea, Cardiff, Newport,

Oxford, Reading, Croydon and London to be precise.

The group: The eight-strong team, half of whom are partners, is based in both Wales, where Mark Bolt and Emyr Lewis are based, and the Thames Valley, where Alison Sarsfield-Hall, who heads the Intellectual Property Group, is based.

The work: One type of client which the firm has significant experience in advising is educational institutions, with both Morgan Bruce and Cole & Cole having them. Although mainly devoted to traditional IT work, this side of the practice does encompass digital media issues, particularly in relation to use and abuse of email and the Internet, with universities often having large numbers of users registered for these services.

In Cardiff, Emyr Lewis is building a practice in advising on the impact of digital television. Relatively few firms are advising on this topic, which could be very significant for any producers and broadcasters of television content. Old contracts may not be up to scratch where digital licensing and broadcasting is concerned, and these are issues which the firm has been looking into, especially in respect of bilingual broadcasting, which may not be catered for.

In Oxford, Alison Sarsfield-Hall has built up a client base which includes a range of computer companies, involved in areas such as distribution and development among others, with the firm advising on matters relating to e-commerce.

One area of particular focus is CD-ROM publishing, notably in relation to medical CD-ROMs, although the firm has also advised computer games clients.

Key contacts: Mark Bolt, Emyr Lewis, Mike Lindsey, Alison Sarsfield-Hall.

Sample clients: withheld

This firm would suit: In pre-merger days, Morgan Bruce was identified as one of the leading IT firms in the South-West, and that reputation has been carried forward for Morgan Cole. The main thrust of the digital media practice, however, comes from the firm's Thames Valley offices, and any client looking for intellectual property expertise combined with a digital media practice in that area would be well advised to give this firm a go. In Wales, Emyr Lewis is one of the few lawyers in this field to offer legal services through the medium of Welsh – competitive advantage for local start-ups.

Website: www.morgan-cole.com - links directly to www.cole-and-cole.co.uk. Currently being updated after the merger between Morgan Bruce and Cole & Cole, some eight months ago now, the site gives the most basic of information – namely contact details for the respective heads of each department and bullet-points for areas covered by each department. Archive newsletters cannot be ordered directly, but you can request for any updates to be sent as and when they are released. Not very inspiring yet – but an update is promised (no ranking – site being updated)

For more information see pages 62, 78, 232, 233, 244

Nabarro Nathanson ☎

Large/medium-sized London-based firm with an excellent reputation for property. Also has significant presence in Sheffield and Reading.

The group: Nabarros operates, in common with most firms, a cross-disciplinary 'matrix' system across traditional department boundaries. Paul Golding is London head of the IT, communications and new media industry group, which can count eight lawyers in total. It is fair to say that Nabarros comes at convergence from the carrier end of practice, with strength particularly in IT, but also in telecoms.

The work: As with many broad commercial firms, the amount of e-commerce work is growing as the industry grows. Key recent work includes advising IMG, host managers of the Manchester United website; advising Dutch national airline KLM on Internet ticket sales and the UK hydrographic office in relation to a joint venture with its Norwegian equivalent on a European-wide underwater mapping service. Other notable e-work includes acting for Netstore, Glass' Information Services and Financial Times Business Information.

Key contacts: Sara Ellacott, Paul Golding, Rosemary Martin-Jones

Sample clients: IMG, KLM, UKHO, Netstore, Glass' Information Services

This firm might suit: We would judge Nabarros a good choice for players in the IT industry, particularly on the supplier side (whether software or hardware) but also, increasingly, for general corporate users exploring the possibilities of e-commerce. Although not a publicly-stated 'core area' for the firm, its cv is pretty impressive, even compared to some much larger firms.

Given the firm's ability to manipulate its cost base across offices, clients may find Nabarro Nathanson a less expensive choice than many City firms, with the added advantage of having a presence so close to the beating heart of the UK's IT industry.

Website: www.nabarro.co.uk
A good sense of web-convention (such as animated banner advertising for an article on email dangers) characterises the Nabarros site, which makes some other legal sites look very dry. The site is easy to navigate and contains a good deal of regularly updated legal information, nicely organised, with

interested parties able to subscribe to an email briefing. Search engine is quick, but 'digital media' and 'e-commerce' both came up blank. Seminars, publications and profiles are all easily accessible. Refreshingly, all lawyers (not just partners) are profiled and there are maps of all Nabarros' offices. ★★★

For more information see pages 60, 66, 76, 79, 226

Nicholson Graham & Jones

Nicholson Graham & Jones is a medium-sized firm based in the City.

The group: Consisting of four partners, five qualified solicitors and one trainee solicitor, the firm's digital media expertise is housed in the IP and IT group, with an additional cross-departmental IT group. The non-contentious practice is led by Sarah Kirk, while Peter McBride leads the contentious practice.

The work: The group's work covers a broad base of IP, IT and media, although the firm appreciates that some telecoms experience will be necessary in order to push the practice as far forward as possible. Current and recent work includes; drafting website linking contracts, contracts for the reformatting of websites to interactice television services, e-commerce contract terms and conditions, domain name disputes and cybersquatting, data protection, and online software downloads.

The nature of the practice has developed over the last 12 months, moving away from more traditional IP rights. The majority of the practice is, however, still user-based, and generally involves advising a small client in deals with much larger players on the other side.

On regulatory matters, the firm has been advising in relation to digital radio multiplex services. Corporate finance is also an area which has grown recently, in respect of digital media issues.

The contentious practice is growing in anticipation of a future increase in the workload, especially where jurisdictional and data protection matters are concerned – often in conjunction.

Key contacts: Sarah Kirk, Peter McBride, Richard Talbot

Sample clients: withheld

This firm might suit: Nicholson Graham & Jones believes that there are several factors which mark it out as a good choice for digital media work: it offers full legal service, it is less expensive than many of its City rivals, and is versatile and able to develop a digital media and e-commerce practice from the knowledge base of its commercial IP lawyers. Not a stand-out choice, but competent and relatively commercially-minded.

Website: www.ngj.co.uk

Legal services

Fairly efficiently laid out with all the basic information (groups, location, partner profiles, some recent deals, information on Globalex) easy enough to get to. However, beyond the surface there is not much in the way of information and structure. Department brochures, and some newsletters can be ordered through the site. ★★

Norton Rose

City firm Norton Rose has long been recognised for its expertise in the banking and financial markets sector, a field in which it is generally recognised to be one of the leading forces in the UK.

The group: The firm's intellectual property and technology department is led by Chris Ryan. The three partners in the group (Ryan, Richard Barratt and Keith Hyman) spend between one quarter and one-fifth of their time on digital media issues, with the rest of the department comprising ten assistants and three other fee-earners.

The work: With the firm's specialisation in banking and finance, it is no surprise that Norton Rose has been advising on legal issues relating to electronic share dealing and the use of network technology in financial services for some time, and as you might expect it is this type of work which makes up the bulk of the practice. The new media practice is, for the most part, an offshoot from the firm's heavyweight finance and corporate finance practices.

Aiming for the sort of work which probably could not be handled by most niche digital media practices, Norton Rose has been advising on the whole in deals involving a wider corporate, finance, and regulatory knowledge. Partners from other departments, such as corporate finance, advise a range of new media clients. Corporate partner Edward Lukins, for example, has recently acted for Global Internet and The Internet Technology Group on major transactions.

Encryption and security are obvious areas for the firm to exploit – central as they are to the concept of electronic trading and the flow of financial information over remote networks – and it is no surprise that Norton Rose has focused on these areas. Lawyers at the firm are regular speakers on these topics, and the firm has advised several clients, such as the operators of the Switch card scheme, owners of bill payment systems, and has been involved in several schemes relating to Mondex, which despite not finding much favour in this country is becoming an accepted standard in other European nations. The firm has also advised on the recent and successful set up and launch of the easyeverything Ltd chain of Internet cafes.

Key contact: Richard Barratt

Sample clients: The Internet Technology

Group, easyeverything Ltd

This firm might suit: Banks and financial institutions should look closely at this firm. A few other firms may have better banking practices, and some other firms may offer more comprehensive new media services, but as a combination of experience in one area and a desire to branch into an offshoot of that area, Norton Rose's digital media practice, particularly for closed and open trading systems (including, of course, e-commerce), is a worthy combination.

In addition to its large and established clients, though, Norton Rose feels that unlike other firms of a similar size or corporate oriented culture, it is relatively flexible in its billing towards smaller, less-developed clients. In fact, clients such as small web developers are welcomed with an 'acorns to oak tree' style approach.

Website: www.nortonrose.com
The lack of a search engine means the visitor seeking information about digital media/Internet will have to do a bit of hunting – try Media & Communications in Practice Areas. News needs a bit of updating (the most recent thing was a Budget briefing – six months after the event, while older pieces dated back to January 1998) and a peculiar glitch saw us stuck in a partner profile when we tried to re-access the Practice Areas part of the site. Publications are available, although disappointingly few in electronic form. ★

☕	**Face to face interview**
☎	**Telephone interview**

Olswang ☕

The first firm to set up a multimedia practice (in 1986) and the first law firm to start talking about convergence, Olswang has grown from its roots as an entertainment practice to become a formidable force in the converging industries.

The group: The firm's investment in new personnel over the last few years has been dedicated to creating what it sees as the full service firm for the converging industries. From a standing start it has built up its intellectual property practice (via Andrew Inglis and Paul Stevens, formerly of Nabarro Nathanson), its telecoms practice (recently via telecoms regulatory guru Colin Long) and has even sought to expand its presence in competition law (via a Brussels office and the recruitment of a senior solicitor from Freshfields) as its activities for a host of clients takes it into territory requiring a broader, deeper practice requiring more specialist advice.

The work: Having neatly positioned itself as a firm for convergence before most other law firms had even heard of the term,

Legal services

independent editorial assessment independent editorial assessment independent editorial assessment independent editorial assessment

Olswang has effectively captured a huge amount of dm work for a range of Internet names (such as UUNet and Demon Internet), broadcasters (such as BiB (Open), Two-Way TV and Microsoft WebTV) and media companies (such as Bloomberg).

Given the way the Internet is going (or was at time of going to press), the landing of Freeserve as a client has to position Olswang squarely at the top of the ISP market.

The expansion of e-commerce into other industries has seen Olswang active away from its traditional media base.

Flicking through a list of Olswang's TV clients is rather like thumbing through a TV guide: Granada, BBC Worldwide, Nickelodeon, MTV Europe, Channel 4, Channel 5, Discovery...1998 saw the firm on the other side from BSkyB and Ondigital on numerous occasions.

Altogether, the firm has one of the most impressive cvs seen by the research team.

Key contacts: John Enser, Andrew Inglis, Colin Long, Kim Nicholson, Selina Potter, Paul Stevens, Victor Timon, David Zeffman

Sample clients: BiB, Bloomberg, Channel 4, Channel 5, Demon Internet, Discovery, E-Trade UK, Freeserve, Microsoft WebTV, MTV Europe, Nickelodeon, Pangolin International, Two-Way TV, UUNet

This firm might suit: Olswang can lay claim to be the firm closest to covering all the bases on convergence, and its consistent growth means it can service the largest clients on the spectrum of dm issues (although games is, to date, an area of relative weakness). The recent addition of the Brussels office, and of Colin Long in particular, has closed an important gap for the firm.

Its recent growth has not been at the expense of cohesion, however. The firm has always been tightly run, and seems to have taken care to recruit around its vision, as opposed to the pursuit of more opportunistic recruitment.

While its corporate muscle does not approach that of Clifford Chance, for instance, it has been getting involved on much larger deals than would hitherto have come to it. The fact that large, international clients use it in Europe speaks of the capability of the firm to perform even without the major network of international offices proferred by its larger brethren.

Although it remains primarily a content practice, one senses that the turning wheels of the global economy will tend to favour an Olswang as time goes on, although the pressure to keep ahead of the trailing pack will remain. It does need to guard against complacency, though: an assumption that having one of the finest practices in this area will mean that it sells itself is not good enough – clients need to be kept more aware of the firm's clear prowess.

Nonetheless, at time of writing, Olswang can do what very few others come close to: the mobilisation of an entire firm to serve dm clients. Recommended.

Website: www.olswang.co.uk
Bouncing bunny on the homepage, which gives one the suspicion that the site is not updated as regularly as it might be (the bunny and nearby daffodils being very appropriate for spring, less so for summer, which was when we investigated. A colourful site, easily navigable (although the search facility was being upgraded when we investigated), with a lightheartedness missing from virtually every other law firm site (among the inclusions are a guide to Covent Garden, where the firm is based, a selection of lawyer jokes and film reviews where the producers are Olswang clients). Legal update material is well organised and in Q&A format, making it instantly more appealing, along with a glossary of legal terms. The site also contains information on clients, with links to their sites. ★★★★

For more information see pages 59, 60, 64, 66, 67, 69, 70, 72, 74, 201, 223, 238, 249

Osborne Clarke

Having now outgrown its Bristol roots, Osborne Clarke is steadily becoming a force on the London scene. Recent recruitment drives have seen the firm grow to its current size of 60 partners. This rapid expansion has seen the firm's London offices receive plaudits in a number of areas, of which interactive services and digital media is one.

The group: Digital media and IT are both areas which have seen some of the most rapid recent expansion for Osborne Clarke. The IT and telecoms department has been strengthened by the addition of several well known names from rival new media departments, including Paul Gardner from Titmuss Sainer Dechert, and Rory Graham from Bird & Bird. The firm's intention has been to cover as many bases within the converging industries as any firm can, by drawing in partners from a range of disciplines. The partner count now stands at two at the London and Reading offices, with a further five solicitors also in the group, although this figure does not include lawyers from other departments. Were they to be included the number would rise substantially. A recent addition to the team is Frank Jennings – formerly a member of the in-house legal team at software publisher Psygnosis. As the guide went to press, Ashley Winton (ex-Kemp & Co) joined the firm and David Schollenberger left to go in-house at Choice Hotels International.

The work: The digital media practice at Osborne Clarke is among the most rounded of any to be found in UK firms, described as 'excellent' by clients. The recruitment of Paul Gardner from Titmuss

Legal services

Sainer Dechert last year brought to the firm a partner with an established reputation in the computer games field, with clients such as Electronic Arts, and Activision among others on the publisher side, and developers such as Milestone, Simis and Eurocom in his canon. One of the department's flagship clients is Yahoo! Since Osborne Clarke began advising the search engine and now GeoCities owner, a constant flow of similar clients have also sought the firm's assistance.

The firm also has an active relationship with 3i plc.

Key contacts: Andrew Braithwaite, Paul Gardner, Rory Graham, Simon Rendell, Ashley Winton

Sample clients: 3i, Activision, EA, Eurocom, Milestone, Simis, Yahoo!

This firm might suit: Although lacking the heavyweight punch of the very top firms in this area, Osborne Clarke's aggressive march on the world of communications and media should not be discounted. The lawyers at the head of the various elements of the practice have extensive experience at other major firms, and have now all come together at a firm which is more forward-thinking than some of its peers. Although the department seems to lack some of the cohesiveness which the very best digital media firms have, this is perhaps the only current factor keeping Osborne Clarke from being among the true elite. The addition of new resources (such as Ashley Winton) may speed this progress.

For a firm of its size, Osborne Clarke has some pretty impressive clients. It is a firm more receptive to smaller clients than many others, and has forged links in a number of areas with industry players – such as the Y2K link with IT supplier Lorien plc. Despite now seeing itself as a London firm, Osborne Clarke can't quite disown its Bristol roots, and the atmosphere in the firm does seem to reflect its origins. Indeed, the digital media practice is not limited to the London office, with a thriving practice recently established in the Thames Valley to capture the relatively untapped but important market in that part of England.

Website: www.osborneclarke.com
Modern, if slightly offbeat site (the inclusion of naif illustrations is rather bizarre...), which presents the firm as three-pronged. Choosing the IT/Telecoms prong will lead the browser to information about the partners, and some decent articles, available in either text format, pdf or via snail mail. The only slightly disappointing feature is that the 'pricing partnership' trailed in the Welcome section doesn't actually say anything about prices (except the usual flexible, transparent, oh, and can you remember to pay on time, please). ★★★

For more information see pages 60, 61, 62, 67, 68, 73, 78, 224, 226

Oxley & Coward ☎

Rotherham based Oxley & Coward is a relatively small firm with a distinct focus on Information Technology. In addition to this main focus area, the firm also concentrates on NHS and private client work.

The group: The much admired and respected John Yates (the firm's managing partner) heads the firm's IT practice, with assistance from four other partners, and six assistant solicitors.

The work: The technology practice at Oxley & Coward is still very much IT-driven, and over the last 12 months has not genuinely developed from this root into a digital media practice. This has, however, been a deliberate policy of the firm, rather than a failing. The firm's main clients in this area, which tend to be drawn from the supplier side, include Kewill Group plc, and a large software services provider. The firm is much more likely to be found acting for e-commerce software suppliers, or companies establishing e-commerce projects for their business, than new media companies and e-commerce operators themselves.

Having said all this, however, Oxley & Coward has advised on a few new media ventures, advising for instance on IP issues and branding, and essential contractual matters.

Key contact: John Yates

Sample clients: Kewill Group plc, MBA Direct, Ultimate Sun

This firm might suit: The firm's location means that the legal fees will be normally lower than those of comparator firms in Leeds, London, or Manchester, while the strength of the IT practice means that if you are after solid IT advice based on industry knowledge, with the potential to expand into digital media work, this is a dependable choice of firm.

Smaller clients may also benefit from the firm's 'Stop The Clock' service, which guarantees a fixed rate for a given project, and includes two days of free consultation at the client's office, one establish the scope of the work, and one to appraise the success implemented advice.

Website: www.oxcow.co.uk
An attractive, easy-to-navigate site with some nice features, including a gallery-style profile area (which profiles assistants, trainees and legal executives as well as the partners) and some detail on the firm's services (including Stop The Clock). Although the search engine returned nothing on 'digital media' or 'e-commerce', a list of articles available in the Know How section lists Internet, data protection and computer misuse, among others. There is even a wine review section for light relief. ★★★

For more information see pages 77

Paisner & Co ☎

City firm Paisner & Co can be found on Fleet Street. Although the firm does not lead any markets, it has a sound, broadly-based practice in commercial and corporate law, as well as property, litigation, employment, and insurance departments.

The group: Linda Fazzani heads the computer, media and intellectual property group, and is one of four partners in the group. The other three partners have all joined the firm since the beginning of 1998; Laurence Kaye joined from the Simkins Partnership, and has a strong Internet and web-based practice,while both Mimi Curran and Jonathan Cameron left West End media firm Mishcon de Reya to help broaden Paisner's digital media remit.

The work: The group now represents a wide range of clients on digital media matters, using media and IP as the main approach into the area. Broadly speaking the work now splits into two main areas, one of which is traditional media advice, on contracts and litigation for the publishing, film and TV industries, while the other is the developing digital media side of the practice.

In this latter field, Paisner & Co has been advising a range of clients, including ft.com, BAFTA interactice, This is Britain, and upmystreet.com. Other clients include Apax, with Paisner's advising the Venture Capital House on an investment into UK based online auction site QXL. The firm probably has as many new media clients as most in fact. One of the major clients is the recent MCPS/PRS alliance, which Paisner has advised – having acted for the Performing Rights Society in the past – on contracts relating to a license application system for musical works to be traded across the Internet.

The firm has also been involved for Great Universal Stores Home Shopping, in relation to negotiations with British Interactive Broadcasting.

Key contacts: Jonathan Cameron, Mimi Curran, Linda Fazzani, Lawrence Kaye, Adam Rose

Sample clients: Aladdin Knowledge Software, Apax, BAFTA Interactive, FT.com, The Beenz Company, Unipower Systems, UpMyStreet.com,

This firm might suit: Paisner & Co places believes that there are three strands to a successful digital media practice – understanding of and involvement with a client's business, understanding of the technology, and a comprehension of the traditional industry from which the new company's business has emerged. So far the firm seems to be satisfying its clients with this mix of skills and abilities, and, with the arrivals of three partners to the department in just over a year, the group is looking more substantial than it did the same time last year. Moreover, it seems to be realistic about its abilities: 'Paisner know that they are on a learning curve as well as we are and are more than willing to admit it,' said one client. (Commentary ranged from 'fantastic' to 'adequate', so it is clear that there is work to do on ensuring consistent excellence, but the indicators are good).

Although the practice seems to be biased towards the media side, it is worth noting that Paisner & Co has a good IT practice, led by Linda Fazzani, which works in combination with the media and IP practice.

Website: www.paisner.co.uk
An attractive site with some nice features: partner profiles, for instance, have a built-in message section, and a list of clients is provided. Information on computer and media law is relatively easy to find, although there is no search engine, and there is a good selection of publications available to order as well as an email 'e-Brief' plus the usual press releases. ★★

For more information see page 72

☕	**Face to face interview**
☎	**Telephone interview**

Rakisons ☕

Rakisons has been quietly carving itself a respectable practice advising hi-tech clients since its inception in 1979. Now with a complement of around 40 lawyers, including 14 partners, in addition to IT, telecoms and new media work the firm's main areas of work are in corporate/commercial and corporate finance, litigation, and commercial property, with a focus generally on the hi-tech and Internet sectors.

The group: At present the firm's communications and technology group comprises a total of four partners and three solicitors, although this figure is subject to fluctuation, depending on the workload at any one time. In addition to dedicated lawyers in this group, a number of other lawyers at Rakisons also advise on digital media issues.

The work: Developing alongside the firm's IT and telecoms practice, with particular strength in the latter discipline, Rakisons' digital media practice has grown over the last 12 months, advising a range of new clients. Among these are two major software companies, and several international communications companies.

Rakisons has a good international communications practice, which has seen the firm advise in jurisdictions such as Tanzania and Georgia and the Gabon. Although strictly speaking this is not pure digital media work, it has given the firm insights into systems set-up and

Legal services

regulatory issues.

Current work also includes advising on the public listing of an Internet company, a domain name acquisition, investment advice for a number of Internet start-ups, and continuing advice to more established digital media companies.

Key contacts: Peter Carey, Paul Hosford, Christopher Hoyle, Daniel Preiskel, Gerald Wakefield

Sample clients: Band-X, Governments of Tanzania, Georgia, Gabon, Internet Technology Group

This firm might suit: Rakisons is a firm which appears to be modelled on the US firms entering the London market rather than its fellow UK law firms. The twin approach of commercial and technology advice (including financing) to this specific sector has been successfully pioneered by a number of the leading firms in this area, and to some extent, Rakisons appears to have the capability to follow suit.

Seeing its lawyers as business advisors rather than just as legal advisors, Rakisons hopes to be able to operate closer relationships with its clients.

The firm's size is another factor which it perceives as an advantage. Although it means that enormous projects may be out of the firm's reach at the moment, the firm's current size does allow it some of the benefits afforded by smaller firms – namely a more personal service, lower costs, and a greater flexibility.

Website: www.rakisons.co.uk
Quite stylish, if basic, brochure site, with partner profiles and somewhat scant information about the firm's services, although no specifics on clients or deals. No publications or articles are available from the site. ★

For more information see pages 62, 72, 76, 202, 217, 228

Robert Muckle ☎

One of Newcastle's major law firms, Robert Muckle is a 12 partner firm, with a total of 50 fee-earners and an additional three associates and two consultants.

The group: The firm's practice is currently led by Mary Anne Macharg – taking over from Nick On who left earlier this year – who joined the firm from McGrigor Donald in September 1998. The IP / IT unit comprises three partners – the other two being Roddy Gordon and Hugh Welch, and a further two assistants.

The work: Digital media by no means makes up the majority of the firm's work in the arena, with more resources concentrated on IP and IT. This has not prevented Robert Muckle from advising on deals such as an online e-commerce training module, in this case, for the

Northern Colleges Network. Other work has included advising a large local authority on all IT matters – including problems of email and Internet use policies.

Key contacts: Roddy Gordon, Mary Ann Macharg, Hugh Welch

Sample clients: Northern Colleges Network

This firm might suit: Competent shortlist candidate for clients in the Newcastle area and North of England.

Website: www.robertmuckle.co.uk Confusingly directs the user to www.database.co.uk, which lists a number of competitor firms, but says nothing about Robert Muckle (no rating).

Rowe & Maw

A medium-sized City firm, Rowe & Maw, by its own partners' admission, is not a trumpet-blowing firm.

The group: Adopting a cross-disciplinary 'virtual team' of lawyers, the firm has drawn together members of various seemingly disparate groups to form its practice in this area, in common with other practices. Rowe & Maw is looking to use the experience of its corporate department relating specifically to communications and media work as leverage into a digital media practice. The firm's insurance group has embraced the digital revolution with use of its Fastrack system, perhaps a good indication of the firm's direction and potential.

The work: The firm has advised on a number of deals in the digital technology field, including advice on interactive television services. Additionally, perhaps because of its combination of corporate and new media expertise, the firm advised in an outsource involving two major players – namely the C&W outsource to IBM. The firm has also been advising Netgravity – a company specialising in providing tools for calculating Internet advertising efficiency.

Key contacts: Peter Dickinson, Mark Prinsley, Michael Webster

Sample clients: CWC, C&W, Netgravity, EMI

This firm might suit: Rowe & Maw is generally well-respected in many areas of mainstream corporate life, both by clients and by larger firms, which often refer to Rowe & Maw when they are conflicted out of acting on a particular deal.

Clients looking for decent advice on new projects, ventures, or joint ventures, but who are intimidated by the larger City firms (and their rates) should include Rowe & Maw on their shortlist and will find the firm calmly confident, discreet and reassuring.

Website: www.roweandmaw.co.uk Not the most appealing site (over-heavy

Legal services

ment independent editorial assessment independent editorial assessment independent editorial assessment independent editori use of shadowing on the homepage creates a blurry effect) but containing a huge mass of information in the way of press releases, group information, articles and some of the lengthiest partner profiles around. The sheer volume of it all makes the site somewhat of a maze to navigate at times (a search engine would help), but if information is what you want, this has a ton of it. The inclusion of the annual review is a nice touch. ★★★

For more information see pages 63, 67, 70, 220, 241, 251

Shaw Pittman

Originally a Washington firm, Shaw Pittman now also has offices in New York, Virginia and London, with the last of these established as recently as last year. With a focus on vertical market sectors, technology is one of four areas the firm advises in, the others being business and finance, disputes and government regulation. In opening a London office, the firm hopes to capture the market for advising UK and European technology companies on issues in the UK and Europe.

The group: The London office now features a complement of four partners and a further five assistants. Advising specifically in the technology sector, the work is divided internally into eight categories: IT and telecoms outsourcing, business process outsourcing, IP-related transactions, agreements between suppliers and customers, re-negotiation, restructuring and dispute resolution, Internet law and practice, Y2K compliance, data protection regulation and practice.

The work: The firm's practice in the area of e-commerce and the Internet could be a growing source of work, as use of the Internet both by consumers and businesses increases over the coming years. Shaw Pittman lawyers are currently advising on a number of innovative new media related projects, which are still under wraps, and therefore too sensitive to name. However, issues arising from these projects include data protection, jurisdictional conflicts (particularly in relation to payment methods and tax issues), consumer laws, and project outsourcing.

With its US-inspired commercial focus, Shaw Pittman has made good progress in the short space of time since the inception of the London office.

Key contacts: Andrew Dunlop, Margaret Harvey, Christopher Holder, Alistair Maughan, Andrew Moyle

Sample clients: withheld

This firm might suit: Technology sector companies with a view to expanding into new territories, either the UK or Europe, or even the US – where the firm has a strong technology presence – would find this firm's knowledge of their business helpful indeed.

With a particular expertise in financing technology company ventures and listings, Shaw Pittman would be a good choice for a firm looking for expertise on both sides of the Atlantic, with advice given by a committed team of technology specialists.

Website: www.shawpittman.com Disappointingly, for the UK client, there is no London-specific information about Shaw Pittman on the US site, aside from a number of partner and associate profiles of those lawyers based in London. Aside from that, the site is extensive, with a wealth of legal information, links and, interestingly, a list of how to subscribe to an array of cyberlaw e-zines (no rating).

For more information see page 63

Sidley & Austin ☎

With principal areas of focus in banking, structured finance, tax, corporate finance, and property, Sidley & Austin's technology practice is in a good position to benefit from the knowledge base of these other specialisms. The firm was originally established in Chicago in 1866, and opened its London office in 1974.

The group: The firm's information industries group comprises some ten lawyers, of whom two are partners. Of the remaining eight, six are assistants and the other two are trainees. John Edwards is head of the department – notably, he is also the managing partner of the London office. In general the department's lawyers spend one quarter of their time dealing with digital media issues.

The work: Clients range from large communications companies, such as Nokia, to UK based ISPs, such as Demon Internet. During the last 12 months, the firm has advised on several impressive deals involving these clients. For Nokia, Sidley & Austin has been acting on a global basis in the pursuance of online infringers, while the firm has also advised the Post Office on the use of encryption software, with particular reference to the importation of that software. Approvals have been achieved from 25 countries worldwide for that import.

On the Internet side, the group has advised a US-based Portal company on European issues centring on the registration of domain names, and potential challenges to domain names registered by other parties. Domain names have represented a good source of work for Sidley & Austin over the last year, and the firm has advised on several domain name disputes, as well as advising the companies responsible for the registration of domain names on issues relating to government attempts to seize control of the names.

Other work over the last 12 months has included some commercial matters, with the firm advising web designers and consultants on contractual documentation and IP strategy.

Key contacts: Gill Andrews, John Edwards

Sample clients: Demon Internet, Nokia, Post Office

This firm might suit: Another of a crop of good American firms active in digital media work, Sidley & Austin has a comparatively long-established London office, advising in a range of industries. The firm has a longstanding reputation for telecoms work in particular, and a growing international reputation for all things cyber-related.

Website: www.sidley.com
After a bit of hunting around on the US site, London was found, although the information is rather scant (unless you're looking for a training contract as a lawyer). The one significantly impressive feature of the site is an entire area devoted to the Cyberlaw group, with articles and profiles and an impressive client/experience list (including representing Microsoft, Peapod, Real Networks and the American Medical Association). (no rating)

For more information see pages 63, 69

Simmons & Simmons

A top ten City firm providing a general service to major clients, Simmons & Simmons has perhaps more than most of its kind focused on specialist areas, such as intellectual property, telecoms, employment and environment work, thanks to market-leading lawyers in each area. Its recent history is one of turbulence, but 1999 has so far been reasonably kind to it, particularly in its growing communications practice which continues to forge ahead.

The group: The firm can field some seven partners and around 20 other lawyers on dm issues, chief among them those from the communications practice, where Chris Watson and Tom Wheadon are key players in particular.

The work: It is fair to say that the firm's digital media practice has its origins in its increasingly successful telecoms carrier practice, but this has broadened with exposure to the issues thrown up by new media, such as charges for online services (where the firm has advised Scottish Telecom), charges for Internet access and the industry standard peering agreement (Internet Technology Group) and data protection (London Electricity, Telewest). With the benefit of a strong banking practice, the firm also has experience in online banking and trading.

Key contacts: Paul Barton, Jeremy Morton, Christopher Watson, Tom Wheadon

Sample clients: Scottish Telecom, Telewest, Internet Technology Group, London Electricity

This firm might suit: Simmons & Simmons' carrier practice has grown considerably over the past few years with the firm's recent recruits serving to further bolster its reputation in this area, and the group has scored some notable successes on the regulatory front, both in court and on the marketing stage, ensuring that it is a name to be reckoned with.

The telecoms carrier and regulatory strength, however, serves somewhat to overshadow a presence on the content side, not particularly focused on traditional media clients, but on content in the wider e-commerce sense, spun from the firm's impressive banking and industrial client base.

Simmons' lawyers also display a degree of lateral thinking, not just about their solutions to legal problems, but in their approach to business models generally, which gives an added dimension to the service – something, frankly, the research team encountered infrequently on its travels. In the words of one client the firm is 'consistently expensive, but very proactive and gives very good advice', and other clients contacted by the research team were equally impressed, citing 'specialist advice' and the 'best information available'.

Although devotees of the legal press will have noticed a fraying round the edges at Simmons & Simmons in recent times, the reputation and track record of the relevant individuals is such that local difficulties should have no impact on the group's ability to serve clients, and the firm's underlying strength in corporate and banking remains largely intact to more than cover the bases on the deal front. Recommended.

Website: www.simmons-simmons.com
A functional site, with plenty of information on the firm, including CVs of the various departments and details of clients, something which is absent from many law firm sites. The site is easy to navigate, with many embedded links in the clearly-written text (although a Home button on each page would have been welcome). Examples of the artwork the firm owns have been used to enliven the pages, although the lack of animation (perhaps a rotating 'gallery' of the works?) leaves it still rather stiff, as does the absence of partner profiles. ★★★

For more information see pages 60, 61, 64, 66, 67, 69, 72, 74, 75, 203, 215, 238, 251, 253

Face to face interview

Telephone interview

Legal services

Legal services

Sinclair Roche & Temperley ☎

Sinclair Roche & Temperley is one of few firms in the UK specialising in international trade and transport legal advice. In addition to London, the firm has offices in several locations worldwide

The group: The firm's IT law group is headed by senior associate solicitor Scott Singer. A former computer programmer, Singer devotes all his attention to IT law. A further four partners also advise in IT, IP and new media issues, but this is generally only part of their overall workload.

The work: The firm's practice in this area, which is dominated by IT, rather than digital media, can be broadly divided into two discreet sections. The first is advice to clients of the firm as a whole; clients which tend to be large businesses in international trade, and banks and insurance companies. The route into digital media advice for these clients comes from an appreciation of the importance of their IP rights.

The second side of the practice is advice for IT clients, such as software houses, computer hardware manufacturers. Work tends to be of the licensing and procurement vein, although relevant to new media is advice on encryption technologies, which Singer has been advising on for a number of years now.

E-commerce has also featured on Sinclair Roche & Temperley's radar in recent times, most notably in respect of the Bolero initiative. The firm has advised clients in relation to bills of lading, which may be fundamentally affected by this initiative. Another piece of ongoing digital media advice relates to a domain name dispute.

Key contact: Scott Singer

Sample clients: Withheld

This firm might suit: Although more of an IT practice than digital media, Sinclair Roche & Temperley is a good choice for those involved in international trade.

Website: www.sinclair-roche.com
A pleasantly designed homepage offers the user the usual range of options. Partner and departmental profiles are here, as are a number of articles, although none, sadly, centering on digital media issues. The search engine does yield ten results for a search on "e-commerce" (none for digital media), although these turn out in the main to be partner profiles. The links provided may prove useful. Attractive if somewhat lightweight. ★★

SJ Berwin & Co ☎

SJ Berwin is a relatively young firm, only established 17 years ago, which has risen from its original complement of four lawyers to its current count of well over 200 lawyers. SJ Berwin's remarkably rapid growth is, in the firm's view, attributed to a style reliant upon quality delivered quickly.

The group: The media and communications group is at the core of the firm's digital media practice. It comprises a total of four partners and six assistant solicitors, and is led by Nigel Palmer. In a wider context, the firm has established a cross-departmental communications group which involves a further six partners and 30 assistants.

The work: Having established a cross-departmental group to capitalise on the growing interest in e-commerce, SJ Berwin has begun to grow the client base to justify such a move. Clients are drawn from a range of industry sectors, as you might expect from a firm with a department covering so many of the firm's overall practice areas.

The communications group has been instructed by clients such as NSM Atkiengesellscaft – a premier global supplier of jukeboxes, which SJ Berwin has advised in relation to remote ISDN-driven jukebox networks and Lionhead Studios.

Having a strong corporate finance practice, and especially in the field of private equity has put SJ Berwin in an ideal position from which to create a digital media practice. One recent corporate deal saw the firm acting for Sports Internet Group plc on its acquisition of Planetfootball.com for £24m, reputed to be the first sale of an Internet content provider in the UK. The firm has also advised a series of venture capital houses active in the digital media sector.

Key contacts: Tim Johnson, Robb Klein, Nigel Palmer

Sample clients: Advent, Amadeus, Apax Partners, Atlas Venture, Lionhead Studios, NSM Atkiengesellscaft, Sports Internet Group plc

This firm might suit: SJ Berwin has for some time had a strong venture capital practice, in the main for equity providers but a cross-fertilisation from both sides of the venture capital equation ensures all-round capability in finance raising for technology companies.

The firm has, for the moment, eschewed the creation of a major stand-alone digital media practice, favouring instead a broad base of commercial technology sector knowledge. Whether this lack of genuine specialism will count against the firm remains to be seen, although for commercial advice in this sector the firm is not considerably behind some of the leading players.

Website: www.sjberwin.com
An eclectic, almost surreal site compared to those of other law firms, significantly marred for this reviewer by the fact that it booted up two Explorer windows, one of which was totally inert and the other lacking any navigation aids whatever. We tried it on another PC and again the two

windows came up, but this time there were some helpful little Java applets telling us where to go. Want to join SJ Berwin? Head for the Hubble Space Telescope. Want the foreign offices? Click on the Global Positioning System. Partner profiles? Why, Fermat's Theorem, of course. A different approach, certainly, but the glitches and eclectic overall feel rather got in the way. ★★

Slaughter and May

Arguably the finest corporate law firm in the UK, Slaughter and May has maintained an untarnished reputation for excellence in mergers and acquisitions and privatisation work particularly. Unlike many of its rivals, it has eschewed marketing and promotion to the extent that its media-shy stance has become legendary in the legal profession. Its rather slower development of an international network than many of its rivals has led many in the profession to speculate as to whether the firm really has a long-term future in a global marketplace, but much of this speculation is in fact based upon nothing other than envy.

The group: Despite a conservative attitude to marketing generally, Slaughter and May has been quietly active developing business in this area, via conferences and seminars in particular. One recent advancement (and quite revolutionary for the firm) was the establishment of a cross-disciplinary e-commerce group.

In terms of strength, the firm can field two partners (Nigel Swycher and Chris Hickson, who are both broadly experienced in IP/IT matters) and 13 other solicitors in total (no full-time digital media practitioners).

The work: Examples of work include acting for publishing clients such as EMAP which is expanding into electronic publishing; for Psion on its major Symbian joint venture project; and for BIB (now Open) on the establishment of its interactive digital television services.

Key contacts: Elizabeth Barrett, Chris Hickson, Mike Rebeiro, Nigel Swycher

Sample clients: British Interactive Broadcasting (Open), Psion/Symbian, EMAP

This firm might suit: Go to Slaughter and May and the one thing you will never compromise on is quality. One could draw parallels with premium consumer goods or services, but they would not convey the level of devotion to quality which is displayed at Slaughter and May. Of course, this devotion has its price: Slaughter and May is one of the most expensive choices of law firm that one could make (although if one factored in the unknowable expense – ie the cost of getting it wrong – then the firm would arguably come out much better).

The firm's e-commerce experience, also, will not suit every client. We would recommend the firm without hesitation for major corporate deals and for major projects requiring a huge amount of dedication and fastidiousness from the lawyers working on it. However, its exposure to a huge volume of day-to-day e-commerce activity seems, at this juncture, relatively limited, and its litigation experience does not match those of most of its rivals. It is likely that as e-commerce grows, the currently underpartnered IP/IT department will become a more powerful force within the firm. One to watch.

Website: www.slaughterandmay.com
The site would not work on the review computer we used, but in deference to the firm, we tried it on Internet Explorer 4.0. Not, it has to be said, really worth upgrading your browser for – minimal, anonymous fare, couched in a conservative, almost retro design. There are no partner profiles, only contact names; no substantive information about the firm's credentials and nothing to hold the casual browser (although there is a reasonable selection of articles). Disappointing. ★

For more information see pages 65, 67, 74, 204

Tarlo Lyons

Tarlo Lyons' four main practice areas are media and entertainment, IT and telecoms, commercial property, and gaming and licensing regulation – the last being a respected niche the firm has taken. Of these, the firm has recently concentrated of late on IT, and intends to build a strong practice round its capability in this area, which is both contentious and non-contentious. Having experience in advising media clients in film and television amongst others could prove to be a useful combination for this medium sized (22 partners) firm as the media and technology industries converge.

The group: Led by Andrew Rigby on the non-contentious side, and Nick Arnold – who heads the firm's dispute resolution department – in contentious matters, Tarlo Lyons' media and technology practice areas are at the core of the firm's work. The IT and telecoms practice numbers 15 lawyers, 12 of whom focus almost exclusively in those areas. The aim of the digital media practice is to utilise the knowledge of the IT group by advising media clients in their new digital ventures.

The work: A variety of users and suppliers are advised in IT matters, and this translates into the digital media and online practice. Interactive television software, allowing more user choice over broadcasts, and digital projection of films are just two of the many issues covered by the practice, which also includes advising on the first ever truly digitally made and broadcast television series.

In the last 12 months the firm has moved into the financial services sector, advising on of online banking services, nationally and globally.

The firm's gaming practice is another which has helped to expand breadth of the digital media practice. The possibility for online gambling and lotteries has attracted the attention of a plc, which has instructed Tarlo Lyons on a number of betting issues, both on and off-line.

Key contacts: Robert Carolina, George Gardiner, John Mawhood, Lawrence Phillips, Andrew Rigby

Sample clients: withheld

This firm might suit: Clients frightened by the thought of being one of hundreds of similar clients in a large City firm may find they are more comfortable being advised by Tarlo Lyons. Having a smaller number of easily-defined and in general complimentary practice areas means that the firm feels it is able to concentrate its energies more effectively towards clients in those areas.

Tarlo Lyons does not have an extensive corporate department, although in addition to its core areas you will find a decent commercial property practice.

As with many firms of its size, and many firms advising in this area, Tarlo Lyons is keen to attract small and medium-sized companies to its services, by offering flexible billing structures, designed to meet the needs of companies who more often than not are far from cash-rich, with a view to retaining growing clients.

Website: www.tarlo-lyons.co.uk
Quite basic site, with not much in the way of human content (no partner profiles or pictures). There is a definite accent on IT matters, which will guide the client in the direction of articles and publications. French and German clients will find several introductory pages in their native tongues. ★★

For more information see pages 76, 218, 224, 235, 242

Taylor Joynson Garrett

A medium-sized City corporate firm, traditionally strong in intellectual property, Taylor Joynson Garrett took a decision two years ago to focus on technology and lifesciences, with the result that the last two years have seen steady recruitment in all disciplines.

The group: Digital media work in the firm centres on the IT/telecoms group, which gives some indication of how TJG approaches convergence. The firm has some eight partners active in the field, most notably the endearingly 'techie' Glyn Morgan, Kiran Sandford (a recruit from Speechly Bircham), Simon Walker (corporate partner, ex Manches & Co) and the energetic David Kent, who is largely responsible for the impressive flow of inward-bound work from the US which comes to the firm. Of note also are telecoms guru Ted Mercer and IP partner Gary Moss, both of whom have excellent personal reputations.

The work: Aside from the more traditional IT and IP work, which TJG can boast by the barrowload, the firm has been active in a number of key dm areas. Inward-bound US work has given the firm valuable experience on set-ups from scratch of established US clients but which have no presence in the UK. The firm is acting for a number of the Internet's hottest new stocks as they expand from the US into Europe, although the sensitivity of some of the work is such that TJG lawyers are reluctant to talk in detail about it for the moment (although examples include ebay, e-gain and e-Toys).The firm also acts for a number online publishers and enterprise software providers as well as for a major push technology provider. It has also been active for a number of encryption providers. On the financial services side, experience includes acting for a major credit company on Internet fraud issues.

The recruitment of Simon Walker was key in kicking off the firm's presence in the burgeoning computer games industry, in that he brought in star UK games company Eidos (which the eminent publisher uses for large transactional work). However, the firm has also, crucially, acted for Sony Computer Entertainment Europe in relation to its anti-piracy programme against the rechipping of its PlayStation consoles. Another interesting niche has been work on geographic information systems, where the firm has acted for both supplier and user clients.

Key contacts: David Kent, Glyn Morgan, Kiran Sandford, Simon Walker

Sample clients: Cadcorp, ebay Inc, e-gain, Eidos, eMusic.Com, Entertainment Europe, e-Toys, on board info Ltd, Sony Computer StartIT.com plc

This firm might suit: Clearly, TJG is an attractive choice for US clients and for US referrers of work (the firm claims the legal work on one-sixth of US work coming into the UK in this sector), and this seems to spring as much from a willingness internally to think and act more like a US West Coast law firm as it does from David Kent's energetic capture of work in the US. As the firm develops its thinking along these lines (and the degree to which that thinking permeates mainstream disciplines such as corporate and property), its focus on technology disciplines is bound to harden.

The firm covers the bases across most of convergence and can certainly talk 'techie' with the best of them. Where it has a distinct edge over some of its smaller rivals is in the corporate back-up to its vision. Its too-shy corporate department still accounts for a third of the firm's turnover, and its experience is such that it can field a good team on a broad range of transactions – most importantly of all, that it actually has corporate lawyers who do nothing but corporate work with the technology-related industries. With this kind of added-value corporate service, at a less expensive tariff, TJG also provides an alternative to the larger City firms on transactions in the converging industries.

Clients seem satisfied: 'I couldn't be more pleased with the work they do for us... they may not be one of London's largest law firms, but they are certainly one of the best,' says one; 'They are real specialists in this field and that's why we employ them,' according to another.

On commercial dm work, it is fair to say that the firm's client base tends to focus on the supplier, rather than user side, although its experience for a huge number of household names on traditional IP work should give it an 'in' acting for major brand owners on dm-related issues.

If the firm has a fault, it is that it has, to date, failed to properly mobilise its resources as regards its profile publicly and among its peers. Having said that, its concentration on recruitment and on ensuring its stream of US work continues will be of considerable benefit when the firm decides to come out fighting with a vengeance. Recommended.

Website: www.tjg.co.uk

Among the most stylish of all the law firm sites we reviewed, easy to navigate, with among the most detailed partner profiles encountered. Some of the text, particularly with regard to services provided, looks suspiciously lawyer-written (over-long, stilted) but otherwise the site is clear and easy on the eye. A significant amount of legal update material is available and is well-organised, although there is no search engine. ★★★

For more information see pages 59, 63, 64, 66, 68, 69, 70, 73, 74, 76, 205, 231, 245, 250

Taylor Vinters ☎

Cambridge-based Taylor Vinters is one of several firms in and around the city to specialise in, among other areas, advice to the hi-tech industries. Taking advantage of the wealth of local clients in industries such as biotechnology, the Internet, computer technology, Taylor Vinters has built this into a practice which already includes areas as diverse as commercial property, personal injury, bloodstock, and charities.

The group: The innovation and technology group, headed by Tom McGuire, has seen significant growth in the last 12 months, and the group has swelled from its previous count of two partners (Tom McGuire and Michael Womack), to include two assistants,

David Rainford and Sophie Kelley. Of the four lawyers in the group, only McGuire spends a significant amount of his time (just under half) on digital media work, with the figure for the other three averaging at around 25 per cent. However, unlike many departments where this is the case, at Taylor Vinters non-digital media work is probably more closely linked with the digital media work, with the practice complimentary to the firm's biotechnology practice. The cross-over links many kinds of work, with the possible exception of patent work, where industry specialisation is needed.

The work: The innovation and technology group's client base is drawn from all over the UK, including clients in Scotland, although the majority are to be found in East Anglia. Clients on the whole tend to be of the very cutting-edge flavour, with Taylor Vinters advising clients such as AT&T Laboratories Cambridge Ltd – previously known as Olivetti Research Ltd before being bought out by AT&T – on both commercial issues and IP issues.

Key contact: Tom McGuire

Sample clients: AT&T Laboratories Cambridge Ltd

This firm might suit: One of a few firms in East Anglia of any note, Taylor Vinters should be shortlisted by any client looking for legal advice from that part of England. Located in the heart of silcon fen's hi-tech industry, and just outside the Cambridge Science Park, Taylor Vinters is a firm which prides itself on this proximity to the industries it is advising, and in the technical know-how of its practitioners – Tom McGuire, by way of example, was a robot engineer prior to training as a lawyer – so anyone wanting to instruct lawyers who can speak their language could do a lot worse.

Website: www.taylor-vinters.co.uk
A basic, reasonably attractive brochure website, quite light on content. ★

For more information see pages 77

Theodore Goddard

A medium-sized City firm with a reputation for corporate, banking and entertainment work.

The group: Theodore Goddard's IT Law group, which co-ordinates digital media and e-commerce work within the firm, has seen significant growth in the last few years. Head of the group, Arnold Segal, has a good public profile including many conference appearances, seminars and authorships. Another lawyer with a good public profile is the charming, effective Rafi Azim-Khan (described as 'absolutely excellent' by one client), who has considerable experience in branding and advertising issues, and who was

Legal services

engaged in dm work pretty much full-time during the research process for the guide. As the guide went to press, we learned of the departure of consultant John Angel to Clifford Chance, which is a blow to the group.

Although the firm does not hold itself out as a telecoms specialist, the recent addition of former Oftel lawyer Edward Pitt and Susannah Shephard, formerly with the European Commission, has bolstered the firm's presence and expertise at this end of convergence. Its response to the challenge posed by convergence, in the creation of a complex skills-services matrix (operated by many other firms but rarely with the sophistication and breadth of skillset seen at TG), indicates the seriousness with which the firm treats the subject, though its forays into web-based delivery systems for legal services have been, to date, modest.

The work: Theodore Goddard has succeeded in marrying a traditional reputation for 'soft' content issues, such as music and advertising, with a harder IT practice, giving it a broader perspective than some firms its size. Its recent association with Integralis Network Systems and insurance brokers Nelson Hurst – to provide the Cyberliability Service – and its experience acting for Western Provident in the landmark Norwich Union email case has given it an edge in advising on the email/intranet liability frontier. Otherwise, the firm has been active on a variety of e-commerce issues including the sale of music on the Internet and intranet licences. One major coup saw the firm advising News International on the set-up of CurrantBun.com.

Its long history acting for clients in the music industry and the recent addition of recognised games lawyer Arnold Segal give it a good general content practice.

Key contacts: Rafi Azim-Khan, David Engel, Paul Renney, Arnold Segal

Sample clients: Dialog, Ericsson, Quantum International, Syzygy, Western Provident

This firm might suit: Theodore Goddard can offer a broad range of services to clients both in the IT industry and in the 'user' base of general corporate life. Its corporate department is sturdy, less expensive than larger rivals and with a good reputation, and its spread of related services (tax, employment, pensions etc) is reliable if unremarkable. Where it scores is in the expertise of the individual lawyers within particular industry sectors – IT, games, music and advertising in particular. Although it cannot offer the spread of international offices of some major City rivals, it has good associations overseas. Its Cyberliability Service is one example of how the firm can innovate successfully. One to watch.

Website: www.theodoregoddard.com
The TG website was one of a few visited by the research team with any serious degree of interactivity – a marketing

gimmick which can win the visitor champagne, weekends away or gift vouchers via a system of lucky numbers. Design is slightly dated compared to many of the other major firms, but the overall feel is bright and relatively inviting. Description of practice areas is kept to a minimum and a wealth of legal developments come via the Law Channel section (although this neat idea is not carried through in a graphical way) – the lack of a search engine reduces the client-friendliness of this section, though. ★★★

For more information see pages 60, 61, 65, 66, 72, 73, 206, 214, 242, 245

Thomas Eggar Church Adams

Thomas Eggar Church Adams was established just over one year ago, from a merger between two small practices – Thomas Eggar Verrall Bowles, and Church Adams Tatham. The 50-partner firm has its London office in Holborn, but also has its roots in the South of England, with offices in Horsham, Winchester, Worthing and Reigate. The combined firm has strengthened its hand in many areas, notably commercial property.

The group: Digital media work is handled as a part of the firm's general commercial practice, this part of it led by Mike Camps, previously of the Thomas Eggar Verrall Bowles side of the firm. With both constituent firms having had IP practices, the main difference between the two lay in the client base. Church Adams had a concentration of larger commecial clients, while Thomas Eggar acted for a number of SMEs.

The work: Although digital media is not a core area for the firm, it is an area which TECA has realised will inevitably form part of the practice for existing commercial clients. It is through this method that Philip Kraus, a partner in the IP practice, first became involved in digital media, advising an existing client on a large-scale electronic banking venture.

The firm's work covers a broad range of digital media issues, from advising on web development agreements, to ISP liabilities and domain name disputes. The firm is a member of e-centre.

Key contacts: Mike Camps, Philip Krauss

Sample clients: withheld

This firm might suit: Any commercial client in the South of England which needs e-commerce advice as an add-on to general commercial and corporate legal services might do well to shortlist TECA.

Website: www.teca.co.uk
Quietly impressive. Reasonably stylish site, with one important feature to the digital client. Under Free Information, a number of general Internet/web-related questions are answered (to a degree), which is more than many firms can claim, and certainly

better set-out than the majority of legal advice offered on websites. Information on the firm's services is easy to access and comprehensive. Otherwise, the site is standard law firm fare (profiles etc), although well-presented for all that.
★★★

For more information see pages 79, 232

Titmuss Sainer Dechert ☎

Acting for a strong retail client base, Titmuss Sainer Dechert has historically been known for its commercial property practice. An alliance with American firm Dechert Price & Rhoads was initiated in 1994, which has given the firm a trans-atlantic impetus to go with its existing relationships within Europe.

The group: The firm's commercial department houses the digital media practice, which is staffed by a complement of two partners and two other solicitors. Work undertaken in this area covers a broad range of IP and commercially-related issues, as well as advice on computer games agreements – a part of the practice which has continued in a low-key manner over the last twelve months since the departure of Paul Gardner, who headed that side of the contract. It should be pointed out that both Renzo Marchini and Simon Tracey, the group's two assistant solicitors, have experience in the computer games field.

The work: As with many firms in this area, Titmuss Sainer Dechert is actively pursuing e-commerce clients, and with its strong retail client base the firm may be in an excellent position to capitalise on one of the more prominent areas of this fast-growing industry. Aside from running seminars in conjunction with a number of existing clients, the firm has advised on a number of e-commerce projects, with particular reference to the regulation of trading online.

In addition to non-contentious commercial advice, the firm has also been active in litigation, advising a number of clients. Among these are has been Entranet, an e-commerce consultancy and site developer. Titmuss Sainer Dechert also advised in a significant computer games dispute between Psygnosis and Perfect Entertainment. The firm acted for the developer, Perfect Entertainment, the dispute arising over a claim for unpaid invoices and royalties.

Key contacts: Peter Crockford, Simon Leonard, Renzo Marchini, Simon Tracey

Sample clients: Entranet, Perfect Entertainment

This firm might suit: TSD is a friendly, relaxed firm, somewhat smaller than many of its local rivals. The relatively small size of the team means that although the firm will not necessarily be the best placed for advising on mega-deals, a client can be assured that he will generally be instructing the same solicitors on a regular basis.

In an area such as e-commerce, which broadly speaking can be split vertically into a range of industry specialisms, it will often be prudent to select a firm with expertise in one of those industry sectors. This means that Titmuss Sainer Dechert would be a solid if unadventurous choice for clients looking to instruct on online consumer retail issues, for instance.

Website: www.titmuss-sainer-dechert.com A colourful homepage, which confronts the browser with 'Lawyers – who needs them?', the theme of TSD's brochure. The site is an attractive one and has several neat gimmicks (such as being able to send an Internet postcard and a Snakes & Ladders game for trainees (although with some depressing 'snakes' such as 'forgetting to post the senior partner's pools coupon' which is hardly an encouragement to join the modern legal profession...), as well as the usual partner profiles, publications and information about practice areas. No search engine though. ★★★

For more information see page 64

Travers Smith Braithwaite ☎

City firm Travers Smith Braithwaite has one of the leading corporate finance practices in the country for its size, and, despite lacking the sheer weight of numbers of some of its competitors, advises many impressive clients in that area.

The group: The firm's intellectual property and information technology practice is part of the overall company commercial group, and comprises many partners from a range of commercial disciplines. Generally speaking three partners have IP as their main focus, with partner Alistair Wilson at the head of this team, although lawyers from the firm's tax, employment, and corporate finance departments also advise in this area.

The work: On the whole the work is focused towards the commercial and contractual side of the hi-tech sector. Concentrating on the skills present within the firm, most deals have involved advising as part of the corporate or commercial process (for instance, advising the shareholders and management team of Internet Network Services in the sale to Cable & Wireless). Having a strong corporate finance practice has led the firm to advise on several flotations of hi-tech companies.

Travers' e-commerce credentials are based around a long-standing relationship which has seen the firm

Face to face interview

☎ **Telephone interview**

advise on the electronic share dealing system, CREST.

Key contacts: Nick Aleksander, Alistair Wilson

Sample client: CREST

This firm might suit: Essentially, Travers Smith Braithwaite's digital media practice consists of commercial and corporate advice to technology sector clients. Although Alistair Wilson and his team can and will advise on intellectual property issues, this is by no means the mainstay of the practice, so if IP rights are your only major asset, then perhaps this isn't the firm for you. If, on the other hand, you are likely to need strong corporate and corporate finance advice, coupled with advice on commercial agreements but don't want to approach the large City firms which specialise in those areas, then you could do a lot worse than choose to instruct Travers.

Website: www.traverssmith.co.uk
Not much for the client here, but plenty for the potential recruit. The briefest of marketing-brochure sites. ★

For more information see pages 214, 253

Walker Morris ☎

Walker Morris is one of a group of excellent Leeds-based firms which have flourished in Yorkshire's recent legal renaissance.

The group: Walker Morris' intellectual property group is 11-strong, headed by partner Patrick Cantrill. The group, which is teamed with the firm's information technology and telecommunications group, forms part of the overall commercial practice.

The work: Walker Morris acts for a relatively broad range of clients, and this is reflected in the list of clients which instruct the IP and IT groups. Retail clients are joined by companies investigating the possibilities offered by online financial trading and a former public utility.

This last client has not, strictly speaking, been a digital media client of the firm to date. Rather, it is one of the firm's IT clients, and it is this more traditional work which dominates the practice, with some admittedly impressive deals coming the firm's way. The digital media practice has developed out of both this and Walker Morris' IP practice, into a commerical and contractual practice. From the intellectual property perspective comes domain name advice, an area the firm has been active in, recently settling a dispute on behalf of a client.

Key contact: Patrick Cantrill

Sample clients: withheld

This firm might suit: For a firm of its size, Walker Morris has good stature, consistently punching above its weight in terms of the corporate work it has been able to bring in. The same has not been overly apparent of its digital media practice as yet, but some of the building blocks do seem to be in place.

Website: www.walkermorris.co.uk Stylish-looking homepage, but bubbling with Javascript errors on our test machine. That aside (better get v 4.0 if you haven't already), this is not a bad brochure-site, with some nice features. The addition of the words 'have fun' to the exhortations on the homepage, for instance, at least doffs its cap to a more human approach than many other firms' starchy efforts. There are many of the usual features, publications to order and profiles, as well as an 'Ask Us' feature allowing submission of basic questions. Descriptions of work areas are a little wordy, but contain information on recent experience, which is welcome. There is no search engine so head for IT or IP. ★★★

For more information see pages 77, 217

Weil Gotshal & Manges

Weil Gotshal & Manges is one of a number of US firms which has opened London offices in the past few years. In America, and in the firm's office in Brussels, the focus is on the hi-tech sector, providing a range of services to clients within that sector. The recent addition of ex-Clifford Chance corporate partner Mike Francies means that compared to the same time 12 months ago, Weil Gotshal & Manges can claim to have a more comprehensive product to offer technology clients, including regulatory and corporate finance lawyers – recruited on the whole from major City UK law firms.

The group: As the technology sector forms the overall focus of the firm, many of the lawyers in the firm are involved in advising technology sector clients. Advice includes transactional work and acquisitions, although there is currently no real IP practice at the firm.

The work: The aim of the hi-tech group's practice is to advise on the full range of issues relating to the technology sector, a line which follows the lead of several of the more successful digital media firms. Focusing on corporate, finance, intellectual property and regulation for this sector, recent work includes advising ISPs on both content liability and corporate and finance issues. Much of the work is drawn from the corporate and finance fields, and includes advising on several substantial technology sector share offerings. On the regulatory side, the year's major client has been AOL, and its subsidiary AOL Bertelsmann. Weil, Gotshal also advised this client on a

Legal services

independent editorial assessment independent editorial assessment independent editorial assessment independent editorial assessment substantial acquisition, namely that of Compuserve, and on the creation in 1998 of the joint venture between AOL, Bertelsmann, Canal Plus and Cegetel.

Key contacts: James Chesterman, Mike Francies, David Naylor

Sample clients: AOL, AOL Bertelsmann, Cisco, Futurenet, Intel, Matsushita, News Corporation

This firm might suit: Like other American firms in London, Weil Gotshal & Manges claims to offer an alternative style practice, not just because of its technology sector focus, but also because of its US heritage, giving the client-lawyer relationship a slightly different spin. There is no doubt that the firm has built an impressive practice in a relatively short space of time, aiming for the high end of the market. With regulatory knowledge in Brussels assisting an impressive London finance practice, Weil Gotshal & Manges is definitely one to go for if you like your firms modern, and capable of covering the UK, Europe and US bases.

Website: www.weil.com
Disappointingly, London does not even have its own page on the US-based site, so no information was forthcoming (no rating).

For more information see pages 63, 70, 72, 207

Wiggin and Co ☎

Wiggin and Co is a small commercial firm based, within easy reach of London, in Cheltenham. The firm has an excellent private client practice, in addition to its communications practice, which, it should be said, is among the strongest and most focused outside London.

The group: Wiggin and Co's media department, headed by Tim Osborne, consists of three partners – in addition to Osborne the other two partners are Sean James and Shaun Lowde. A further four solicitors and one trainee make up the remainder of the department. The lawyers in the media department spend a varying amount of time on digital media work, and for the most part it forms the bulk of their work.

The work: Wiggin and Co has established for itself a niche in the television and digital television market, advising a number of clients from that sector. The firm is one of few to be currently active in this area, and of those firms, has probably the most impressive national client base. Wiggin and Co has advised a number of joint ventures in this industry on issues such as carriage contracts and regulatory conditions, the most notable of which is perhaps that between the BBC and Flextech. This saw Wiggin and Co advise on carriage contracts for ONDigital's digital terrestrial platform. The firm has also advised Flextech on its interactive channels and services.

Key contacts: Sean James, Caroline Kean, Shaun Lowde, Tim Osborne

Sample clients: BBC/Flextech jv, Flextech

This firm might suit: Wiggin and Co has many features to recommend it: it is outside London, but has recruited a series of City-trained lawyers; the client-facing attitude is a throwback to the dominance of the private client practice, giving a very personal touch; Wiggin and Co will be cheaper (in general) than City firms; and the broadcast practice is almost peerless in the UK. Certainly outside London there is no comparable firm.

The firm is very much playing to its strengths at the moment, and, while realising that as the digital broadcast market diversifies and broadens, leading to a reduction in the firm's dominance in that area, is content for the time being to continue to act for the major players.

If you are looking at the digital broadcast market in any shape or form, then this is a solid choice for legal advice.

Website: www.wiggin.co.uk
The website was under reconstruction at time of going to press, but the firm assures us it will be operational by the end of the summer (no rating).

For more information see pages 62, 72, 209, 228, 229, 23, 240

Willoughby & Partners (Rouse & Co International) ☎

Willoughby & Partners (internationally Rouse & Co International) is a niche firm based in the Docklands area of London (with an office in Oxford) which specialises in intellectual property advice. Often acclaimed for its strength in that field, the firm has won several awards.

The group: Headed by Bina Cunningham, the Internet and New Media group consists of four partners and 11 other fee-earners. In Oxford Ben Goodger leads the way for the non-contentious side of the practice.

The work: With a total focus on intellectual property rights, Willoughby's global client base includes many of the leading brand owners across the widest imaginable industry spectrum. Major media companies, interactive games companies, IT companies, and many others have been advised on a range of issues from electronic publishing to electronic merchandising rights and data protection. Sadly, it is the firm's policy not to publicly announce client details, but its client list is impressiveness.

Willoughbys has a very strong reputation for its fierce style of litigation. Its comprehensive service includes investigation services to proactively monitor the market for potential infringements of a client's brand, advice to distributors on IP rights preservation, and rights clearance work.

While being a global practice – with offices in China, Indonesia, Vietnam, Hong Kong and Dubai – the only move away from IP that the firm has taken is a slight venture into IT related advice, although only one partner at the firm has been handling this side of the practice.

Key contacts: Bina Cunningham, Ben Goodger

Sample clients: withheld

This firm might suit: Simply put, Willoughbys has one of the best intellectual property practices in the UK, advising on the protection of both national and international IP rights. In addition to this the firm has a strong litigation practice, and on top of that is the natural progression into protecting IP in the wired world, which Willoughbys has adopted in a clear and planned fashion.

If you are concerned about protecting your intellectual property above all else, then Willoughbys is an excellent choice for any client, large or small.

Website: www.iprights.com
Impressive-looking, modern site (though annoyingly we couldn't access the site map with our 3.0 browser) focusing entirely on IP rights. Clearworld magazine (the firm's e-zine) provides a vast amount of general information and advice including hot IP news. There is little about the people at the firm, which is a mite disappointing, and navigation is not totally watertight. Nonetheless, the site performs admirably on a number of levels. ★★★

For more information see page 64

Wragge & Co ☎

Possibly the number one firm in Birmingham, Wragge & Co leads the way in the West Midlands in a number of disciplines, and has a practice to rival many City firms. Wragges is known and respected for its work both in the Midlands and further afield.

The group: The computer and IT group is led by Bill Jones, practising exclusively in those combined disciplines, of which digital media is an integral part. The group has recently had two promotions to partner level (with three in total now) – a reflection of the firm's confidence in the ability and experience of its lawyers – which gives it more clout. It is difficult to establish precisely how much of the group's work is strict digital media work, as there is a certain amount of overlap with more traditional IT areas, but the combination of the two is the sum of the practice. Another relevant partner appointment is that of Nick Smith, a corporate lawyer specialising in IT sector mergers and acquisitions.

The work: The practice appears to be very much corporate and communications driven, with Wragge's acting for a number of major names in the communications sector. Among these are Birmingham Cable, naturally a local client (and one of the largest telephony providers in the UK, to boot), and AT&T, not so local, but its presence on Wragge's books is a measure of the ability of the firm to draw in major clients.

Recently, Wragge & Co has also gained new instructions on two exciting e-commerce ventures – one from a US client, and one UK based - by major companies in their respective fields of banking and travel.

Key contacts: Patrick Duxbury, Bill Jones, Sarah Sasse

Sample clients: AT&T, Birmingham Cable, Kalamazoo

This firm might suit: Anyone thinking of advising a firm within a 100-mile radius of Birmingham should shortlist Wragge & Co, and if you're looking for a City-quality firm based outside the Square Mile, then this is the one for you. The firm has a very impressive single office practice, staffed by knowledgeable practitioners, with broad skill-sets. In addition to being able to advise on IT and new media issues, the firm has a comprehensive all-round practice.

Website: www.wragge.co.uk

Modern-looking website with an innovative navigation bar (in the form of a horizontal radio dial). Publications are available to order (although, irritatingly, you can only order one newsletter at once via the form, and the codes to order the firm's Briefing Notes were not in evidence), there are partner profiles and some basic information about the firm's services, as well as some helpful facts and figures. One nice touch is a Daily Alert, pointing the browser in the direction of newspaper articles of legal interest. ★★★

For more information see pages 64, 77, 210, 229

Face to face interview

Telephone interview

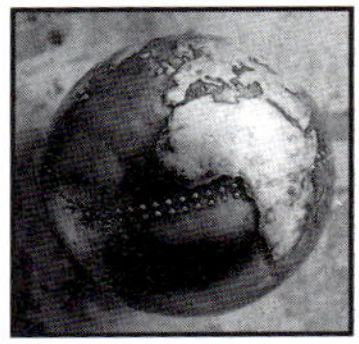

Where do I find a law firm?

A full telephone and address list of all the firms recommended in this book, including full profiles of many firms

Law firms

Addleshaw Booth & Co
Sovereign House,
PO Box 8 Sovereign Street,
Leeds LS1 1HQ
Phone: 0113 209 2000
Fax: 0113 209 2060

Allen & Overy
One New Change,
London EC4M 9QQ
Phone: 020 7330 3000
Fax: 020 7330 9999

Ashurst Morris Crisp
Broadwalk House,
5 Appold Street,
London EC2A 2HA
Phone: 020 7638 1111
Fax: 020 7972 7990

Baker & McKenzie
100 New Bridge Street,
London EC4V 6JA
Phone: 020 7919 1000
Fax: 020 7919 1999

Berwin Leighton
Adelaide House, London Bridge,
London EC4R 9HA
Phone: 020 7760 1000
Fax: 020 7760 1111

Bevan Ashford
35 Colston Avenue,
Bristol BS1 4TT
Phone: 0117 923 0111
Fax: 0117 929 1865

Biddle
1 Gresham Street,
London EC2V 7BU
Phone: 020 7606 9301
Fax: 020 7606 3305

Bindman & Partners
275 Gray's Inn Road,
London WC1X 8QF
Phone: 020 7833 4433
Fax: 020 7837 9792

Bird & Bird
90 Fetter Lane,
London
EC4A 1JP
Phone: 020 7415 6000
Fax: 020 7415 6111

Bird Semple
249 West George Street,
Glasgow,
Scotland G2 4RB
Phone: 0141 221 7090
Fax: 0141 204 1902

Biddle

Media & publishing group

Biddle

1 Gresham Street, London EC2V 7BU
Phone: 020 7606 9301 **Fax:** 020 7606 3305
Website: www.Biddle.co.uk **Email:** Kim.Walker@Biddle.co.uk
Head of group: Kim Walker
Other offices: Biddle is a member of Logos, a group of law firms with offices throughout the European Union, www.Logos-eeig.com
Firm: 33 partners, 33 assistants, 15 other fee-earners
Unit: 2 partners, 3 assistants

"Biddle is a highly progressive City business law practice with a particularly strong reputation in IT and the media. Already well regarded for its integrity and professionalism, Biddle's strategy is to provide a genuine City based alternative for commercial clients who are looking for a first class service. The firm's hallmark is the ability to advise on and implement precise and imaginative legal solutions to clients' business objectives in a user-friendly manner."

Recent highlights

- Advising a bidder on the IT, contractual and intellectual property issues arising on the proposal to digitise The British Library.
- Advising on development agreements for an interactive digital television channel.
- Advice to clients on the implications for e-commerce on the Copyright in the Information Society Green Paper and the proposals regarding encryption and electronic contracting.
- Content advice, copyright and trade mark notices and disclaimers for websites.
- Preparing terms and conditions and contractual procedures for online ordering of goods from websites.

Related services

Computer games	✓	E-commerce	✓	Internet	✓	Multimedia publishing	✓
Digital TV	✓	'Hard' IT	✓	Litigation	✓	Telecoms	✓

Bird & Bird

Digital Media & E-commerce

BIRD & BIRD

90 Fetter Lane, London EC4A 1JP
Phone: 020 7415 6000 **Fax:** 020 7415 6111
Website: www.twobirds.com **Email:** info@twobirds.com
Head of department: Mark Haftke/Graham Smith
Other offices: Brussels, Hong Kong
Firm: 51 partners, 112 assistant solicitors
Unit: 19 partners, 27 assistant solicitors

"Digital media and e-commerce expertise is threaded through the firm. Aside from our dedicated digital media group, all our lawyers – many experts in their own fields – understand the application of e-commerce in their industry sectors. We deliver solutions to match our clients' innovation across a wide range of services."

Recent highlights

- **Carlton Online:** advising on establishment of Jamba.com and popcorn.com and linking deals for them.
- **EMAP Metro Online:** advising this organisation on various content and linking deals.
- **Last Minute Networks Ltd:** advising on the set up and financing of its online travel and entertainments business.
- **Lloyds/TSB:** setting up the legal framework for their Internet banking product.
- **Out There News Ltd:** acting for an Internet news and analysis agency in its deal with AOL to set up their site as part of the AOL service.
- **Planet Online:** advising on 'Dixons' Freeserve' Internet deal and similar transactions.
- **QVC:** acting as QVC's (the home shopping channel) main UK counsel in respect of its satellite up-links/telecoms requirements.
- **The Electronic Telegraph:** advising on various Internet and interactive television deals.
- **Video Networks Ltd:** advising on development and launch of this video on demand service trialing with BT and Kingston Communications.

Related services

Computer games	✓	E-commerce	✓	Internet	✓	Multimedia publishing	✓
Digital TV	✓	'Hard' IT	✓	Litigation	✓	Telecoms	✓

key contacts

Bird Semple

Bird Semple TechMedia

BIRD SEMPLE TechMedia

Napier House, 27 Thistle Street, Edinburgh EH2 1BS
Phone: 0131 459 2345 **Fax:** 0131 459 5600
Web: www.birdsemple.co.uk **Email:** techmedia@birdsemple.co.uk
Head of department: Norman Oliver
Other offices: 249 West George Street, Glasgow G2 4RB
Firm: 19 partners, 39 assistants, 8 other fee-earners
Unit: 2 partners, 6 assistants

"Technology is all about change. People in the digital and new media sectors keep pace with change. When they need help, they are right to expect advisers who are up to speed. To meet these expectations, Bird Semple has set up TechMedia. Bird Semple TechMedia can provide legal solutions to meet all the needs of new media, media and technology businesses.

What's different about TechMedia?

Bird Semple TechMedia has specialists with experience in all the areas which are relevant to new media, media and technology companies. These specialists can assist companies in these sectors to find creative solutions which suit their needs. This is an innovative sector which requires innovative solutions delivered by flexible and dynamic advisers. Bird Semple TechMedia's specialist lawyers only carry out work for technology and media companies. The concentration on these sectors gives the lawyers a greater insight in to the industries and what makes them different."

Recent highlights

- *Inner Workings v Microsoft.* Bird Semple TechMedia, succeeded in obtaining an undertaking from Microsoft Corporation after Inner Workings alleged an infringement of intellectual property rights in its registered trade mark – Lemon Dog. Microsoft agreed not to use their Rocky the dog character on any packaging, advertising, or promotional material for Office 2000. Microsoft also agreed not to publish Rocky on any website.

- **VC Funding for Red Lemon Studios.** Bird Semple TechMedia advised Red Lemon in relation to their raising of early stage expansion finance. The funding was provided by 3i, Scottish Development Finance and Bank of Scotland.

- TechMedia has also advised Red Lemon on publishing agreements with Eidos and Red Storm and in relation to development agreements with Sega.

Related services

Computer games	✓	E-commerce	✓	Internet	✓	Multimedia publishing	✓
Digital TV		'Hard' IT	✓	Litigation	✓	Telecoms	✓

key contacts

Bristows

Intellectual property/corporate - digital media

BRISTOWS

3 Lincoln's Inn Fields, London WC2A 3AA
Phone: 020 7400 8000 **Fax:** 020 7400 8050
Web: www.bristows.com **Email:** info@bristows.co.uk
Digital Media contacts: Paul Cooke, Matthew Warren, David Wilkinson, Philip Westmacott

Firm: 20 partners, 40 assistants, 27 other fee-earners
Unit: 10 partners, 10 assistants

"Bristows' high profile in intellectual property has led to the firm advising a wide variety of clients on both litigation and transaction based digital media matters. The firm has a thriving practice in the area of digital interactive entertainment, computer games, e-commerce and the Internet."

Recent highlights

- Advising a major magazine publisher on CD-Rom and online publishing.
- Advising Panasonic on a digital satellite interactive television joint venture (BiB).
- Acting for Digital Image Design on corporate/publishing issues and other leading figures in the computer games industry.
- Ongoing advice for a major airline on the development of e-commerce systems.
- Pre and post-publication libel advice for one of the UK's leading magazine publishers.
- Competition law advice for a worldwide cable and satellite channel.
- Advising a national television broadcaster on licensing digital television technology.
- Acting for Revolution Software in relation to its agreements with Virgin interactive.
- Advising on European distribution of CD's and videos by e-commerce.
- Acting for Phillips in connection with a dispute over CD technology.
- Advising on Internet service provider on the launch of a new Internet service.

Related services

Computer games	✓	E-commerce	✓	Internet	✓	Multimedia publishing	✓
Digital TV	✓	'Hard' IT	✓	Litigation	✓	Telecoms	✓

Briffa & Co
Business Design Centre, Upper Street,
Upper Street, Islington Green,
London N1 0QH
Phone: 020 7288 6003
Fax: 020 7288 6004

Bristows
3 Lincoln's Inn Fields,
London WC2A 3BP
Phone: 020 7400 8000
Fax: 020 7400 8050

Brobeck Hale and Dorr
Hasilwood House, 60 Bishopsgate,
London EC2N 4AJ
Phone: 020 7638 6688
Fax: 020 7638 5888

Cameron McKenna
Mitre House, 160 Aldersgate Street
London EC1A 4DD
Phone: 020 7367 3000
Fax: 020 7367 2000

Charles Russell
8-10 New Fetter Lane,
London EC4A 1RS
Phone: 020 7203 5000
Fax: 020 7203 0200

Clark Holt
1 Sanford Street, Swindon SN1 1QQ
Phone: 01793 617 444
Fax: 01793 617 436

Clifford Chance
200 Aldersgate Street,
London EC1A 4JJ
Phone: 0171 600 1000
Fax: 0171 600 5555

Cobbetts
Ship Canal House,
King Street, Manchester M2 4WB
Phone: 0161 833 3333
Fax: 0161 833 3030

Davenport Lyons
1 Old Burlington Street,
London W1X 2NL
Phone: 020 7468 2600
Fax: 020 7437 8216

Davies Arnold Cooper
6-8 Bouverie Street,
London EC4Y 8DD
Phone: 020 7936 2222
Fax: 020 7936 2020

Denton Hall
5 Chancery Lane, Clifford's Inn,
London EC4A 1BU
Phone: 020 7242 1212
Fax: 020 7404 0087

Dibb Lupton Alsop
125 London Wall,
London EC2Y 5AE
Phone: 0345 262 728
Fax: 0171 600 1650

Dickinson Dees
St Ann's Wharf, 112 Quayside,
Newcastle upon Tyne NE99 1SB
Phone: 0191 279 9000
Fax: 0191 279 9100

DJ Freeman
43 Fetter Lane,
London EC4A 1NA
Phone: 020 7583 4055
Fax: 020 7353 7377

Denton Hall

Media, information & technology group

DENTON HALL

MEMBER OF THE DENTON INTERNATIONAL GROUP OF LAW FIRMS

Five Chancery Lane, Clifford's Inn, London EC4V 1BU
Phone: 020 7242 1212 **Fax:** 020 7404 0087
Website: www.dentonhall.com **Email:** info@dentonhall.com
Head of department: Nicholas Higham
Other offices: Almaty, Brussels, Beijing, Dubai, Gibraltar, Hong Kong, Istanbul, Moscow, Singapore and Tokyo; Denton International associated offices in Austria, France, Germany, Denmark, Norway, Sweden and Spain
Firm: 138 partners, 215 assistants
Unit: 11 partners, 14 assistants

“Denton Hall has been at the cutting edge of technology law since the initial explosion of the internet in the mid 1990s. We are ideally placed at the crossroads of media, information and technology, areas in which we have the leading practitioners, to guide clients on the opportunities and threats presented by convergence of these areas and the multitude of commercial issues it raises.”

Recent highlights

- Advising Bertelsmann on its joint venture arrangements with AOL for AOL/Bertelsmann online and Compuserve online services in Europe.
- Advising Teletext on the launch of its digital television services.
- Advising BDB/OnDigital on aspects of the launch of its digital television service.
- Advising Revolution Software on its game development work.
- Advising Sibelius Software on licensing arrangements for musical scorewriter software used by professionals around the world.
- Ongoing work for Springboard Internet Services on online services and electronic commerce issues.
- Working with Europay International on its smart card certification services.
- Advising a European government on e-commerce legislation.
- Working with Encyclopaedia Britannica on a series of online service projects.

Related services

Computer games	✓	E-commerce	✓	Internet	✓	Multimedia publishing	✓
Digital TV	✓	'Hard' IT	✓	Litigation	✓	Telecoms	✓

Donne Mileham & Haddock
100 Queens Road,
Brighton, East Sussex BN1 3YB
Phone: 01273 329833
Fax: 01273 747500

Edge Ellison
18 Southampton Place,
London WC1A 2AJ
Phone: 020 7404 4701
Fax: 020 7831 9152

Eversheds
Senator House,
85 Queen Victoria Street,
London EC4V 4JL
Phone: 020 7919 4500
Fax: 020 7919 4919

Field Fisher Waterhouse
41 Vine Street,
London EC3N 2AA
Phone: 020 7481 4841
Fax: 020 7488 0084

Freshfields
65 Fleet Street,
London EC4Y 1HS
Phone: 020 7936 4000
Fax: 020 7832 7001

Garretts
180 Strand, London WC2R 2NN
Phone: 020 7344 0344
Fax: 020 7438 2518

Hamiltons
42B Independent Place,
London E8 2HE
Phone: 020 7923 7823
Fax: 020 7923 0758

Hammond Suddards
7 Devonshire Square,
Cutlers Gardens,
London EC2M 4YH
Phone: 020 7655 1000
Fax: 020 7655 1001

Harbottle & Lewis
Hanover House, 14 Hanover Square,
London W1R 0BE
Phone: 020 7667 5000
Fax: 020 7667 5100

Henry Hepworth
5 John Street,
London WC1N 2HH
Phone: 020 7242 7999
Fax: 020 7242 7998

Herbert Smith
Exchange House, Primrose Street,
London EC2A 2HS
Phone: 020 7374 8000
Fax: 020 7374 0888

Hobson Audley Hopkins & Wood
7 Pilgrim Street, London EC4V 6DR
Phone: 020 7450 4500
Fax: 020 7450 4545

Keeble Hawson Moorhouse
Old Cathedral Vicarage,
St James Row, Sheffield S1 1XA
Phone: 0114 272 2061
Fax: 0114 275 0243

Kemp & Co
Sadlers House, Gutter Lane,
London EC2V 6BR
Phone: 020 7600 8080
Fax: 020 7600 7878

Freshfields

Communications and media group

FRESHFIELDS

65 Fleet Street, London EC4Y 1HS
Phone: 020 7936 4000 **Fax:** 020 7832 7001
Website: www.freshfields.com **Email:** email@freshfields.com
Principal contacts: Rachel Brandenburger, Avril Martindale, Dinah Nissen
Other offices: Amsterdam, Bangkok, Barcelona, Beijing, Hanoi, Ho Chi Minh City, Hong Kong, London, Madrid, Milan, New York, Paris, Rome, Singapore, Tokyo and Washington. In Germany we are represented through Deringer Tessin Herrmann & Sedemund's offices in Berlin, Cologne and Frankfurt and we operate joint offices in Brussels and Moscow.
Firm (worldwide): 231 partners, 925 assistants
Unit (worldwide): 40 partners, 80 assistants

"This exciting and fast changing area requires innovative legal advice. We provide solutions to digital media and e-commerce legal issues which enable our clients to meet their commercial goals worldwide. Our well-known team regularly advises on data protection, web-site development, encryption, electronic banking and licensing. We have also resolved a number of international cyber-piracy and domain names disputes."

Recent highlights

Advising:

- Many financial sector clients on electronic banking and trading systems.
- On the development of a cross utility platform for the secure and guaranteed electronic transfer of commercial information.
- On the roll-out of digital television and interactive services.
- On various high profile domain names disputes.
- On the legality of tele-shopping and internet auctions under EU legislation.
- A multinational telecommunications operator in relation to the European Commission e-commerce and copyright initiatives.
- A large media company on ITC regulations on concentration and ownership of digital TV channels.

Related services

Computer games	✓	E-commerce	✓	Internet	✓	Multimedia publishing	✓
Digital TV	✓	'Hard' IT	✓	Litigation	✓	Telecoms	✓

Herbert Smith

IP/IT

HERBERT SMITH

Exchange House, Primrose Street, London EC2A 2HS
Phone: 020 7374 8000 **Fax:** 020 7374 0888
Web: www.herbertsmith.com **Email:** mark.turner@herbertsmith.com
Head of department: Bill Moodie
Other offices: Bangkok, Beijing, Brussels, Hong Kong, Jakarta, London, Moscow, Paris and Singapore.
Firm: 147 partners, 330 assistants, 160 other fee-earners
Unit: 6 partners, 17 assistants, 4 other fee-earners

“Herbert Smith is a premier international law firm operating from the City of London and offices around the world. We are the forefront of developments in electronic commerce, advising leading companies on website design, contracts and payment on the internet, regulation of business online and e-commerce issues generally. Our expertise covers intellectual property, retail sales, financial services and promotional activities.”

Recent highlights

- Acting for WH Smith on their agreement with Microsoft to set up the new WH Smith portal, WH Smith Online.
- Advising leading insurance companies on the marketing and sale of financial products across the Internet.
- Advising on the BiB project for BskyB, which plans to provide a range of interactive services (eg home shopping, job search and educational features) through broadcast television and a telephone line return path.
- Acting for The Learning Company, the leading US software publisher, and its subsidiaries Mindscape and Broderbund on various issues in connection with their European CD-Rom publishing activities.
- Advising Psygnosis Sony's subsidiary, which is one of the world's leading computer games manufacturers, in litigation matters.
- Acted for GAME Plc, advising on its £148m flotation.

Related services

Computer games	✓	E-commerce	✓	Internet	✓	Multimedia publishing	✓
Digital TV	✓	'Hard' IT	✓	Litigation	✓	Telecoms	✓

key contacts

Kemp & Co

IT & multimedia

Saddlers House, Gutter Lane, London EC2V 6BR
Phone: 020 7600 8080
Fax: 020 7600 7878
Website: www.comlegal.com
Email: info@comlegal.com
Firm: 2 partners, 5 assistants, 2 other fee-earners

KEMP & CO

“ Kemp & Co was established in November 1997 as 'a law firm for the .com world.' The practice specialises in computer information and communications work for major supplier and acquirer clients, with a particular emphasis on digital media, e-commerce and convergence. Our key objective is to lawyer the convergence of the computer, information and communications industries to the highest level in Europe. ”

Recent highlights

- Digital Media and e-commerce work is running at a third of practice turnover.
- The practice's turnover has risen strongly in the 18 months since launch: monthly fees billed were at the rate of £50,000 in the first six months, £90,000 in the second six months and £120,000 in the third six months.
- We have grown to nine lawyers, with two more contracted to come.

In terms of clients:

- See the firm's review of 1998 on our website at www.comlegal.com
- We act as outside counsel to Microsoft on their Expedia online travel service product on a European basis. Expedia has recently overtaken Amazon.com in terms of revenues generated to be the largest web-based business.
- We act for a number of leading financial information companies (like FTSE International and Primark) who make an increasing number of internet related consultancies including etech associates, netdecisions, Netlife UK, Sightlines and SmartMoves.
- We act for the well known Internet and e-commerce investors Christopher Sharples and David Taylor.

Related services

Computer games	✓	E-commerce	✓	Internet	✓	Multimedia publishing	✓
Digital TV		'Hard' IT	✓	Litigation		Telecoms	✓

Linklaters & Alliance

Communications/intellectual property & technology

LINKLATERS
& ALLIANCE

One Silk Street, London EC2Y 8H2
Phone: 020 7456 2000 **Fax:** 020 7456 2222
Website: www.linklaters.com **Email:** rdune/jbrown@linklaters.com
Head of group: Robyn Durie/Jeremy Brown
Other offices: Alicante, Amsterdam, Antwerp, Bangkok, Berlin, Brussels, Cologne, Frankfurt, Gothenburg, The Hague, Hong Kong, Leipzig, Madrid, Malmö, Moscow, Munich, New York, Paris, Prague, Rotterdam, São Paulo, Shanghai, Singapore, St Petersburg, Stockholm, Tokyo, Warsaw, Washington DC
Firm: 209 partners, 875 assistants and other fee-earners
Unit: 12 partners, 60 assistants and other fee-earners

“Linklaters & Paines is one of the member firms of Linklaters & Alliance, the largest integrated legal practice in Europe. All of the member firms of Linklaters & Alliance have leading practices within their own countries and internationally, enabling us to provide clients with a unique service – access through a single source to high quality, integrated legal advice on a global basis.”

Linklaters & Paines' digital media and e-commerce practice resides within two departments of the firm: the Communications group headed by Robyn Durie, and the Intellectual Property & Technology group, headed by Jeremy Brown. The two practice groups work together on a range of digital media and e-commerce matters, with their combined expertise covering the following areas:

- Digital TV
- E-commerce
- 'Hard' IT
- Internet
- Litigation
- Multimedia publishing
- Telecoms

Recent highlights

- Working on the initial offering of Telecom Eireann.
- Drafting an electronic commerce law for Bermuda.
- Handling the IT aspects of the flotation of a software company.

Related services

Computer games	☐	E-commerce	✓	Internet	✓	Multimedia publishing	✓
Digital TV	✓	'Hard' IT	✓	Litigation	✓	Telecoms	✓

key contacts

Lovell White Durrant

Computers, communications & media unit

LOVELL WHITE DURRANT

65 Holborn Viaduct, London EC1A 2DY
Phone: 020 7236 0066 **Fax:** 020 7248 4212 **DX:** DX Box 57
Web: www.lovellwhitedurrant.com **Email:** information@lovellwhitedurrant.com
Other offices: Beijing, Brussels, Chicago, Ho Chi Minh City, Hong Kong, Moscow, New York, Paris, Prague, Singapore, Tokyo, Washington DC
Firm: 170 partners, 449 assistants, 252 other fee-earners
Unit: 6 partners, 11 assistants, 4 other fee-earners

"The CCMU was set up over three years ago as a focus for digital media work. The unit advises on aspects of Internet law including advertising, gaming, intellectual property, establishing Internet portals, defamation, encryption and e-commerce. It handles the development, content clearance issues and distribution of multimedia products, advises on interactive consumer services including services offered over the Internet, kiosks, and digital interactive television. Our practice includes extensive advice to computer games manufacturers and covers all aspects of information technology and telecommunications for both providers and users of such equipment and services. We also handle litigation in connection with digital media. The firm carries out a significant amount of venture capital and other financing work in relation to the digital media sector."

Recent highlights

- Acting for a broadcaster in relation to the protection of electronic programme guides.
- Advising a computer games manufacturer on games development and infringements over the Internet.
- Advising on a secure smart card project using electronic certificates to generate electronic signatures.
- Advising a major high street bank and one of the national newspapers in relation to their launch of Internet portal services.
- Advising in relation to the establishment of the Global Trust Organisation, a global certification authority network.
- Advising on the establishment of a number of PKI projects, particularly in the financial services sector.

Related services

Computer games	✓	E-commerce	✓	Internet	✓	Multimedia publishing	✓
Digital TV	✓	'Hard' IT	✓	Litigation	✓	Telecoms	✓

key contacts

LAWRENCE GRAHAM
190 Strand, London WC2R 1JN
Phone: 020 7379 0000
Fax: 020 7379 6854

LEDINGHAM CHALMERS
1 Golden Square, Aberdeen AB10 1NY
Phone: 01224 408408
Fax: 01224 408400

LINKLATERS & ALLIANCE
One Silk Street,
London EC2Y 8HQ
Phone: 020 7456 2000
Fax: 020 7456 2222

LINNELLS
Greyfriars Court,
Paradise Square, Oxford OX1 1BB
Phone: 01865 248607
Fax: 01865 728445

LOVELL WHITE DURRANT
65 Holborn Viaduct, London EC1A 2DY
Phone: 020 7236 0066
Fax: 020 7248 4212

MACLAY MURRAY & SPENS
151 St Vincent Street, Glasgow G2 5NJ
Phone: 0141 248 5011
Fax: 0141 248 5819

MACROBERTS
152 Bath Street, Glasgow G2 4TB
Phone: 0141 332 9988
Fax: 0141 332 8886

MANCHES & CO
Aldwych House, 81 Aldwych, London
WC2B 4RP
Phone: 020 7404 4433
Fax: 020 7430 1133

MARRIOTT HARRISON
12 Great James Street, London
WC1N 3DR
Phone: 020 7209 2000
Fax: 020 7209 2001

MASONS
30 Aylesbury Street, London EC1R 0ER
Phone: 020 7490 4000
Fax: 020 7490 2545

MCNEIVE
26 Cowper Street,
London EC2A 4AP
Phone: 020 7253 0535
Fax: 020 7253 0537

MILLS & REEVE
Francis House,
112 Hills Road,
Cambridge CB2 1PH
Phone: 01223 364422
Fax: 01223 355848

MORGAN COLE
Bradley Court
Park Place, Cardiff CF1 3DP
Phone: 01222 385385
Fax: 01222 385300

NABARRO NATHANSON
50 Stratton Street,
London W1X 6NX
Phone: 020 7493 9933
Fax: 020 7629 7900

NICHOLSON GRAHAM & JONES
110 Cannon Street,
London EC4N 6AR
Phone: 020 7648 9000
Fax: 020 7648 9001

Masons

Information & technology group

30 Aylesbury Street, London EC1R 0ER
Phone: 020 7490 4000 **Fax:** 020 7490 2545
Website: www.masons.com **Email:** info@masons.com
Head of group: Rob McCallough
Other offices: Bristol, Brussels, Dublin, Glasgow, Guangzhou, Hong Kong, Leeds, Manchester, Singapore
Firm: 86 partners, 187 assistants, 70 other fee-earners
Unit: 9 partners, 20 assistants, 8 other fee-earners

MASONS
M
Solicitors
& Privy Council Agents

“The e-commerce revolution is with us. It is pervasive and challenging. With an established and well regarded commercial information and technology group, Masons helps our clients seize the opportunities and overcome the legal hurdles.”

Recent highlights

In the past year we have assisted clients both nationally and internationally with:

- PC and Internet banking.
- Data collection and data protection.
- Meditating online auction systems dispute.
- Website and content agreements, customer policies, weblinking.
- Online licence and data agreements.
- Internet and email policies.
- Help desk agreements.
- Knowledge and electronic document management.
- Data warehousing.

Related services

Computer games	✓	E-commerce	✓	Internet	✓	Multimedia publishing	✓
Digital TV	✓	'Hard' IT	✓	Litigation	✓	Telecoms	✓

Norton Rose
Kempson House, Camomile Street,
London EC3A 7AN
Phone: 020 7283 6000
Fax: 020 7283 6500

Olswang
90 Long Acre, London WC2E 9TT
Phone: 020 7208 8888
Fax: 020 7208 8800

Osborne Clarke
Hillgate House, 26 Old Bailey,
London EC4M 7HS
Phone: 020 7809 1000
Fax: 020 7248 9934

Oxley & Coward
34-46 Moorgate Street,
Rotherham S60 2HB
Phone: 01709 510999
Fax: 01709 512999

Paisner & Co
Bouverie House, 154 Fleet Street,
London EC4A 2DQ
Phone: 0171 353 0299
Fax: 0171 583 8621

Rakisons
Clements House,
14-18 Gresham Street,
London EC2V 7JE
Phone: 0171 367 8000
Fax: 0171 367 8001

Robert Muckle
Norham House, 12 New Bridge Street West,
Newcastle upon Tyne NE1 8AS
Phone: 0191 232 4402
Fax: 0191 261 6954

Rowe & Maw
20 Black Friars Lane,
London EC4V 6HD
Phone: 020 7248 4282
Fax: 020 7248 2009

Shaw Pittman
Regis House, 45 King William Street,
London EC4R 9AS
Phone: 020 7337 9400
Fax: 020 7337 9401

Sidley & Austin
1 Threadneedle Street,
London EC2R 8AW
Phone: 020 7360 3600
Fax: 020 7626 7937

Simmons & Simmons
21 Wilson Street, London EC2M 2TX
Phone: 0171 628 2020
Fax: 0171 628 2070

Sinclair Roche & Temperley
Royex House, 5 Aldermanbury Square,
London EC2V 7LE
Phone: 0171 452 4000
Fax: 0171 452 4001

SJ Berwin & Co
222 Gray's Inn Road,
London WC1X 8HB
Phone: 0171 533 2222
Fax: 0171 533 2000

Slaughter and May
35 Basinghall Street,
London EC2V 5DB
Phone: 020 7600 1200
Fax: 020 7600 0289

Olswang

OLSWANG

90 Long Acre, London WC2E 9TT
Phone: 020 7208 8888 **Fax:** 020 7208 8800
Email: olsmail@olswang.co.uk **Website:** www.olswang.co.uk
Firm: 41 partners, 68 assistants, 23 other fee-earners

"Olswang is different. Forward thinking, Olswang is about realising potential, the potential of our clients, the potential of all of our people, the potential within every situation in which our clients find themselves.

And our aim is simple. To be the preferred law firm of leading companies in the media, communications and technology sectors. We know the players, we know the business and above all, we understand the issues.

Being different has brought rapid growth. Olswang is a 250+ strong team committed to providing innovative solutions through legal excellence."

Recent highlights:

- Advising Freeserve in relation to all matters for the launch and the ongoing operation and growth of its ISP service including the largest deal to date in the UK for a content partner.
- Advising Head New Media Ltd in its partnership with The Lowe Group.
- E-Trade UK Ltd on its European launch of its online real time brokering services.
- Advising BMP Interaction, one of the leading advertising agency's interactive divisions, on projects with clients including Britvic (Pepsi UK website) and Vauxhall.
- Advising a major start-up Internet sports provider, Pangolin International Ltd, on corporate finance and commercial matters including its branding and rights acquisition programme.
- Advising Bloomberg LP on its launch of interactive TV services in France.

Related services

Computer games	✓	E-commerce	✓	Internet	✓	Multimedia publishing	✓
Digital TV	✓	'Hard' IT	✓	Litigation	✓	Telecoms	✓

Rakisons

IT & telecoms group

RAKISONS

Clements House, 14-18 Gresham Street, London EC2V 7JE
Phone: 020 7367 8000 **Fax:** 020 7367 8001
Email: rakisons@rakisons.co.uk **Website:** http:/www.rakisons.co.uk
Head of department: Chris Hoyle
Firm: 13 partners, 20 assistants, 2 senior consultants
Unit: 3 partners, 6 assistants, 1 senior consultant

"Rakisons is a commercial law firm founded in 1979 with an international practice. The firm's aim is to provide a complete range of first class legal services for the business world. The firm has grown steadily in reputation in technology law and has a leading regulatory and commercial telecoms practice."

Recent highlights:

- Acting for Panavision Inc in its £40m acquisition of Samuelson Group plc.
- Acting for NASDAQ-listed telecoms operator, IDT Corp inc, on the acquisition of capacity as an original owner on a $1bn-plus submarine transatlantic cable project.
- Acting for a leading Internet service provider on its UK and EU telecoms regulatory matters including obtaining the first telecoms licence granted to an Internet service provider. Rakisons also advised the client on obtaining the first ever US s.214 telecoms licence for a UK ISP.
- Acting for Band-X, the first Internet bandwidth exchange, playing a key role in turning a completely new concept into one of the most talked about telecoms developments during 1997.
- Acting for Virgin Vie Ltd on its start-up in-sourcing project with ICL.
- Acting for a leading international telecoms company on an Internet defamation litigation.
- Acting for Internet Technology Group plc on a double reverse takeover on AIM of Global Internet Ltd and Ballnatray Holdings plc.
- Acting as UK & EU counsel for NASDAQ-listed telecoms operators on high yield debt offering.
- Winning mandates to advise governments in Georgia, Tanzania and Gabon on telecoms regulatory issues.
- Acting for an Internet based provider on a public listing.
- Obtaining first L34.1 voice licence in France, as well as licences throughout EU.

Related services

Computer games	✓	E-commerce	✓	Internet	✓	Multimedia publishing	✓
Digital TV	✓	'Hard' IT	✓	Litigation	✓	Telecoms	✓

key contacts

Simmons & Simmons

Communications practice

SIMMONS & SIMMONS

21 Wilson Street, London EC2M 2TX
Phone: 020 7628 2020 **Fax:** 020 7628 2070
Website: www.simmons-simmons.com **Email:** enquiries@simmons-simmons.com
Other offices: Abu Dhabi, Brussels, Hong Kong, Lisbon, Milan, New York, Paris, Rome, Shanghai
Firm: 147 partners, 753 other fee-earners
Unit: 21 partners, 35 assistant solicitors

“E-commerce and digital media are integral parts of Simmons & Simmons' communications practice, reflecting the increasing convergence of telecommunications, IT and media. Our clients include internet service providers, major corporations engaged in electronic commerce, banks, providers of content for interactive services, software businesses and regulators. These clients come to us because of our:

- integrated communications practice;
- industry understanding and proximity;
- international capabilities; and
- outstanding reputation in intellectual property, sector regulation, corporate finance, banking, commercial, dispute resolution and tax.”

Recent highlights

- Advising the Internet Service Providers' Association on its complaint to OFTEL over BT's introduction of BT ClickTM.
- Advising one of the major web portals on transborder data flow arrangements and online services.
- Creating a dispute resolution system for a group of leading banks doing business to business internet trading.
- Working on a strategically important project for high-speed PC Internet access to innovative content.
- Helping the proprietors of one of the largest integrated Internet content businesses acquire a leading games site business.

Related services

Computer games	✓	E-commerce	✓	Internet	✓	Multimedia publishing	☐
Digital TV	✓	'Hard' IT	✓	Litigation	☐	Telecoms	✓

key contacts

Slaughter and May

Electronic commerce

SLAUGHTER AND MAY

35 Basinghall Street, London EC2V 5DB
Phone: 020 7600 1200 **Fax:** 020 7600 0289
Website: www.slaughterandmay.com
Other offices: Brussels, Hong Kong, New York, Paris, Singapore
Firm: 109 partners, 500 assistants

"Since its foundation in 1889, Slaughter and May has grown steadily without merger. We aim to provide a professional service of the highest quality combining technical excellence with commercial understanding and a practical constructive approach. Our clients have always expected and received innovative and positive support. To this extent, electronic commerce poses no new challenge."

Recent highlights

- Acting for Open Interactive (formerly BIB) on corporate and IT aspects of its interactive digital TV service.
- Acting for Psion in relation to the establishment of Symbian, the joint venture with Nokia, Ericsson and Motorola.
- Advising in relation to the privatisation of INMARSAT (satellites).
- Advising EMAP On Line on its Internet/new media ventures including the award winning *bargainholidays.com*.
- Acting for numerous companies in the financial services sector on Internet ventures and activities.
- Advising in relation to domain name disputes, defamation matters and cross border Internet disputes.

Related services

Computer games	✓	E-commerce	✓	Internet	✓	Multimedia publishing	✓
Digital TV	✓	'Hard' IT	✓	Litigation	✓	Telecoms	✓

key contacts

Taylor Joynson Garrett

IT/Telecoms group

Carmelite, 50 Victoria Embankment, Blackfriars,
London EC4Y 0DX
Phone: 020 7353 1234 **Fax:** 020 7936 2666
Website: www.tjg.co.uk **Email:** enquiries@tjg.co.uk
Head of group: Glyn Morgan
Other offices: Brussels, Bucharest
Firm: 77 partners, 110 assistants, 57 other fee-earners
Unit: 8 partners, 14 assistants, 2 other fee-earners

"Taylor Joynson Garrett is a major City law firm. It offers a full service to its corporate clients across all commercial disciplines and has long been regarded as one of the leaders in intellectual property. An experienced and respected team deals with corporate, IT, telecoms and digital media and e-commerce issues to assist clients in advances in technological fields, advising and protecting inventors, manufacturers, suppliers and users."

Recent highlights

- Continue to act for Eidos plc in various transactions, including the purchase of Crystal Dynamics Inc for £28.5m, and also in relation to their subscription free access to online Internet service in conjunction with Easynet.
- Acting for Sony Computer Entertainment Europe in relation to its anti-piracy programme against the re-chipping of PlayStations so as to allow the playing of counterfeit discs.
- Acting for Multex.com, Inc, the largest provider of online financial information to institutions and investors.
- Advised Cadcorp, a geographical information systems company, on a wide range of commercial contracts including standard terms and conditions and distribution agreements.
- Currently dealing with the first wave of major US inbound Internet companies including ebay, Inc, e-gain, e-Toys and four other well known major US e-companies in their UK start up, e-commerce activities and joint ventures.
- Advising a further 34 US Internet companies in their UK e-commerce activities, ventures, distribution and logistics.
- In addition, the firm runs a series of successful seminars aimed at clients in the digital media and e-commerce field.

Related services

Computer games	✓	E-commerce	✓	Internet	✓	Multimedia publishing	✓
Digital TV	✓	'Hard' IT	✓	Litigation	✓	Telecoms	✓

Theodore Goddard

E-commerce group

150 Aldersgate Street, London EC1A 4EJ
Phone: 020 7606 8855 **Fax:** 020 7606 4390
Website: www.theogoddard.com
Email: paulrenney@theodoregoddard.co.uk
Head of group: Paul Renney, Arnold Segal, Rafi Azim-Khan
Other offices: Brussels, Jersey, Paris and associates worldwide
Firm: 54 partners, 90 assistants, 28 other fee-earners
Unit: 7 partners, 10 assistants, 2 other fee-earners

THEODORE GODDARD

“City law firm, Theodore Goddard, has provided businesses with a full range of legal services and advice since 1902. With over 170 lawyers focused in specialist groups the firm advises on all aspects of business related law. The e-commerce group brings together multi-departmental specialists to make up a team able to advise on all aspects of electronic trade, including acknowledged experts, Arnold Segal (eg IT contracts and computer games), Paul Renney (eg digital content distribution and site contracts) and Rafi Azim-Khan (eg e-shopping/trade, contracts and net advertising). The group has been particularly busy over the last 12 months advising on every aspect of e-commerce, including domain names, site creation, encryption, online terms of trade, contracts with third parties, hypertext link and cyberlibel liability, online gaming, lottery and betting, distance selling regulation, webvertising and e-commerce 'audits' of online ventures. Our clients range from multinational broadcasters/publishers and manufacturers to online startups.”

Recent highlights

- Complete e-commerce 'audit,' substantive report and ongoing advice regarding all aspects of electronic promotion, marketing, communication and trade for General Motors.
- Advising News International on the full range of issues regarding its freeserve ISP venture (currantbun.com) with various partners, including online terms, disclaimers, contracts, terms of trade, domain names and all other matters for ISP operations.
- Advising an educational publisher on its freeserve ISP, again covering all issues.
- Advising novel online music business venture, including on issues relating to online trade, ticket purchase, contracts with designers, games companies and top artists.
- Advising a major gaming company in relation to Internet gaming and betting services and products.

Related services

Computer games	✓	E-commerce	✓	Internet	✓	Multimedia publishing	✓
Digital TV	✓	'Hard' IT	✓	Litigation	✓	Telecoms	✓

key contacts

Weil, Gotshal & Manges

Digital Media & E-commerce group

One South Place, London EC2M 2WG
Phone: 020 7903 1000 **Fax:** 020 7903 0990
Web: www.weil.com **Email:** weil.london@weil.com
Key contacts: Michael Francies (020 7903 1170), David Naylor (020 7903 1151)
Other offices: Brussels, Budapest, Dallas, Houston, New York, Miami, Prague, Silicon Valley, Warsaw and Washington DC.
Firm: 210 partners, 490 assistants, 150 other fee-earners
Unit: 18 partners, 70 assistants, 8 other fee-earners

WEIL, GOTSHAL & MANGES

“Weil, Gotshal & Manges provides corporate,commercial and finance advice under US and UK law to companies of all sizes in this sector. We have particular expertise in digital media, e-commerce and IT/telecom, the firm is highly regarded in each of these fields.

The Practice: Our lawyers have a real understanding of our clients' technologies and products and a genuine enthusiasm for the sector. They are supported by the full resources of the international law firm with particular expertise in New York, London, Silicon Valley and Brussels.

Our US and UK law experience spans high-technology venture capital transactions, public offerings, high yield debt issues, acquisitions, mergers and joint ventures, through to content liability and regulation, hard and soft intellectual property, data protection and electronic privacy issues and all forms of digital media and e-commerce commercial agreements.”

Clients

- AOL Bertelsmann
- Bell Atlantic
- Berg Electronics
- CBS
- Disney
- Cisco
- Comverse Technology
- Futurenet
- GE Capital
- GIGA Information Group
- Intel
- Matsushita
- News Corporation
- Texas Instruments

Related services

Computer games	☐	E-commerce	✓	Internet	✓	Multimedia publishing	☐
Digital TV	☐	'Hard' IT	✓	Litigation	✓	Telecoms	✓

key contacts

Tarlo Lyons
Watchmaker Court,
33 St John's Lane,
London EC1M 4DB
Phone: 020 7405 2000
Fax: 020 7814 9421

Taylor Joynson Garrett
Carmelite, 50 Victoria Embankment,
Blackfriars, London EC4Y 0DX
Phone: 020 7353 1234
Fax: 020 7936 2666

Taylor Vinters
Merlin Place, Milton Road,
Cambridge CB4 4DP
Phone: 01223 423444
Fax: 01223 423486

Theodore Goddard
150 Aldersgate Street,
London EC1A 4EJ
Phone: 020 7606 8855
Fax: 020 7606 4390

Thomas Eggar Church Adams
Fulwood House, Fulwood Place,
London WC1V 6HR
Phone: 020 7242 0841
Fax: 020 7831 9609

Titmuss Sainer Dechert
2 Serjeants' Inn, London EC4Y 1LT
Phone: 020 7583 5353
Fax: 020 7353 3683

Travers Smith Braithwaite
10 Snow Hill, London EC1A 2AL
Phone: 0171 248 9133
Fax: 0171 236 3728

Walker Morris
Kings Court, 12 King Street,
Leeds LS1 2HL
Phone: 0113 283 2500
Fax: 0113 245 9412

Weil, Gotshal & Manges
One South Place, London EC2M 2WG
Phone: 020 7903 1000
Fax: 020 7903 0990

Wiggin and Co
The Quadrangle, Imperial Square,
Cheltenham GL50 1YX
Phone: 01242 224114
Fax: 01242 224223

Willoughby & Partners
(Rouse & Co International)
The Isis Building, Thames Quay,
193 Marsh Wall, London E14 9SG
Phone: 020 7345 8888
Fax: 020 7345 4555

Wragge & Co
55 Colmore Row, Birmingham B3 2AS
Phone: 0121 233 1000
Fax: 0121 214 1099